The
Healing Plants Bible

A GODSFIELD BOOK

The
Healing Plants
Bible

Helen Farmer-Knowles

The definitive guide to herbs, trees and flowers

An Hachette UK Company
www.hachette.co.uk

First published in Great Britain in 2010 by
Godsfield, a division of Octopus Publishing Group Ltd
Endeavour House, 189 Shaftesbury Avenue, London, WC2H 8JG
www.octopusbooks.co.uk

ISBN 978-1-84181-390-5

A CIP catalogue record for this book is available from the British Library.

Printed and bound in China

10 9 8 7 6 5 4 3 2 1

This book is not intended as an alternative to personal medical advice.
The reader should consult a physician in all matters relating to health
and particularly in respect of any symptoms that may require diagnosis
or medical attention. While the advice and information are believed to be
accurate and true at the time of going to press, neither the author nor
the publisher can accept any legal responsibility or liability for any error
or omissions that may have been made.

Contents

Introduction

What are healing plants?

Plants *are* life. Our lives depend upon the survival of the plant life that surrounds us. They not only create our wondrous environment, which feeds and heals both body and soul, but without them nothing is sustainable on our beautiful planet; plants are the bedrock of our evolution, civilizations and cultures. In addition, among the world's species of flowering plants, which are estimated to number around 250,000–400,000, there are many 'healing plants' that can help us physically, mentally and spiritually.

Part of a fire-starting kit, a Birchback cylinder was used by Ötzi, 'to hold embers wrapped in maple leaves'.

The use of plants for healing has a long history. Europe's oldest Copper Age (Chalcolithic) natural male mummy, nicknamed 'Ötzi the Iceman' (or Frozen Fritz) and dating from around 3300 BCE, was found in 1991 in the Schnalstal glacier in the Ötztal Alps near Hauslabjoch, on the border between Austria and Italy. Ötzi's stomach contained a primitive 'first-aid' antiseptic wound-healing moss known as *Sphagnum imbricatum*. Among his effects he carried a small leather pouch containing herbs and two birch fungi, which incorporate antibiotic substances that can produce hallucinations. They may

have had a spiritual use, because from its outset herbalism intertwined medicine with mystery and magic.

Tapping the power of plants

Modern science continues to identify powerful healing properties that come from plants. There are at least 120 distinct chemical substances derived from plants that are considered important drugs currently in use around the world. With more than 50 per cent of the estimated plant species found on earth coming from the rainforests, the campaign against deforestation there has

Rainforests are researched to find natural remedies and constituents that can be made into pharmaceutical drugs.

added urgency, plus global preservation of plants vanishing into extinction. Scientists continue to probe the rainforests and other isolated parts of the globe in search of plants that will yield their secrets and medicinal values in order to heal humankind. This book explores the many different therapeutic aspects of plants, ranging from the medicinal and edible healing plants to the trees with healing energies, the plants used for spiritual healing and the flower essences.

The history of healing plants

All over the world, birds and animals appear to know instinctively the best remedy for what ails them, and even domesticated animals seem to retain part of this ability. Their innate aptitude to choose healing plants has developed from hard-won inherited learning by means of trial and error, with speedy adoption of what actually works; for them the herb *itself* is their physician.

Less intuitive, humans have the advantage of learning and logic, but the basis of our knowledge about nature's healing plants was originally gained through observation of animals' natural 'testing' in the wild. Our dogs, cats, birds, horses and mammalian predecessors were by example our first true-life herbalists and teachers.

Before the written word recorded the accumulative knowledge and practical healing applications of plants, description of all their uses was verbal. Science was in its unsophisticated infancy and so, where the results lacked proper explanation, some of what occurred in plant healing was attributed to magic.

Earliest records

Tablets from ancient Sumeria reveal that their medicines were made from plant and mineral compounds mixed with liquids or solvents, such as wine, beer, honey or plant or vegetable oils. Babylonian clay tablets dating from 3000 BCE recorded imports of herbs. In 2005 nearly 1,000 such clay tablets, found in modern-day Iraq and covering the period *c*. 2000 BCE–150 BCE, yielded remnants of a standard diagnostic handbook used for centuries to train and inform doctors, as well as treatments using plant, animal and mineral materials.

Within and around that same period, parallel cultures in China, Egypt and India

This ancient Indian Manuscript depicts Hanuman's quest to the Himalayas to find the four healing plants to cure Rama's brother Lakshmana.

made written records of mainly medicinal herbs. Today's traditional Chinese medicine began with the most important Chinese herbal text *Huang Ti Nei Ching* (*The Yellow Emperor's Classic of Internal Medicine*), which was allegedly authored by the legendary Chinese sovereign Huang Ti in around 2,697 BCE. Herbalism remains an important aspect of traditional Chinese medicine today, with herbs being prescribed according to the principles of traditional Chinese medicine, including the five-element theory *Wu Xing* and energy rebalancing.

Ancient Egyptian medicine refers to the practices of healing that were common in that country from about 3300 BCE until the Persian invasion of 525 BCE, and these also involved 'magic'. However, its most famous text – the *Ebers Papyrus*, dated to *c*. 1550 BCE – sensibly remedied asthma with 'a mixture of herbs heated on a brick so that the sufferer could inhale their fumes'.

India's traditional medicine, Ayurveda, which was first described in Vedic religious scriptures in around 1200 BCE, features both herbs and diet as being of central importance, and several prominent Ayurvedic herbs (such as turmeric, cardamom and coriander seeds) are still used worldwide in Indian cooking today. As with traditional Chinese medicine, Ayurvedic herbalism aims to bring about a rebalancing of energy in the body to achieve optimum physical, mental and spiritual health.

On the other side of the world, in Mesoamerican civilizations dating from 2000 BCE to the time of the conquest of Mexico by Spanish conquistador

Hernando Cortés in 1519, the doctors of the Aztec empire used many herbs, including cocoa leaves and other natural resources, to prevent, treat and cure ailments and diseases. Much later, in mid-17th-century North America, immigrant European settlers discovered the Native Americans' medicinal plant remedies, which they incorporated into their own system before eventually returning to their countries of origin.

This woodcut from 'On the Properties of Things' 1520 (original c.1230–1240) shows herbs being sorted for distillation and concoction of medicines.

Doctrine of Signatures

Based on the idea of sympathetic magical correspondences, the Doctrine of Signatures is an ancient concept that was found worldwide. In the Doctrine of Signatures, a plant's shape, colour, markings, texture and scent all have significance – mandrake roots, for example, are held to resemble the human body and to have supernatural powers. This philosophy was commonly held from the time of its initiation in Pliny's *Historia Naturalis*, Dioscorides's *De Materia Medica* and Galen's *De Simplicius*, and remains reflected in the common names of plants whose coincidental shapes and colour suggest that they might heal corresponding parts of the body, such as lungwort (*Pulmonaria officinalis*). The concept, developed and published by Paracelsus in the 16th century, was further disseminated by Jakob Boehme and elaborated in mainstream medical texts into the 19th century; it also had some influence on the development of homeopathy.

Plant medicine continued to be important throughout the Middle Ages, with monasteries and village wise women maintaining and developing herbalism as a healing art. The 16th and 17th centuries were an era of herbals (illustrated books describing the characteristics of healing plants), among which John Gerard's *The Herball or General History of Plants* (1597) and Nicholas Culpeper's *The English Physician Enlarged* (1653) were considered especially important. The illustrated Aztec herbal known as *The Badianus Manuscript* was also translated into Latin in the 16th century.

Herbalism today

The emergence of pharmacology, and the discovery of how to manufacture healing pharmacological agents in the 18th and 19th centuries, caused a decline in the use of herbalism. However, it never completed disappeared. In Britain, for example, professional herbalism survived through the establishment of the National Institute of Medical Herbalists in 1864. In other countries, such as China, use of traditional herbalism continued to run alongside the practice of Western pharmacology.

The concept of the New Age, which began in the 1960s, resulted in an unexpected resurgence in herbalism and complementary medicine during the 1980s, including a revival of Edward Bach's Flower Remedies and the creation of their offspring, Flower Essences, to treat mental states and correct emotional imbalances, alongside

The scented pleasures of choosing an essential oil to treat body, mind and spirit.

the resurrected and now hugely popular art of aromatherapy.

Today plants are regaining respect, as science begins to gather evidence for the specific healing properties of herbs and foods. At last, ancient folk knowledge is being supported by scientific evidence and launching a new era of healing.

How to use this book

This book introduces you to some of the most important healing plants from around the world, but it is not intended as a guide to prescribing herbal treatment or for curing ailments and disease. It is meant as an inspirational reference source to help you learn more about all aspects of phytotherapy – the science of healing with plants.

Where to find the plants

For ease of reference, the plants have been grouped into the chapters listed below. However, there is necessarily some overlap, with some plants having a medicinal use as well as being edible, for example. Consult the index if you don't find a plant in the chapter where you'd expect to find it.

Many vitamins, minerals and anti-oxidants are found in plant foods. One way of harnessing these benefits is to make a herbal infusion.

- **Healing and medicinal herbs** (pages 16–107) explores herbs used in traditional Western herbalism, as well as those from traditional Chinese medicine and Ayurveda. In this chapter, the profiles explore the history of the plant's use in herbalism and provide a guide to the parts that are used medicinally, general treatment principles and key therapeutic benefits.

Gathering and separating aerial parts from roots of medicinal plants before drying and storage.

- **Edible healing plants** (pages 108–247) provides the latest findings concerning phytonutrients (see pages 112–114) – the beneficial vitamins, minerals and antioxidants that are found in many readily available plant foods.

- **Healing energies of trees** (pages 248–303) is a guide to the vibrational or energy medicine that is present in trees, and to the way that ancient societies and cultures have viewed the particular energy of trees.

- **Plants for spiritual healing** (pages 304–349) explores the plants that are traditionally used for spiritual healing. These include cacti used by shamanic healers, as well as plants that are sacred to a range of spiritual traditions.

- **Flower essences** (pages 350–375) offers advice on the use of Bach Flower Remedies, Australian Bush Flower Essences and Flower Essences Services for the treatment of common ailments.

Under each plant profile, you will find both the common name of the plant and its full botanical (Latin) name (the latter given in italic type). You will also find its family name and a brief description of the plant.

Throughout the book, and particularly in the chapter on healing and medicinal herbs, a range of pharmaceutical and medical terms are used. These are explained in the glossary (pages 376–383).

Cautions

Plants can be powerful medicines, and cautions for their use are noted throughout. This book is not a substitute for medical care – always consult your medical practitioner when considering treatment, and advise him or her if you are taking any kind of herbal supplement.

Healing and medicinal herbs

Principles of herbalism

Although many important conventional drugs derive directly from herbs, herbal medicine remains the only readily accessible medical option for 80 per cent of the world's population. It is also increasingly being used by many people in the West as a first option for simple self-medication or in complementary medicine.

The principles of herbalism are based on the innate healing power of herbs and their affinity with the person using them. When herbs or their natural plant substances (botanicals and extracts) are used for medication to restore physiological balance, it is important for the herbalist to have a full understanding of the nature of the illness and, via consultation and assessment, to take into consideration the 'whole' person being treated, alongside the potential healing aspects of the chosen herb itself. Its importance grows as herbal medicine becomes more popular in the West.

Due care and caution must be taken in the selection of herbs – including their provenance and condition at the point of use – because plants (whether organic or otherwise) contain chemical compounds that may either deteriorate or cause side-effects in the person being treated.

A holistic and preventive approach

The strength of herbal medicine lies in its ability to treat the person holistically, and in its aim to prevent (as well as help to cure) illness. Herbs can be used to aid resistance to disease through nutrition and immunological support, whereas orthodox medicines have little or no preventive ability and their use is purely remedial, *after* the onset of illness.

Medicinal herbs are generally used for uncomplicated ailments, benign chronic conditions and persistent complaints, rather than for grave diseases, although in some serious illnesses herbs may be used as an additional therapy under professional monitoring, such as for the aftermath of chemotherapy.

A doctor in hospital practising Traditional Chinese Medicine, the mainstream medical care in China, weighing herbs for eastern remedies.

How to use medicinal herbs

The quality of the herbs used for healing is very important, as are accurate identification and appropriate use of the correct plant species. Understandably the effectiveness of herbs and their preparations depends upon these, before any form of extraction occurs.

Collection

To avoid degradation and mould, gather herbs in dry weather, after evaporation of the morning dew. Pick only flawless leaves or other herb parts in their prime. Before storing herbs, spread them out to dry in a well-ventilated atmosphere.

Storage

Store both home-dried and bought herbs in airtight jars, away from sunlight. Label jars with the name of the herb and date of collection. A herb's aromatic strength and colour are a guide to its freshness, when a date is not available.

Uses of herbs

The botanicals, essences and essential oils of medicinal herbs are all used, in toiletries, perfumery and proprietary preparations. These include capsules, elixirs, extracts, incense, liniments, mixtures (liquid and dry), oils, ointments, powders, soaps, tablets, vapour rubs and (floral) waters. Below are descriptions of the main types of internal and external remedies that you are likely to encounter.

Internal remedies

Internal remedies are taken orally, delivered by mouth through the alimentary tract, which may be used for internal or external effects.

Herbal infusion: Herbal infusions are made by steeping plants in near-boiling water and leaving them covered for five to ten minutes. The strained liquid may be used internally or to make external applications, such as an eye wash, when cooled.

Depending on the material used to make them, herbal teas can stimulate, relax or sedate.

Herbal tea/tisane: An infusion, made as described above from material other than 'tea' (*Camellia sinensis*), such as berries or flowers. To be taken internally. Used to stimulate, relax or sedate.

Maceration: A preparation made by soaking herbal material in water for 12 hours, or by leaving herbal material in vegetable oil or an organic solvent in the sun for a minimum of two weeks (the solar method). Used in cooking oils or added to topical applications, such as creams.

Tincture: An extract of herb parts infused in alcohol, or herb essences added to alcohol (such as brandy, vodka or rum 80–100 per cent proof), though glycerine and water extraction methods are also used; multi-use tinctures are taken orally in homeopathy and naturopathy, or may be added to topical products.

Suspension: A mixture in which fine solid or liquid particles are suspended in a fluid. For example, you can create a suspension by adding a tincture to a base lotion, instead of using the more concentrated tincture direct.

Aromatherapy massage with aromatic plant essential oil and fixed oils promotes either specific or a general sense of well-being

External remedies

External remedies are medications that are applied topically to a certain area of the skin, with limited area effects or they are absorbed into the bloodstream.

Balms, creams, lotions, oils, salves: Made with water-extracted botanicals and/or macerated extracts; they are also used in massage oils and other healing topical applications.

Compress: A pad soaked in a heated decoction (see below) or infusion (see page 20), applied as hot as possible to the affected body part, covered with plastic or other thermal wrapping and left in position until cooled.

Decoction: Extracts of bark, chips, roots and seeds simmered for 15 minutes, then strained, to produce a stronger liquid, for purposes other than ingestion.

Essential oils: Extracted from plants, essential oils can be added to hot water for inhalations or added to a bath. They can be diluted in a carrier oil for aromatherapy massage, or added to balms, creams, lotions and salves.

Poultice/plaster: A soft, moist mass (a pulp or paste) soaked in a decoction or infusion. It is usually heated and then bound with a cloth or bandage to the affected body part (for example, around a splinter or infected area) and left until cooled. Reapply as necessary to 'draw out' the abscess or splinter.

Whole herbs: Used in cooking or consumed as foods; they may be whole or powdered, or dried or fresh leaves or other plant parts. Leaves or other parts of herbs can also be added to hot water for steam inhalations (see opposite) or wrapped in a muslin cloth and used for a steam bath.

How to make a herbal steam inhalation

A quick and easy way of using herbs to treat colds, coughs and sore throats is by making a steam inhalation. Before selecting a herb or essential oil for use, check the plant profile for any cautions. You will need a large bowl or basin, boiling water, a handful of herbs or 3–4 drops of essential oil and a large towel. Suggested herbs include eucalyptus and peppermint (herb or oils) or sage (oil).

1 Pour boiling water into the bowl until it is filled halfway. Immediately add the herbs or 3 drops of the essential oil.

2 Lower your face over the bowl, close your eyes and 'tent' a towel covering your head and basin to trap the steam. Breathe the healing warmth and aroma in and out through your nose for five to ten minutes.

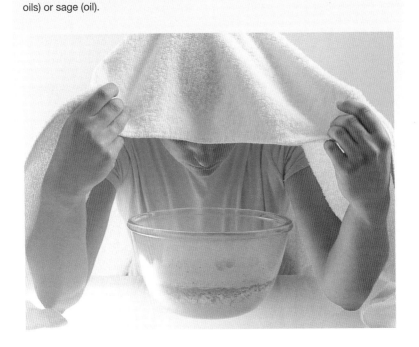

Safety guidelines

Safety is essential when dealing with any medical product or treatment – be it conventional or herbal. To this end, the World Health Organization (WHO) has been actively involved in developing guidelines to regulate the quality and safe use of herbal medicines across the world.

The WHO is aware there is widespread use of traditional medicine in all developing countries, while the use of complementary and alternative medicine is increasing rapidly in developed countries. The EU Directive on Traditional Herbal Medicinal Products has also played a role, requiring that traditional over-the-counter herbal remedies be made to assured standards of safety and quality, and that regulations are standardized across Europe.

Suggested safety guidelines

When using healing and medicinal herbs, it is a good idea to bear in mind the following guidelines:

• **Treat herbs with respect:** Herbs are medicines and they should be treated with the same measure of respect as prescription drugs. They are a route to improving health and boosting immunity, and are beneficial when used regularly in moderation (including edible herbs within a balanced diet) alongside exercise and a healthy lifestyle. The pharmaceutical terms used throughout this chapter to describe the effects of herbs are explained in the glossary (pages 376–383).

• **Remember that 'natural' does not automatically mean 'safe':** Highly concentrated essential oils, which are a natural herbal derivative, must be diluted and used according to the instructions. Bear in mind that some people are allergic to entire plant families, such as Asteraceae (the daisy family).

• **Consider age and bodily vulnerability:** Babies, those who are contemplating pregnancy or who are already pregnant, and the elderly should not take herbal remedies unless they are prescribed by a qualified practitioner.

• **Follow the recommended dosage:** More is not necessarily better, so do not exceed a stated dose. Herbs can be harmful in over-large or prolonged dosages, or addictive after a long period of inappropriate usage. Some herbs are poisonous or may have toxic side-effects. Follow professional guidance so the dosage is tailor-made to your needs as an individual, your medical history, the illness being treated and the need to avoid aggravating any condition – including past ones – or creating a new one.

• **Don't self-medicate:** Self-medication should be for only minor ailments such as coughs and colds or cuts and bruises.

• **Respect any cautions:** Plants (organic or otherwise) contain chemical compounds that may deteriorate or cause side-effects when used on their own or in combination with other herbs, or may have interactions or contraindications with orthodox drugs. The use of some herbs may be prohibited for specific illnesses.

• **Tell your doctor:** Tell your doctor what herbal medicines you are taking.

Safety is an important consideration when choosing which plants/ herbs to combine. While their scents may appear compatible, there may be unforeseen interactions.

Horse chestnut

Botanical name *Aesculus hippocastanum*

Family Hippocastanaceae

Description: Horse chestnut is native to northern and central Asia and central Europe. This large deciduous tree can grow up to 36 m (118 ft) tall, and has showy white or dusky-red flowers. The fruit is a green, leathery and prickly capsule that splits in three to reveal nut-type seeds.

Parts used: Seeds (fruit), bark, seldom leaves, buds (in Bach Flower Remedies, pages 356–357).

History: In Eastern countries, ground horse chestnuts were used in horse and cattle fodder. When correctly and thoroughly processed, the leached, pulverized seeds yield a wholesome starchy porridge that was once important in the diet of some Native American peoples.

Main therapeutic properties: For centuries the seeds, leaves, bark and flowers of horse chestnut have been used for a variety of conditions and diseases, as an alterative, analgesic, anti-inflammatory, astringent, diuretic, expectorant, febrifuge, haemostatic, narcotic, tonic, vasoprotector, vasoconstrictor, and vulnerary.

The bark has tonic, narcotic and febrifuge properties and is used as an infusion in intermittent fevers; the infusion is also applied externally to ulcers. The seed extract has been used in the treatment of rheumatism and neuralgia, in rectal complaints and for haemorrhoids, as well as for chronic venous insufficiency. Although scientific evidence concerning deep-vein thrombosis (DVT) is lacking, small studies have found that standardized horse-chestnut seed extract containing about 16–20 per cent of aescin (escin), the active component of the herb, is as effective as wearing compression stockings.

Recent research has suggested that beta-aescin (beta-aescin) may be a candidate for use in anti-leukaemic drugs. German research into a combination of aescin and troxerutin, a flavanol, has been developed for treating inner-ear perfusion problems. And encouraging results have demonstrated the potential use of an extract in anti-wrinkle cosmetics.

Cautions: Properly processed horse-chestnut seed extract is generally considered safe. However, raw horse chestnut's seeds, leaves, bark and flowers contain esculin, which is poisonous to animals (including humans), so home-made preparations of the herb should not be used. The extract can cause some side-effects, including itching, nausea and gastrointestinal upset.

Aloe vera

Botanical name *Aloe vera*
Family Aspholdelaceae

Description: Aloe vera is one of 250 species of aloes worldwide. Aloes are indigenous to eastern, southern and northern Africa and Madagascar and have been introduced into the West Indies and other tropical countries, where they grow wild. Aloes have also naturalized and flourish in the Mediterranean basin, with a natural range spanning Algeria, Morocco, Tunisia, and the Canary and Madeira Islands. Aloe vera is a perennial, semi-tropical succulent, with strong, fibrous roots and numerous thick and fleshy, serrated green to grey-green leaves (when grown commercially, the plants are harvested every six to eight weeks by removing three to four leaves per plant).

Parts used: Leaves' gel and juice

History: Sumerian tablets dated 2200 BCE, found in the city of Nippur, show that aloe vera's leaf was used as a laxative. By 1550 BCE, the Egyptian *Ebers Papyrus* tells us that the leaf was ground up, mixed with other medicinal components and boiled, then used in 12 healing formulas, both internally and externally. Around 400 BCE the sap was boiled down for domestic use and exported via Arab traders throughout western Asia. Concurrently the plant came to be known as the 'silent healer' by Hindus, and the 'harmonic remedy' by ancient Chinese physicians. It was (and is) grown and used in India as a healing agent both internally and externally.

Main therapeutic properties: The plant is mainly used for skin products and the digestive system and is antidiarrhoeal (the latex), antimicrobial (the gel and latex), antiretroviral and antiviral (gel), astringent (gel), bactericidal (gel), detoxifying (gel and latex), emollient (gel), fungicidal (gel), anti-inflammatory (gel and latex), laxative (purgative), stimulant (latex), skin-regenerative (gel), stomachic and tonic (juice), vermifuge (latex) and vulnerary (gel). The juice is an edible treatment.

Aloe vera's clear gel contains Vitamins A, B_1, B_2, B_{12}, C and E; and the minerals calcium, chromium, copper, magnesium, manganese, potassium, sodium chloride and zinc. It also contains 20 out of 22 essential amino acids.

Traditionally, and primarily, aloe's latex was used as a laxative and vermifuge; later it was used for constipation and haemorrhoids, as well as for pre- and post-operative cleansing.

The gel of aloe vera has been used externally to treat cuts, burns, skin wounds and sores, and ulcers and eczema, though its wound-healing efficacy is controversial. It may help some people with ulcerative colitis (an inflammatory bowel disease), although abdominal cramps and diarrhoea have been reported with oral use.

There is good scientific evidence for the use of aloe extract to treat genital herpes and psoriasis, and of aloe lotion (applied topically) to treat dandruff. Aloe is also used in hundreds of skin products as a moisturizer, including lotions and sunblocks. Aloe vera is an exceptional plant in that it continues to release oxygen and absorb carbon dioxide in the dark, making it suitable for growing in bedrooms.

More research is required, but there is evidence for aloe's use in treating cankers. Research in China in 2008 and in Taiwan in 2003 indicates that aloe may reduce the risk of and help treat lung cancer. Oral aloe may also help type-2 diabetes, as is shown by studies undertaken in Mexico in 2007 and Korea in 2009. A polysaccharide from aloe leaf rind has also been found to impair the ability of viruses (including retroviruses like HIV) to infect healthy T-cells.

The plant has an analgesic action, producing at least six antiseptic agents, among which lupeol and salicylic acid in the juice are effective painkillers. Medicinally, aloe's anti-inflammatory fatty acids, cholesterol and phytosterols and campersterol are thought to assist in skin ailments and digestive conditions.

The US Food and Drug Administration (FDA) has approved aloe as a natural food flavouring. Canada has approved it as an over-the-counter laxative, France as traditional medicine and the German Commission E as an over-the-counter drug. Aloe also appears in the Japanese and British Pharmacopoeias.

Cautions: The topical use of aloe vera is not associated with significant side-effects, although it may affect those with allergies to the onion family. During pregnancy, oral use is not recommended, and the dried juice of aloe leaves should not be consumed by mothers who are breastfeeding.

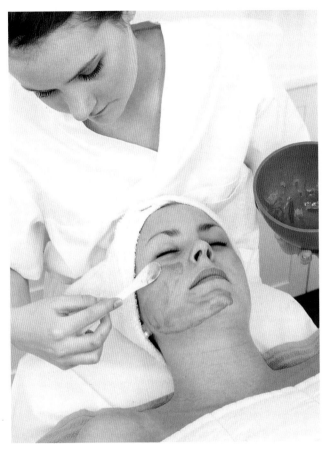

One of the primary uses of aloe vera is for skin products because of its bacteria-fighting and skin-regenerative properties.

With chronic use or abuse, a potassium deficiency may develop. Diarrhoea caused by the laxative effect of oral use of aloe vera can decrease the absorption of many drugs. It should not be taken by those with irritable bowel syndrome (IBS) or haemorrhoids. Diabetics should be cautious about taking oral aloe vera, which may lower blood glucose levels and interfere with therapy.

Angelica

Botanical name *Angelica sinensis*

Family Apiaceae

Description: Angelica is a member of the parsley, carrot and celery family. *A. sinensis* is native to China and Japan, where it is now cultivated. It is a perennial aromatic herb that may grow as tall as 2.5 m (8 ft). Its small white flowers are arranged in groups of flat, umbrella-like clusters that bloom in midsummer. It has thick, yellowish-brown branched roots that have many medicinal uses.

Parts used: Rhizomes, part of the roots.

History: Known as 'Chinese angelica' or *dong quai* in traditional Chinese medicine, angelica is one of the most popular plants for women and has been used in China for thousands of years, as well as in Korean and Japanese medicine. It has been called 'female ginseng', based on its use for gynaecological disorders and cardiovascular and blood conditions. In the late 1800s an extract called Eumenol became popular in Europe as a treatment for gynaecological complaints, leading to modern investigation and research into this subject.

In esoteric terms, angelica's root powder, also known as 'Holy Ghost root', is widely thought to be powerful guardian and healer and to provide strength to women. It has been used by some to ward off evil and bring good luck in health and family matters.

Main therapeutic properties: Angelica is an unusual vegetarian source of Vitamin B_{12}, as well as of phytosterols, flavonoids and numerous other useful components. It has analgesic, anti-inflammatory, antispasmodic and sedative effects.

Angelica is still widely used in traditional Chinese and Korean medicine for gynaecological ailments, such as dysmenorrhoea and uterine bleeding, and in premenstrual-syndrome formulas, as well as for menopausal problems, fatigue, mild anaemia, high blood pressure and as a tonic. It is also used as an aphrodisiac.

It may improve menopausal hot flushes and cramps, dizziness, blurred vision, sleeplessness, nerve debility and

osteoporosis. However, there have been mixed scientific results regarding the phytoestrogens that angelica may contain, and it is not in itself a replacement for oestrogen. Its ability to relieve menstrual difficulties may come from its power to subdue spasms in the internal organs. Chinese research has discovered that *dong quai* stimulates the production of oxygen-carrying red blood cells throughout the body, thus increasing energy and fighting fatigue.

Cautions: Fair-skinned individuals may become more sensitive to sunlight because Angelica root contains 'psoralens'. Do not use angelica if you are pregnant, breastfeeding or you suffer from chronic diarrhoea or abdominal bloating. Men with prostate cancer and women with endometriosis, breast cancer or uterine or ovarian cancers should also not take angelica. Angelica should not be taken two weeks before or after surgery.

Chamomile (Roman and Blue)

Botanical names *Anthemis nobilis* and *Matricaria recutita*

Family Asteraceae

Description: Wild chamomile is now naturalized on almost every continent of the world. Roman chamomile is a perennial ground-cover plant less than 23 cm (9 in) tall, with spreading daisy-like white flowers with a yellow disc floret. Walking on it releases its lovely fragrance and encourages its growth. Blue chamomile is a hardy annual that grows up to 50 cm (20 in) tall, with similar small flower heads. The entire *M. recutita* plant has a pleasantly characteristic aroma described as a pineapple or apple scent, and a bitter flavour.

Parts used: Flowers, oil.

History: The name chamomile (also spelled camomile) is derived from the Greek *chamamimēlon*, meaning 'earth-apple', because of the plants' apple-like scent. Ancient Egyptians dedicated it to their gods (the sun god Ra in particular), calling it the 'herb of the sun', and valued it over all other herbs for its healing qualities. They used it for the treatment of ague (acute fever). The Romans used the herb in beverages, as a tonic and a blood purifier. In the Middle Ages, Roman chamomile was one of the 'nine sacred herbs' of the Anglo-Saxons, known as *maythen*, and was also an ingredient of several love potions.

The discovery of blue chamomile's remedial azulene content, dates back to the 15th century, from the azure-blue distillate obtained in the production of its essential oil; it is this that gives it its name, too. During the 16th century chamomile was used to cure cramp, spasms and convulsions, while in the 17th century the herb was used to stop pain and treat ulcers. The flowers have always been used herbally, generally consumed as a bitter herbal infusion, but in recent times chamomile has mainly been grown to produce essential oil. In Germany, chamomile is so popular that it is known as *Alles zutraut*, meaning 'capable of anything'.

Main therapeutic properties: Both Roman and blue chamomiles are anodyne, anti-inflammatory, antispasmodic, nervine, sedative, stomachic, tonic and a vasodilator. However, *M. recutita* is predominantly anti-inflammatory, as well as analgesic, anti-allergenic, antiseptic, carminative, cholagogue and diaphoretic; whereas *A. nobilis* is a gentler remedy for various problems of the digestive system and a sedative and nervine, and is especially suited to young children.

Roman chamomile is used internally as a tea for anxiety, insomnia, gout and sciatica, and for gastrointestinal

*Blue Chamomile (*Matricaria recutita*), the magical flower that produces cooling and healing blue azulene during distillation.*

conditions. In particular, *M. recutita* is added to baths and applied externally as a wash or compress for skin inflammations, sunburn and other burns. It is a relaxant for tired, aching muscles and is skin-softening.

Blue chamomile has been used for mouth ulcers resulting from cancer treatment, and an investigatory study in America in 2007 has been undertaken into its anti-cancer effects as a herbal remedy in the management of cancer patients. In 2008, Japanese research also clearly suggested that daily consumption of chamomile tea with meals could help prevent the progress of hyperglycaemia and diabetic complications.

conditions such as indigestion, flatulence and diarrhoea. Research shows that the apigenin content of this well-known bedtime calming and relaxing tea is an effective sedative.

Traditionally chamomile tea has been used externally to stimulate wound-healing and prevent infections, and it continues to be used topically for skin

The German Commission E notes that the oil extract of blue chamomile is anti-inflammatory and anti-fever, and studies have verified that several compounds, including bisabolol and chamazulene, contribute to this activity. Chamazulene is highly anti-inflammatory. Bisabolol has been used for hundreds of years in cosmetics because of its perceived skin-healing properties; it is known to have anti-irritant, anti-inflammatory, antifungal, antimicrobial and bactericidal properties. It has a weak, sweet floral aroma and is used in flavourings and various fragrances.

Blue chamomile's sweet, fruity, herbaceous essential oils and Roman chamomile's bright, crisp, fruity, herbaceous essential oils may both be used in aromatherapy for abscesses, allergies, arthritis, boils, colic, cuts, cystitis, dermatitis, dysmenorrhoea, earache, flatulence, headaches, inflamed skin, insect bites, insomnia, nausea, neuralgia, premenstrual syndrome, rheumatism, sores, sprains, strains, stress and wounds.

Cautions: Do not drink chamomile tea or use the oil of either species if you are allergic to the daisy plant family. Do not use chamomile if taking anticoagulants. Avoid chamomile when pregnant and breastfeeding, and don't give to young children. Be aware that both chamomiles may cause drowsiness that could interfere with driving a car or operating machinery.

While this is extremely rare, very large doses of chamomile may cause nausea and vomiting; even more rarely, rashes may occur. The essential oil may cause dermatitis in some individuals. It is not recommended for those with hay fever, asthma or high blood pressure, heart or blood-vessel diseases.

Single flowers of blue chamomile are the strongest medicinally, but contain a potent alkali that can in large doses harm the stomach and bowel lining tissues; the twin-flowered form is usually preferred.

*A 14th-century illustration of 'Chamamilla' (*Matricaria chamomilla*) in an Italian manuscript.*

37

Astragalus

Botanical name *Astragalus membranaceus*

Family Papilionaceae

Description: Astragalus belongs to a large genus of around 2,000 species of herbs and small shrubs belonging to the leguminous (or pea) family, which is now divided into Papilionaceae, Mimosaceae and Caesalpiniaceae families. It is native to Mongolia and north-eastern China and is grown commercially in the latter region and cultivated in the US. Astragalus is a short-lived, sprawling, perennial flowering plant, with pale-yellow blooms producing pea-like pods of seeds in late summer of its first year. Although ornamental, the plant is usually grown for its medicinal value. Herbalists can harvest the root after two or more years of growth, but because each year the existing plants grow more woody, they should be harvested by the fourth year.

Parts used: Roots.

History: The herb was first recorded in the *Shén Nóng Běn Cǎo Jing*, a Chinese book of medicinal herbs written between 300 BCE and 200 CE. Its Chinese name, *huang-qi*, means 'yellow energy or leader', and the root of *A. membranaceus* or *A. membranaceus* var. *mongholicus* is one of the 50 fundamental herbs used in traditional Chinese medicine.

Main therapeutic properties: Astragalus is chiefly an adaptogen, immuno-stimulant and diuretic. The plant is also antibacterial, anti-carcinogenic, antipyretic, cardiotonic, hypoglycaemic, hypotensive, a pectoral remedy, a uterine tonic and a vasodilator.

Extensively employed in modern herbal practice in China, astragalus has been used traditionally to revive *qi* (vital energy), strengthen the immune system and speed up the healing of wounds and injuries. It is taken as a tea or soup, made usually from the dried roots, or in a formula combined with other medicinal herbs.

Primarily, it is a tonic for enhancing metabolism, digestion and organ functions, such as those of the lungs, adrenal glands and gastrointestinal tract. It is also used in prescriptions for general weakness, lack of appetite, shortness of

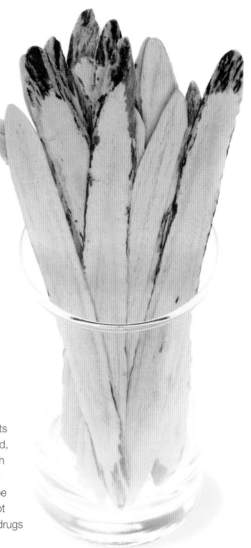

breath, colds and flu, stomach ulcers and diabetes.

Still widely used in China for chronic hepatitis, *A. membranaceus* combined with peony (*Paeonia lactiflora*) has been found in recent research to be effective in animals as a protective liver treatment. And American studies in the 1990s showed the potential benefits of *A. membranaceus* combined with glossy privet (*Ligustrum lucidum*) as a supplementary cancer therapy, particularly for prostate cancer.

Cautions: Although the side-effects of astragalus are not documented, due to its use in combination with other herbs, it is considered safe for most adults, but should not be used by pregnant women. Do not take astragalus with prescribed drugs without professional supervision.

Marigold

Botanical name *Calendula officinalis*

Family Asteraceae

Description: Marigold belongs to a genus of about 12–20 species of annual or perennial herbaceous plants in the daisy family. It is native from the area of Macaronesia's five archipelagos in the North Atlantic Ocean, east through the Mediterranean region to Iran, with a range over southern Europe. A versatile, cultivated, pungent herb that is easily grown in sunny locations and, often self-sown, it is a gardener's fast-blooming favourite. The spicy-scented flowerheads range in colour from pastels to bright yellows and oranges, and are produced from spring, throughout summer and well into the autumn season in temperate climates.

Parts used: Flowerheads/petals.

History: The genus name *Calendula* derives from the Latin *kalendae*, meaning 'first day of the month'. Its common name of marigold refers either to the Virgin Mary or to its old Saxon name of *Ymbglidegold*, which means 'it turns with the sun'. It was used in ancient Greek, Roman, Arabic and Indian cultures as a medicinal herb. The anti-ageing properties of marigold-infused oil were known to the ancient Egyptians and may be related to the flower's high content of carotenes, phytosterols, polyphenols and essential fatty acids.

Main therapeutic properties: The *Calendula* flower is antihaemorrhagic, while the flowers and leaves are antiphlogistic, antiseptic, antispasmodic, aperient, astringent, cholagogue, diaphoretic, emmenagogue, stimulant and vulnerary. Marigold is used for the treatment of skin disorders and pain, and as a bactericide, antiseptic and anti-inflammatory. It is used internally to accelerate wound-healing and to stimulate the liver, gall bladder and uterus, while soothing digestive disorders and clearing infections.

In a suspension or a tincture, marigold is used topically to treat acne, reducing inflammation, controlling bleeding and soothing irritated tissue. The flowers are also used in cosmetics, skin lotions and toiletries such as hair-lightening shampoo, especially for redheads.

Calendula leaves, blossoms and buds have been used in creams and lotions for the treatment of minor cuts, wounds, burns and abrasions for more than 150 years. The crushed stems are used to prepare corns and warts for easy removal.

Cautions: Do not use marigold if you are allergic to the daisy family (Asteraceae). It should also be avoided internally during pregnancy.

Green tea

Botanical name *Camellia sinensis*

Family Theaceae

Description: Botanical evidence shows that Assam in India and southern China are the only two regions in the world with native tea plants, although today *C. sinensis* is cropped throughout Asia, parts of the Middle-East and Africa. This small evergreen, multi-branched shrub with rough grey bark grows up to 9 m (30 ft) high in the wild. The slightly drooping, fragrant white flowers are single or grouped in twos and threes; they give rise to smooth, flattened, rounded, three-celled capsules with a solitary seed in each cell, the size of a small nut.

Parts used: Leaves, shoots (tips only), oil (perfumery/food flavouring).

History: Archaeological evidence suggests that 'tea' made from tea leaves infused in boiling water was consumed by people as early as 500,000 years ago. Southern China became the biggest cultivated commercial tea production area in the world, followed by Assam (India), where tea is described as a gift from the Buddha, while in China its discovery is attributed to the Emperor Shen Nung in 2737 BCE.

The Classic of Tea by the Chinese Lo Yu was written in 780 CE, and in 801 CE tea was introduced to Japan, where it played a dominant role in Buddhist rituals. Each aspect of the elaborate Japanese tea ceremony, *sado*, is linked to aspects of Zen Buddhism. It is also recounted that a 10th-century Sanskrit medical text from Assam, called *Nidana*, mentions leaves called *shamapatra* from which *shampani* was made, being used as a medicine against coughs, colds, drowsiness, headaches, and so on.

'Tea' was first mentioned in European literature in 1559 by a Venetian author, and by an Englishman in 1615. The earliest reference to 'tea-drinking' in India is found in the writings of a Dutch seafarer who recorded tea being both eaten and drunk there in 1598. By 1657 tea was commonly served in England's coffee houses. Notoriously, come 16 December 1773, American colonists protested against the British import tax on tea by staging the Boston Tea Party.

Carl Linnaeus named the plant *Camellia* after the Reverend Georg Joseph Kamel (1661–1706), a Czech-born Jesuit priest and famous botanist and missionary to the Philippines. *Sinensis* means 'Chinese'.

Today, hundreds of millions of people around the world drink tea. The three main varieties of tea – green, black and oolong – come from the same plant, but differ in their modes of processing. Green tea is made from unfermented leaves, oolong tea leaves are partially fermented and black tea leaves are fully fermented.

Main therapeutic properties: Many research studies have suggested that green tea has diverse health benefits as an astringent, antioxidant (100 times more powerful than Vitamin C and 25 times more powerful than Vitamin E), cardiotonic, diuretic, stimulant and virucide. It is also used for flatulence, for regulating body temperature and blood sugar, as a digestive and to augment mental processes.

In traditional Chinese medicine (where it is considered to be one of the 50 fundamental herbs) and in traditional Indian medicine, green tea has been used to treat asthma, angina pectoris, peripheral vascular disease and coronary artery disease.

Today, green tea is usually brewed and drunk as a revivifying beverage or used as extracts. The tea and its extracts may protect against certain heart diseases (atherosclerosis), particularly coronary artery disease, and may lower LDL or 'bad' cholesterol and raise HDL or 'good' cholesterol.

Its polyphenols and epigallocatechin gallate (EGCG) component have been used to prevent and treat a variety of cancers, including breast cancer. Research on EGCG *in vitro* has also shown that it can reverse methicillin resistance in bacteria like *Staphylococcus aureus*, which – if confirmed – would mean that an intake of green-tea extract would enhance the effectiveness of methicillin treatment against some resistant bacteria, such as MRSA.

Recently, green tea has been used to protect the skin from sun damage via its anti-inflammatory and anticarcinogenic properties (polyphenols), both internally as a beverage and, on its way, externally in the form of a spray; its counterpart, white tea, is also employed in skin products.

Green tea also appears to protect the liver from the damaging effects of toxic substances such as alcohol, and against hepatic tumours (in animals). It may aid Crohn's disease and ulcerative colitis, and may also assist diabetics by helping to regulate glucose in the body.

Studies suggest that green tea may aid weight loss by boosting the metabolism and thus burning fat. It is reported that it can help prevent tooth decay. The tea may also possess the ability to destroy and kill bacteria and prevent food poisoning.

Cautions: Although green tea is generally recognized as safe by the FDA, it should be avoided by pregnant and breastfeeding women. Its caffeine content may cause sleep disorders in nursing infants and the tea has been linked to impaired iron metabolism and microcytic anaemia in infants.

Those with heart problems, kidney disorders, stomach ulcers and psychological disorders (particularly anxiety) should not take green tea. If drunk to excess, its caffeine content may cause insomnia, and other medicinal interference.

Tea is native to southern China and Assam in India but today is cropped on tea plantations throughout Asia, parts of the Middle-East and Africa.

Black cohosh

Botanical name *Cimicifuga racemosa*

Family Ranunculaceae

Description: Black cohosh is a glabrous herbaceous perennial plant that is native to Canada and also grows in eastern parts of the US as far south as Florida, and it is cultivated in Europe. It grows from a rhizome to reach 25–60 cm (7–18 in) tall. The distinctly sweet-smelling white flowers each have six petals and are produced in late spring and early summer. The fruit is a dry follicle containing several seeds.

Parts used: Rhizomes, roots.

History: Black cohosh has an extensive

history of use by the Native Americans, who revered it as a specific and multi-remedy for a host of common ailments and conditions. It acquired its alternative common name of 'black snakeroot' from its use as a rattlesnake-bite antidote. The Delaware, Iroquois and Cherokee are all said to have used it to treat gynaecological problems and as an anti-inflammatory for rheumatism. It was also valued as a tonic and diuretic.

Black cohosh was traditionally a family remedy applicable to all ages, with uses ranging from the treatment of fatigue, sore throat and kidney ailments to respiratory infections and depression; it was also a 'root syrup' for children's whooping cough, as well as being used in cases of St Vitus's dance, a disease associated with rheumatic fever that is characterized by rapid, uncoordinated jerking movements, mainly of the face, feet and hands.

Main therapeutic properties: The plant's root is mainly used for women's complaints. It is an abortifacient, alterative, antidote, anti-inflammatory, antirheumatic, antispasmodic, antitussive, astringent, cardiotonic, diaphoretic, diuretic, emmenagogue, expectorant, hypnotic, sedative, tonic and vasodilator.

Also known as 'squaw root', black cohosh is now recognized worldwide for its ability to assist women's menstrual cycle problems, and has been used for menstrual irregularities, premenstrual syndrome, dysmenorrhoea, uterine fibroids and to induce labour. Today it is *the* modern menopause herb, being effective in the reduction of the frequency and intensity of hot flushes and night sweats, and is used to treat vaginal dryness and other menopausal symptoms, as well as vertigo, palpitation and tinnitus. Research also suggests that it may help to avert osteoporosis.

It is promoted as a natural alternative to hormone replacement therapy (HRT) in the menopause. On scientific comparison of the herb's effects and those of oestrogens, a low number of side-effects were reported, including headaches, gastric complaints, heaviness in the legs and weight problems.

Cautions: The long-term effects of this herb are unknown. As a precaution, black cohosh should not be taken by pregnant or lactating women. Although it promotes menstrual flow, it contains tannin, which inhibits iron absorption. It may cause headaches and stomach discomfort, but rarely any harm to the liver. It should not be used without medical supervision.

Echinacea

Botanical name *Echinacea purpurea*

Family Asteraceae

Description: Echinacea or purple cone-flower is a drought-tolerant perennial plant that is native to the US. It has rich purple, composite flowers. The mature, slightly aromatic, sweetish-tasting rhizomes are lifted after four years to be cut and dried for medicinal use. *E. purpurea* is often combined with the fresh root of *E. angustifolia* and *E. pallida* in remedial formulae.

Parts used: Roots, flowering aerial parts (occasionally).

History: Echinacea is traditionally used for a range of infections and malignancies, and is one of several species that were originally used by at least 14 Native American tribes for respiratory ailments and infections. The Plains Indians used it to treat snake bites and other natural poisons, especially wounds. It was also used by the Dakotas as a veterinary medicine for their horses.

In the early 1900s the American medical research group known as the 'Eclectics' – doctors who used primarily botanical medicines and practised with a philosophy of 'alignment with nature' – documented and used echinacea's anti-inflammatory properties. It was found to be effective against liver, stomach and intestinal inflammation, and gained positive reports for treating boils, poison oak, syphilis and gangrene.

In 1887, echinacea was introduced into US medical practice, and *E. angustifolia* was listed in the US Pharmacopeia-National Formulary (1916–50).

During the 1930s the herb's popularity waned and was overtaken by new discoveries in pharmaceutical drugs. At this time echinacea began to be grown and used extensively in Europe, and in Germany in particular research work was begun by Dr Gerhard Madaus. Through a mix-up in seed collection in the States, however, *E. purpurea* instead of *E. angustifolia* became the focus of his modern pharmacological studies.

Main therapeutic properties: *E. purpurea* regained its popularity and is now the most effective detoxicant in Western herbal medicine for the circulatory, lymphatic and respiratory systems. It has also been adopted by Ayurvedic medicine. It is an adaptogen, alterative, excellent antiseptic, mild antibiotic, depurative, digestive, immuno-stimulant and sialagogue.

Echinacea is the now one of the world's most popular herbs and is used principally as an immune-system booster by nourishing the blood, improving circulation and stimulating white blood-cell activity. It is sometimes used in combination products thought to stimulate the immune system. Published evidence supports its benefit when taken as a preventive remedy or at the first signs of sickness, in decreasing the incidence and duration of the common cold. It can also prevent staphylococcus and strep infections.

Cautions: Reported adverse effects are generally uncommon and minor. They include abdominal discomfort, nausea, sore throat, rash, drowsiness, headache, dizziness and muscle aches. Do not use Echinacea if you are allergic to the daisy family (Asteraceae). It is not recommended for children or for breastfeeding or pregnant women. Its use is discouraged for autoimmune diseases or (HIV) infection.

Horsetail

Botanical name *Equisetum arvense*

Family Equisetaceae

Description: Horsetail is a unique perennial plant that is widely distributed throughout the temperate northern hemisphere, including Asia, North America and Europe. It is found in or near watery areas such as marshes, streams or rivers, and in open fields, arable land, hedgerows, roadsides and waste places, usually on moist soil.

Parts used: Aerial parts, stems.

History: The name *Equisetum* derives from the Latin *equus*, meaning 'horse', and *seta*, meaning 'bristle'. The plant was traditionally tied to horse and livestock tails to ward off flies.

The ancient Greek physician Galen recommended horsetail and it was subsequently used by the Romans and various other cultures worldwide. The Greeks used it as a wound-healer, a diuretic and to staunch bleeding. Iraqis employed it as a folk remedy for kidney and bladder problems, arthritis and bleeding ulcers. Having proven effectual for the spitting of blood, in Turkey it was used to treat tuberculosis (consumption).

In the New World, Cherokee natives used horsetail to treat the kidneys. The Chippewa tribe decocted the stems to treat dysuria and the Potowatami people used it to make a diuretic infusion to aid kidney function.

In 17th-century Britain the herbalist Nicholas Culpeper regarded horsetail as being beneficial as a blood coagulant (antihaemorrhagic), and to treat ulcers, kidney stones, wounds and skin inflammation. In the 19th century, horsetail's repertoire was extended to gonorrhoea, prostatitis and urinary incontinence. In the 20th century it was found to be beneficial for dropsy, bedwetting and enlarged prostate.

Main therapeutic properties: Horsetail is now considered an anodyne, antihaemorrhagic, antiseptic, astringent, cardiac, carminative, diaphoretic, diuretic, galactogogue, haemostatic, nervine and vulnerary.

Its main therapeutic component is silicic acid, a mineral that strengthens and tightens connective tissue, which makes its herbal tea particularly valuable for joint injuries, rheumatic damage, skin disorders and gout. It can also be used to aid in the repair of bone, skin and connective tissue.

Horsetail's component equisetonin relieves fluid retention (oedema) and aids the treatment of swellings and urinary-tract infections. However, its equisetic acid is a heart and nerve sedative that is poisonous when taken in abnormally high doses.

In traditional Chinese Medicine horsetail is used for bloodshot eyes and conjunctivitis; and, because it is rich in trace minerals, it is considered a superb semi-regular tonic.

Cautions: Horsetail is generally safe for adults at the recommended dose (not when pregnant), but the correct species must be used. However, it may interact with existing prescription drugs.

On occasion, horsetail can be hazardously high in selenium, which may cause birth defects. Do not use it in pregnancy or if you are weak, have excessive dryness or frequent urination. Check that horsetail products do not contain the enzyme thiaminase, which destroys Vitamin B.

Meadowsweet

Botanical name *Filipendula ulmaria*

Family Rosaceae

Description: Meadowsweet is an aromatic, hardy herbaceous perennial shrub that is native throughout most of Europe. It grows in damp meadows, marshes and ditches, at the margins of ponds and river banks and in open woodlands. It has fragrant, small, whitish-green to creamy yellowish-white flowers.

Parts used: Whole plant, flowers.

History: Meadowsweet is one of the best-known wild flowers, with a long history of herbal use. It was noted for its therapeutic stomachic effects by the famous 17th-century herbalist Nicholas Culpeper.

Although Hippocrates used willow (*Salix alba*) powder, it was the Italian Rafaele Piria who in 1838 first succeeded in obtaining salicylic acid in its pure state from meadowsweet. In 1899 a new drug (acetylsalicylic acid) was formulated by the drug company Bayer, and was originally extracted from meadowsweet flower petals and some unopened buds. They called it aspirin – the name being based on meadowsweet's earlier Latin name *Spiraea*.

Main therapeutic properties:

Meadowsweet contains useful minerals (calcium, magnesium, sodium and sulphur), as well as salicylic acid and several as-yet-unnamed compounds. It is an alterative, analgesic, anticarcinogenic, anticoagulant, anti-inflammatory, antiseptic, astringent, bactericidal, depurative, diuretic, febrifuge, relaxant, sedative, stomachic and tonic.

Herbally, meadowsweet's astringent action, combined with its nutritive profile, is considered to make it safe, mild and effective for diarrhoea in children. However, it is more usually employed as a digestive remedy, for analgesia and in a supportive role for the common cold. The herb's salicylic acid also makes it useful in treating influenza, respiratory-tract infections, arthritis, rheumatism and fevers.

Being renowned for its anti-inflammatory and analgesic properties,

meadowsweet is also regarded – when used as an oil and lotion in massage – as being remarkably helpful to muscle and joint conditions, providing both quick relief and long-term benefits.

Russian research (1990) has found meadowsweet flowers to contain a Heparin-like anticoagulant, and to have antioxidant properties that may be used preventively and for the treatment of free-radical pathological conditions. Its compounds have also been studied for cancers and for cervical dysplasia.

Most recently (2007), French researchers have shown meadowsweet extract to significantly improve the quality of skin that is prone to acne.

Cautions: The FDA has classified meadowsweet as a 'herb of undefined safety'. However, it should not be used for patients with sulphite or salicylate sensitivity, and only with caution by those with asthma. Avoid using meadowsweet during pregnancy and lactation.

Ginkgo

Botanical name *Ginkgo biloba*

Family Ginkgoaceae

Description: The ginkgo tree is a conifer that can reach a height of 40 m (130 ft) and live for as long as 1,000 years. It is native to China, Japan and Korea, with plantations being cultivated in China, France and South Carolina in the US; it also grows in Iran. Its extraordinary leaves, which are bright green in summer, turning gold before dropping in the autumn, are fan-shaped, leathery and smooth, with radiating veins.

Parts used: Leaves, fruit, seeds.

History: External medicinal use of the ginkgo leaf (*bai-guo-ye*) was first mentioned in China in Lan Mao's *Dian Nan Ben Cao* in 1436. Internal use of the leaves was first recorded in Liu Wen-Tai's imperial commissioned work, *Ben Cao Pin Hui Jing Yao*, in 1505.

Main therapeutic properties: Ginkgo leaves are anti-allergenic, anti-asthmatic, antioxidant, antivertigo, circulatory, ophthalmic and a brain tonic. The fruit is anticarcinogenic, astringent, bactericidal, fungicidal, digestive, expectorant, sedative and a vermifuge; the pulp of the macerated fruit is used in the treatment of pulmonary tuberculosis, asthma and bronchitis.

The cooked seed is antitussive, astringent and sedative, and is used in the treatment of asthma, phlegmatic coughs and urinary incontinence; it also stabilizes the cellular process in the formation of sperm. The raw seed is toxic, containing a chemical known as ginkgotoxin that can cause seizures, but anticarcinogenic activity has also been reported.

Ginkgo is an ancient remedy that the Chinese have used for 5,000 years to improve the circulation of blood to the brain. It expands blood vessels, improves peripheral arterial circulation and inhibits clot formation; its flavonoids, including quercetin, are extremely potent scavengers of free radicals. It is particularly useful to the brain for its oxygenating tonic effect, which increases energy and ameliorates the symptoms of cerebral insufficiency, which include anxiety, difficulty in concentrating, absent-mindedness, confusion, lassitude, depressive moods and anxiety.

Today, in Europe and the US, ginkgo supplements are among the best-selling phytomedicines, and an estimated 10 per cent of people with dementia use the herbal extract to improve memory or to treat Alzheimer's disease. However, recent research has been disappointing regarding its use for dementia and it is likely that further research in this area will be required.

Ginkgo is also used for varicose veins, to decrease claudication (leg pain caused by narrowing arteries) and to treat tinnitus and dizziness. Eye disorders have also responded to treatment.

Cautions: Ordinarily, Ginkgo is ideal for long-term use as it generally produces no side-effects. However, large doses can cause diarrhoea, irritability, restlessness, nausea and vomiting. Minor rare side-effects have included stomach or intestinal upsets, headaches and allergic skin reactions. Gingko may interact with existing prescription drugs. Its use when pregnant or breastfeeding is not recommended due to lack of research.

Devil's claw

Botanical name *Harpagophytum procumbens*

Family Pedaliaceae

Description: Devil's claw is a prostrate, sprawling perennial vine with trumpet-shaped flowers and spiky seedpods. It is found chiefly in eastern and south-eastern Namibia and southern Botswana, and is also native to the deserts and dry plains of southern Africa.

Parts used: Tubers.

History: The discovery of devil's claw and its subsequent use in Western medicine stem from G. H. Mehnert, a German colonial soldier who eventually became a farmer. He learned about the herb in Namibia from healers of the San and Nama tribespeople, and made its merits known to the public in 1904. Devil's claw was first exported to Germany, then introduced into Europe in 1953. During the 1970s, scientists demonstrated its efficacy for arthritic treatment. The herb was traditionally regarded as a panacea for all ills, though only 'whole extracts' (not isolated parts of it) have the desired therapeutic effect.

Main therapeutic properties: The key components of devil's claw are iridoid glycosides, which may be responsible for its anti-inflammatory and analgesic properties, which German research in 1976 found comparable to the anti-arthritis drug phenylbutazine.

Other properties of the herb have been listed as analgesic, anti-arrhythmic, antibacterial, anti-inflammatory, antirheumatic, bitter tonic, cholagogue, diuretic, febrifuge, hypotensive, laxative/purgative, sedative and utero-contractant.

In Aboriginal medicine (and often further afield) devil's claw has reportedly been used for fevers, blood diseases, blood purification, bleeding gums (leading to gingivitis), coughs, diabetes, diarrhoea, gonorrhoea, gout, lower back pain, lumbago, pain in pregnant women and for syphilis.

Devil's claw acts as a stimulating appetizer, helps with the digestive system (heartburn, peptic ulcers, constipation), hypertension and raised cholesterol. It is used to treat diseases of the gall bladder, kidneys, liver, pancreas, small joints and tuberculosis. Externally the ointment can heal ulcers, boils, sores and wounds.

In Western medicine, devil's claw is mainly used for joint pain, such as arthritis, osteoarthritis, rheumatoid arthritis and gout; for soft-tissue pain (with proven efficacy for lower back pain); and to reduce menopausal symptoms. It appears to work like cortisone, without the unpleasant side-effects. The British Pharmacopoeia recognizes devil's claw as having analgesic, sedative and diuretic properties, best used for chronic rather than acute pain treatment. The German Commission E lists the herb for treating loss of appetite, dyspeptic complaints and in supportive therapy for bone and joint disorders and pain.

Cautions: The safety of devil's claw in treating young children, nursing women or those with severe liver or kidney disease is not known and the herb should therefore be avoided. Individuals with stomach ulcers or gastritis and pregnant women should also refrain from using it. Those with gallstones should consult a physician before taking it. It is contraindicated with the use of certain prescription drugs, anticoagulants, heart conditions, high blood pressure and for diabetics. The herb may cause an allergic reaction or mild gastrointestinal side-effects, such as diarrhoea and nausea, as well as headaches, ringing in the ears and taste disturbances.

Goldenseal root

Botanical name *Hydrastis canadensis*

Family Ranunculaceae

Description: Goldenseal is a perennial woodland herb with greenish-white flowers, and fibrous rootlets growing out of long rhizomes. It is native to south-eastern Canada and the north-eastern US.

Parts used: Rhizomes and rootlets.

History: Native Americans of the Cherokee, Catawba, Iroquois and Kickapoo tribes used goldenseal root both as a medicine and as a colouring agent. The Cherokee used it for cancer treatment (it was referred to by Professor Benjamin Smith Barton in his first edition of *Collections for an Essay Towards a Materia Medica of the United States*, 1798), for 'general debility' and 'dyspepsy'. The Iroquois made a root decoction for whooping cough, diarrhoea, liver problems, fever, sour stomach and flatulence, and an emetic for biliousness. Mixed with bear's grease, goldenseal root was applied extensively as an insect repellent. It was also used as a diuretic, an appetite stimulant and as a wash for sore or inflamed eyes, as well as to treat skin diseases, ulcers, arrow wounds and gonorrhoea.

Early settlers adopted these uses and goldenseal root was entered into most 19th-century pharmacopoeias. The 'Eclectics' (see page 48) adopted the herb for gonorrhoea and urinary-tract infections.

By 1919, Finley Ellingwood's *The American Materia Medica, Therapeutics and Pharmacognosy* listed goldenseal as being useful for myriad illnesses, conditions and diseases, ranging from constipation to cerebral engorgements of a chronic character and cirrhosis.

Main therapeutic properties: Goldenseal root is alterative, anticatarrhal, anti-inflammatory, antiseptic, astringent, a bitter tonic, laxative agent and a muscle stimulant. It is used for colds and other respiratory-tract infections. As an astringent, it works against microbial infections and inflammation (bacterial and fungal), gastrointestinal-tract infections, such as colitis and duodenal ulcers, and loss of appetite; also as a topical application for the bladder and rectum.

Goldenseal is applied to wounds and canker lesions, and is used as a mouthwash for sore gums, the mouth and throat. It is also used to treat skin and eye infections, infectious diarrhoea, vaginitis and to stimulate the central nervous system. As a 'bitter', it stimulates the appetite and aids digestion.

Most of the research that is popularly attributed to goldenseal is centred on the small amount of berberine it contains but there is cause for controversy regarding the effects of the plant as a whole. Clinical studies suggest that, while it can benefit certain infections, such as acute infectious diarrhoea and some eye infections, the profound historical and anecdotal use and widely experienced efficacy of the whole herb has yet to be proven.

Cautions: Goldenseal is considered safe for short-term use in adults at the recommended dosages. Rare side-effects may include nausea and vomiting. It should not be used when pregnant or breastfeeding; it may be transferred through breast-milk, causing life-threatening liver problems in nursing and/or jaundiced infants. Those with high blood pressure or other cardiovascular diseases and people on certain antibiotics should not use this herb, so consult your healthcare professional.

St John's wort

Botanical name *Hypericum perforatum*

Family Clusiaceae

Description: St John's wort is a perennial with extensive, stout, creeping rhizomes, yellow-green leaves and bright-yellow flowers. The *Hypericum* species is spread throughout the world, except in desert and arctic regions.

Parts used: Flowering tops, stems and leaves.

History: Legend has it that the herb's common name comes from St John the Baptist, whose feast day at midsummer (24 June) occurs when daylight in Europe is at its longest and the plant is in full bloom. Additionally, the petals resemble a saint's halo, and its red sap is said to symbolize the martyred saint's blood.

The first recorded use by classical herbalists of St John's wort for medicinal purposes dates back 2,400 years ago to ancient Greece, when it was used as a sedative, a nerve tonic, a painkiller for arthritis, menstrual cramping and gastrointestinal problems such as diarrhoea and nausea, as well as for ulcers; it was also a treatment for malaria and a balm for insect bites, burns and wounds.

Main therapeutic properties: The herb is considered to be analgesic, anti-inflammatory, antimalarial, antiseptic, antispasmodic, astringent, cholagogue, digestive, diuretic, expectorant, a nervine, resolvent, sedative, stimulant, vermifuge and vulnerary.

Currently, there is positive scientific evidence for the herb's ability to treat mild to moderate depression; it is also used for anxiety and/or sleep disorders. Hyperforin is believed to be the main active constituent responsible for the antidepressant effects of St John's wort extracts, and is also a known effective treatment for viral infections such as herpes. It may also be helpful in the treatment of alcoholism. In addition, hyperforin has been found to stimulate the release of the neurotransmitter norepinephrine, which has led to speculation that it might alleviate the symptoms of attention-deficit hyperactivity disorder (ADHD).

Maceration of the herb's flowering tops, stems and leaves in a fixed oil makes St John's wort oil excellent for massage to relieve inflammation and muscular pain, especially in the neck, shoulders and back.

There is also a practical homeopathic version of St John's wort formulated in the form of a spray, produced under the guidelines of the homeopathic pharmacopoeia of the United States.

Cautions: St John's wort is generally well tolerated, although it may cause increased sensitivity to sunlight, anxiety, dry mouth, dizziness, gastrointestinal symptoms, fatigue, headache and sexual dysfunction – all of which are said to disappear when the herb has stopped being taken. However, St John's wort has significant interactions with a large number of medicines that are in common use, including prescribed drugs and over-the-counter medicines such as paracetamol. People taking any other medicine should seek advice from a healthcare professional before combining it with St John's wort. It is not recommended for children, or for women who are pregnant or lactating.

Chaga

Botanical name *Inonotus obliquus*
Family Hymenochaetaceae

Description: *I. obliquus*, known as clinker mushroom or by the Russian name of 'chaga', is a parasitic tree fungus (particularly of the birch tree), with the appearance of burnt charcoal or a chunk of clinker. Chaga grows prolifically in eastern and northern Europe, particularly in the birch forests of Russia, as well as in Korea, the northern US and Canada. It is black, with a dark-brown fertile portion, and has pores instead of gills.

Parts used: Fungus.

History: The chaga fungus has been used as a folk medicine in northern Eurasia for millennia. The earliest evidence of human use came from the 5,300-year-old 'Ice Man' mummy (nicknamed Frozen Fritz) discovered in 1991, who wore two walnut-sized pieces of birch fungus drilled through the middle and tied to his left wrist by strands of twisted fur.

The herb was documented in 100 BCE by the Chinese monk Shen Nong in the *Shen Nong Ben Cao Jing*. Since the 16th century there have been countless records of chaga being used in folk and botanical medicine in eastern European countries. However, ears pricked up in the West with the publication of Aleksandr Solzhenitsyn's *Cancer Ward* in 1968, in which a country doctor named Sergei Maslennikov noted that his *muzhik* (peasant) patients rarely contracted cancer because they regularly drank chaga tea.

Main therapeutic properties: Although its forte in Russia is as an anticarcinogenic tool (it has been an approved anti-cancer drug in Russia since 1955), chaga is used elsewhere as a herb mainly for gastric disorders and as an anti-emetic, aperient, cathartic, tonic, antioxidant and immune booster.

This 'king of herbs' is highly prized in Siberia for its antibacterial and disinfecting action, and for its anti-inflammatory properties in the treatment of gastritis and other gastrointestinal-tract diseases and conditions. It is also used as a palliative remedy for tumours found in different locations.

As a folkloric medicine, chaga has been used to treat a wide range of ailments, including digestive and liver cancers, tuberculosis and ulcers, influenza, arthritis, fungal growths, skin ailments, liver and biliary colic caused by gallstones, diabetes and tumour growth, and has a reputation for leading to longevity.

In 1958 Finnish and Russian studies of chaga fungus found it to have highly significant effects against breast cancer, liver cancer, uterine cancer, gastric cancer, hypertension and diabetes. Furthermore, in 2005 it was found that the chaga fungus produces indirect anticarcinogenic effects via immuno-stimulation. Research is ongoing on all these fronts. In January 2008 Korean researchers found that chaga may provide a new therapeutic option in the treatment of liver cancer.

Cautions: Infusions of chaga are not toxic, but sometimes allergic reactions may occur. Increased irritability of the nervous system may result if chaga is used for a long period of time or in high dosages so dietary modifications (food without preservatives, smoked or spicy products; limited consumption of meat and fats of animal origin; no alcohol) are advised during such treatment. Chaga is contraindicated for patients being treated with penicillin or glucose given intravenously. A qualified doctor should be consulted for children under the age of four.

Lavender

Botanical name *Lavandula angustifolia*

Family Lamiaceae

Description: Lavender is a strongly aromatic, small evergreen shrub with pinkish-purple flowers. The genus is native to the western Mediterranean region, primarily the Pyrenees and other mountainous regions of northern Spain. The native range extends south to tropical Africa, the Canary Islands, northern and eastern Africa, southern Europe, Arabia and the south-eastern regions of India.

Parts used: Flowering tops, leaves, essential oil.

History: The plant's herbal use has been documented for 2,500 years. It was used in ancient Egypt as part of the mummification process, as a bath additive in Persia, Greece and Rome and as a perfume by the ancient Egyptians, Phoenicians, Persians and other Arabians.

Lavender's antiseptic and anti-inflammatory properties led to the oil being used in hospitals during the First World War to disinfect floors and walls. The word 'lavender' comes from the Latin *lavandus*, meaning 'to be washed'; *officinalis* (syn. *angustifolia*) means 'medicinal', which conforms to lavender's initial medicinal use as an antiseptic, and also reflects its other early applications to aid mental health – for when we 'sanitize' we wash and cleanse, making subjects *sanus*, meaning 'healthy and sane'.

Lavender extracts have remained very popular as a fragrance for toiletry products and as a culinary herb, being used mostly in the French herbal blend known as *herbes de Provence*. Its relaxing scent interfuses pleasantly with either black or green tea; both the flowers and leaves are also used in herbal medicine and taken as a herbal tea.

Main therapeutic properties: Herbally, lavender is considered to be antihalitotic, antiseptic, antispasmodic, aromatherapeutic, carminative, a cholagogue, diuretic, nervine, relaxant, sedative, stimulant, stomachic, tonic and tranquilizer.

Dried lavender flowers that are used to make teas or liquid extracts can be taken

orally as tinctures for conditions such as anxiety, restlessness, insomnia and depression. A lavender infusion can soothe and heal insect bites, while bunches of the herb are said to repel insects.

Generally, it is lavender essential oil that is used for the various conditions and ailments. Scientific evidence from small studies support its aromatherapeutic use for anxiety. Preliminary results indicate that lavender oil, combined with oils from other herbs, may also help with alopecia, the hair-loss complaint.

The oil is used as an antiseptic, and in aromatherapy is diluted with a carrier oil and commonly used as a relaxant in massage therapy and in other remedial products such as bath oils to induce a relaxed state. Lavender oil applied to the temples may soothe headaches. The sweet-smelling oil of *L. angustifolia* is widely used in balms, salves, perfumes, cosmetics and other topical applications.

Although lavender has a sedative-type scent, when used in a work environment it seems to help prevent the deterioration of work performance due to fatigue. Lavender aromatherapy also appears to ameliorate lower-back pain and neck pain. It is frequently used aromatherapeutically to lull a person to sleep, whereby the inhaled floral scent supposedly promotes a mental state of well-being.

Although lavender oil has shown great promise, overall the scientific evidence concerning it is inconclusive. More research is required regarding its efficacy in soothing agitated behaviour in dementia patients and to establish the effectiveness of Perillyl alcohol (POH), which is derived from lavender and may be beneficial to some types of cancer, such as pancreatic, breast and intestinal cancer.

Cautions: Teas and extracts may cause headaches, changes in appetite and constipation. External use of lavender in reasonable amounts is safe during pregnancy and breastfeeding, but ingesting lavender should be avoided at these times.

Concentrated lavender oil must be diluted for topical applications and must not used internally, except under medical supervision. Direct application of lavender oil to the skin can cause irritation and toxicity and increase the skin's photosensitivity; it can also be a potent allergen. Recently it was reported that continuous use of lavender and tea-tree oils caused mammary development (feminism) in young boys. Do not use lavender with other sedative medications.

Fresh lavender can be mixed with macerating oils to make a cleansing preparation.

Lobelia

Botanical name *Lobelia inflata*

Family Campanulaceae

Description: Lobelia, or Indian tobacco, is an annual herbaceous plant that is native to dry places, growing from south-eastern Canada down through the north-eastern US. It has tiny flowers of pale blue-violet, tinted yellow on the inside.

Parts used: Whole plant, especially leaves and seeds

History: Lobelia was introduced into Europe in the mid-1620s. By 1629 the species *L. cardinalia* was known as 'cardinal flower', its colour being compared to the mitres of Roman Catholic cardinals. Both red cardinal flower and the great blue lobelia (*L. siphilitica*) were used as a cure for syphilis.

In the 1800s – long before herbalist Samuel Thomson disseminated the medicinal use of lobelia in the US and was credited with its discovery – the plant was known to the Native North American Penobscot (or Panawahpskek) tribe and was extensively used in New England. Traditionally, the Native North Americans used lobelia for a wide range of conditions, including the treatment of respiratory and muscle disorders, and as a purgative. Lobelia was brought into general professional use by Manasseh Cutler of Massachusetts. In those days, both Thomson and Cutler called it 'emetic weed' and 'emetic herb'.

Main therapeutic properties: Lobelia has a strong therapeutic history. It is anti-asthmatic, antispasmodic, diaphoretic, emetic, expectorant, a nauseant, nervine, relaxant, sedative, sialagogue and stimulant; secondarily it is cathartic, diuretic and an astringent.

The whole plant is active, but the leaves and seeds are more generally used. Indeed, the most potent part of the plant is its seed, which contains the most lobeline, the main ingredient that gives the plant its psychoactive property. Being evocative of ordinary tobacco (*Nicotiana tabacum*) and prized among ethneogen users, lobelia is often used by mystics and others to facilitate 'mind transformation' – for example, in a trance for the purpose of spanning this world and Otherworlds.

Herbally, ointment from the plant may be used externally, or combined with other ingredients to provide a counter-irritant. The topical ointment is used to treat pleurisy, rheumatism, conditions such as tennis elbow and whiplash injuries, as well as boils and ulcers.

Today, lobelia is used to treat bronchial asthma and chronic bronchitis – even with a homeopathic dose, instant relief is felt. It is also used for food poisoning and in smoking-cessation programmes. Its relaxant property features as a nerve depressant, easing tension and panic.

The plant material of *L. inflata* is also burned as an insect repellent to deter mosquitoes and smoke out gnats.

Cautions: Because of its similarity to nicotine, internal use of lobelia is not recommended and may be hazardous to children, pregnant women and those with cardiac disease. Lobelia is not a poison in the ordinary sense of the term, but poisonous symptoms may occur from absorption of it through the epidermis. It is therefore advised that it is administered by a professional practitioner.

Love-in-a-mist

Botanical name *Nigella sativa*

Family Ranunculaceae

Description: Love-in-a-mist (also known as nigella and fennel flower) is a herbaceous annual that is native to western Asia and across the Mediterranean regions. It has delicately coloured, pale bluish-purple or white flowers with green to bluish tips.

Parts used: Seeds, oil.

History: *N. sativa* is one of the most revered medicinal seeds in history. It has been used for centuries, both as a herb and for its 'blackseed' oil, which is especially supportive to the health of populations in Asia, the Middle East and Africa. The herb was used in ancient Egyptian, Greek and Roman medicine, from Hippocrates (*c.* 460–*c.* 370 BCE)

onwards. The seeds are mentioned in the Bible (Isaiah 28:25, 27) and were found in several sites of ancient Egypt, including Tutankhamen's tomb.

In the 1st century CE, love-in-a-mist was mentioned extensively by Pliny the Elder in his *Naturalis Historia*. And the ancient Greek physician Dioscorides recorded that the seeds were used to treat headaches, toothache, nasal catarrh and internal parasites.

Both in ancient and modern times love-in-a-mist has been an important herb in Ayurvedic and Middle Eastern treatments and in Unani practice. Known in Persian as *Shonaiz*, the seed was referred to by the polymath Avicenna (*c*. 980–1037 CE) as a stimulant to body energy and was said to aid recovery from fatigue and dispiritedness.

In German plant encyclopaedias of the 16th to 18th centuries, a series of remedies using love-in-a-mist against head colds and inflammations are recommended, almost unchanged from earlier usage.

Main therapeutic properties: *N. sativa* is anthelmintic, carminative, diaphoretic, digestive, diuretic, an emmenagogue, galactogogue, parasiticide and stimulant.

Its efficacy had not been properly researched until about 40 years ago, but traditional uses range from digestive complaints and skin problems to asthma and infertility, and include treatments for respiratory, stomach and intestinal health, kidney and liver function, as well as circulatory and immune-system support.

Both the seeds and the oil are used as nutritional supplements. The antiseptic seeds, which are used to treat children's intestinal worms, are also commonly used in India to increase lactation. The oil is used topically to treat abscesses, haemorrhoids and orchitis.

There is scientific evidence that, when used externally, this is an excellent skin-care remedy for psoriasis, eczema, dry skin and for the joints and scalp. Studies have shown that the oil helps to reduce inflammation and is fungicidal.

Love-in-a-mist extract is efficacious in regulating blood-sugar levels, and in stimulating bone-marrow activity and the immune cells, important in the prevention and treatment of cancer. The extract shows particular promise for pancreatic cancer medicine on both counts.

Cautions: Love-in-a-mist is generally regarded as safe when taken in the correct dosage. However, its safety in young children, pregnant or nursing women and those with severe liver or kidney disease is not known.

Basil

Botanical name *Ocimum basilicum*

Family Lamiaceae

Description: Sweet basil is a tender, generally low-growing herb, which was originally native to Iran (Persia), India and other tropical regions of Asia. It has white flowers and a powerful aroma.

Parts used: Whole plant, leaves, flowering tops, seeds, oil.

History: Depending on the plant's variety, its essential oils dominate its chemical make-up, traditionally offering many different flavours and scents: anethole (Thai liquorice, anise), camphene (camphor, as in African blue basil), cinnamate (cinnamon), citral (lemon) and eugenol (clove, as in sweet basil).

Main therapeutic properties: Basil is an aromatic, restorative, warming herb that is traditionally used as a febrifuge and antiparasitic, as well as its more targeted use on the nervous and digestive systems as an antispasmodic, bactericidal, digestive, stomachic and tonic. It is taken internally to allay nausea, arrest vomiting and alleviate nervous headaches and non-specific locations of rheumatic pains.

Nutritionally, basil is a good source of pro-Vitamin A (beta-carotene) and magnesium, both of which promote cardiovascular health; and of Vitamin K, for bone growth and blood coagulation. It is also high in potassium and calcium.

The herb's unique active constituents contain flavonoids, including orientin and vicenin. In studies on human white blood cells, these soluble flavonoids have been shown to protect cell structures as well as chromosomes from radiation and oxygen-based damage at cellular level. Research also indicates that basil tincture is significantly anti-inflammatory, and that the aqueous extract is highly antioxidant and shows promise as an anti-platelet aggregant and antithrombotic.

Scientific studies have established that compounds in basil have potent analgesic, anti-cancer, antidepressant, antimicrobial, antioxidant, antispasmodic and antiviral properties; it is also carminative, cephalic, digestive, an emmenagogue, expectorant, febrifuge,

insecticide, nervine, stomachic, sudorific, tonic and stimulant.

Basil is used aromatherapeutically as a tonic for the treatment of nervous disorders, such as stress-related headaches, and has beneficial action on the respiratory tract for infections such as bronchitis and sinusitis or sinus problems/infections. It is also given/used for exhaustion, flatulence, gout, muscular aches, rheumatism, insect bites and as an insect repellent.

Cautions: Basil essential oil may irritate sensitive skin. Use it sparingly, and avoid in all cases of liver problems. When used in excess, its otherwise stimulatory quality may have a stupefying effect. Do not use it during pregnancy or on children under 16 years.

Basil contains *estragole*, which is a carcinogen and teratogen in rats and mice, but experiments indicate it requires human exposure of at least 100 times the norm to become a cancer risk.

Evening primrose

Botanical name *Oenothera biennis*

Family Onagraceae

Description: Evening primrose is a biennial or short-lived perennial. The *Oenothera* genus originated in Mexico and Central America some 70,000 years ago and is native to North America and naturalized in parts of Europe and Asia. As its name suggests, the pale to bright-yellow richly scented flowers open in the evening

and close the following day. The fruits are hairy capsules containing numerous seeds, which are released when the capsule splits into four sections at maturity.

Parts used: Flowers, leaves, root, seedpod, oil.

History: The first evening primrose plants to arrive in Europe reached Padua in Italy from Virginia in the US in 1614 and were described by the English botanist John Goodyer in 1621. In the language of flowers, the evening primrose stands for inconstancy. Whether viewed as a weed or a wonderful ornamental plant, evening primrose lights up the world like brilliant sunshine and lifts the spirits.

The closely related, diminutive Californian 'tufted evening primrose' (*O. caespitose*) was used medicinally by several Native American tribes, including the Blackfoot, Gosiute, Isleta, Navajo, Keyenta and Hopi. It was employed as wet or dry poultices, for sores, swellings, inflamed wounds and to speed healing; as well as for prolapses of the uterus and as a toothache medicine.

Main therapeutic properties: Evening primrose has edible flowers, leaves, root, seedpod and oil, and has anticholesterolemic, astringent, hypotensive and sedative actions. The whole plant has been used to heal asthmatic coughs, whooping cough and gastrointestinal disorders; and its uses are similar to those of *O. caespitose* described above.

Evening primrose oil is extracted from the seed and contains gamma-linolenic acid (GLA), an essential fatty acid that is required by the body for growth and development, and must be obtained from the diet. The oil has been used topically since the 1930s for eczema, and more recently orally for other conditions involving inflammation, such as rheumatoid arthritis, for which there is a growing scientific rationale. It is also used for female conditions such as premenstrual syndrome, menstrual cycle breast pain and menopausal symptoms. A finely ground powder made from the flowering stems is used cosmetically in face masks to counteract reddened skin.

Cautions: Evening primrose oil should be avoided if you have epilepsy. It is recommended that it is not taken in combination with drugs for schizophrenia. Evening primrose may cause headaches, nausea or skin eruptions, but these effects can be lessened by taking it with food.

Asian ginseng

Botanical name *Panax ginseng*

Family Araliaceae

Description: Asian ginseng is a small perennial herb that originated in the damp woodlands of northern China (Manchuria). It has a fleshy tap-root that can take more than five years to mature. The root is medicinal and is graded according to its source and age, the most prized being the older wild-grown roots.

Parts used: Root.

History: The first recorded history of people using ginseng comes from the earliest Chinese empires. This ancient Taoist herb is one of the most famous plants of traditional Chinese medicine. Its name derives from the herbalist philosophy known as the *Doctrine of Signatures* and from a Chinese phrase meaning 'plant shaped like a man' – for when ginseng matures, it resembles the human form.

The botanical name *panax* derives from the Greek *pan*, meaning 'all', and *akos*, meaning 'cure' – referring to the 'panacea' or 'cure-all' of the earth in the form of a man. However, *seng* (with a prefix) is simply a term used by Chinese medicinal root-collectors for the fleshy roots used in tonics.

Although the discovery of ginseng's therapeutic efficacy is lost in antiquity, we know the herb was commonly used by elderly people in the Orient to improve their mental and physical vitality. The earliest mention of ginseng is in the 2,000-year-old herbal of the Chinese monk Shen Nong, since which time it has been used in China to help restore *yang* energy.

Main therapeutic properties: There are two ginseng-processing methods. Ginseng root that is grown for four to six years, then peeled and air- or sun-dried to bleach it to a yellowish-white, is called 'white ginseng'. The form known as' red ginseng', which is harvested after six years, is steam-cured, which gives the roots a glossy reddish-brown coloration, then heat-dried. Practitioners of traditional Chinese Medicine consider that each form has its own particular benefits.

P. ginseng is principally an adaptogen and immuno-stimulant, as well as reputedly being anticholesterolemic, anti-ageing, antifatigue, antioxidant, antistress, emetic, expectorant, hypoglycaemic, a liver-protectant, mental-function-enhancing, a nervine and an overall tonic.

There are more than 18 active chemicals (ginsenosides) in Asian ginseng, which has had its essences extracted for a wide range of ailments. It is purported to aid female menopausal symptoms, including vaginal dryness. It may be helpful for male infertility and erectile dysfunction, and can act as a libido-enhancer.

In the past 30 years extensive research has been carried out on Asian ginseng in an attempt to confirm the countless properties attributed to the herb. Although it is best known for promoting physical and mental vigour (boosting the immune system) and helping to control type-2 diabetes (adult-onset), recent studies have focused on its antioxidant activity, antiviral and metabolic effects, as well as its actions on the nervous and reproductive systems.

European clinical studies have shown that standardized extracts increased visual and auditory stimuli (alertness) and improved visual and motor coordination. Ginseng also increased subjects' respiratory performance, powers of concentration and grasp of abstract concepts.

Even though it is difficult to find scientific verification for all of ginseng's medicinal benefits because studies often give contradictory results, in Germany Asian ginseng products may be labelled as tonics to treat fatigue, reduced work capacity, lack of concentration and convalescence. Much more research is required to do justice to the herb's varied properties, such as its potential to aid those undergoing chemotherapy for various types of cancer, and to validate studies which reported that a herbal combination containing ginseng may improve the symptoms of multi-infarct dementia (caused by multi-mini-strokes).

Cautions: Ginseng appears to be generally safe when used correctly, with rare side-effects. However, its safety in young children, pregnant and nursing women and those with severe liver or kidney disease is not known. It is suggested by some that its use be limited to three months to avoid side-effects. Do not take ginseng without consulting your healthcare provider, or with existing prescription drugs.

A coloured Lithograph, circa 1820, showing the botanical parts of the powerful Asian root, Ginseng.

Long-term use may cause menstrual abnormalities and breast tenderness in some women. In rare instances, it may cause high blood pressure, nervousness and insomnia. If consumed with caffeine, there is risk of gastrointestinal upset (diarrhoea) and over-stimulatory upset. Ginseng should not be used in cases of extreme inflammation; rashes, heavy bleeding and high fevers will be exacerbated by its boost to the circulatory system. People with known allergies to *Panax* species and/or plants in the Araliaceae family should avoid ginseng; signs of allergy may include rash, itching or shortness of breath.

Common sage

Botanical name *Salvia officinalis*

Family Lamiaceae

Description: Common sage grows in derelict land, near human habitation, and in gardens as a herb or an ornamental plant. It was originally native to the Mediterranean, but now flourishes in sunny conditions all over the world. It is a small, scented, shrubby perennial evergreen belonging to the mint family. The blue to purplish-violet or white hermaphrodite flowers grow in whorls. All parts of the plant have a robust odour and a warm, bitter taste, owing to the volatile oil contained in the tissues.

Parts used: Whole plant, mainly leaves, essential oil.

History: The genus name *Salvia* is derived from the Latin word *salvere*, which means 'to be saved'. Since Classical times it has had a reputation for its healing properties and for promoting human longevity: *Cur moriatur homo cui Salvia crescit in horto?* ('Why should a man die while sage grows in his garden?')

The Romans treated sage as sacred and created a special ceremony for gathering it, while early Christians believed that its healing properties issued directly from the Virgin Mary. And throughout the Middle Ages, sage was held in high esteem for its culinary and medicinal properties. In the tenth century Arab physicians also believed that sage promoted immortality, while 14th-century Europeans used the herb to protect them from witchcraft.

During the mid-17th century extremely expensive tea (*Camellia sinensis*) first appeared in England in 1660 and cost £6–10 sterling per pound weight. At this time, however, the Chinese were so enamoured of sage tea that they reportedly traded three cases of tea leaves to the Dutch for one case of sage leaves.

Sage appeared in the London Pharmacopoeia, and the leaves were still entered and officially prescribed in the US Pharmacopoeia in the 1920s, but then the use of sage by medical practitioners faded – although not as a domestic medicine. Today, the esteem with which it was once regarded has not diminished, and in 2001 the International Herb

Association awarded sage the title of 'herb of the year'.

Main therapeutic properties: Every part of the sage plant can be used medicinally, and the fresh, dried whole or powdered herb is available throughout the year. Currently the leaves are mainly used as an alterative, antiseptic, astringent, depurative, digestive, expectorant, febrifuge and tonic. However, in traditional herbal usage sage is also considered antihydrotic, anti-inflammatory, antimicrobial, antispasmodic, diaphoretic, an aromatherapeutic aromatic, carminative, cholagogue, diuretic, expectorant and nervine, as well as an emmenagogue, galactofuge, stimulant, stomachic, sudorific, vasodilator and vermifuge.

Sage has been use in folk medicine as a remedy for colds, diarrhoea, enteritis, excessive perspiration, snake bite, sore throat, toothache, venereal disease and cancer. It was also used externally to clean ulcers, and sores and to stop wounds bleeding.

The herb remains a timeless remedy for inflammations of the mouth, throat and tonsils, its volatile oils soothing the mucous membranes. It is used for gingivitis, glossitis or stomatitis and apthae. As a gargle it is used to treat laryngitis, pharyngitis, tonsillitis and quinsy. In a lotion or salve it is used to treat sores and skin eruptions, and in shampoo to treat and remove dandruff.

Today the leaves are mainly used internally in the treatment of digestive and respiratory complaints, menstrual

An illumination of two women picking sage from the Italian manuscript 'Tacuinum Sanitas' (The Medieval Health Handbook) by Luisa Cogliati Arano.

problems and menopause symptoms, infertility, nervous tension and depression, and as a galactofuge. The German Commission E approved sage leaf for internal and external use. Sage's leaf tea is listed to treat excessive perspiration.

Externally, sage leaves and oil are used medicinally as an anti-inflammatory. The essential oil is employed in perfumery, cosmetics and toiletries as an aromatic and antihydrotic, while the oil appears in toothpastes. Salvin, a preparation of leaves used as an antimicrobial, anti-inflammatory agent, is used to treat oral cavity disease.

Sage has been used for cerebrovascular disease for more than a thousand years and is known to be beneficial to the mind by easing mental exhaustion, soothing the nerves and strengthening concentration abilities. The 18th-century botanist and herbalist John Hill stated that sage slowed the memory's 'rapid decay'. Recently researchers have looked more closely at Spanish sage (*S. lavandulifolia*) for its beneficial effect on brain function and treatment of Alzheimer's disease. In 2001 English researchers found that Spanish sage's essential oil and its montoterpenoids could inhibit the enzyme acetylcholinesterase, which is relevant to the treatment of Alzheimer's.

In 2003 research revealed that the dried root of Chinese or red sage (*S. miltiorrhiza*), or 'danshen', contained active compounds similar to those developed in modern drugs to treat Alzheimer's. In 2005 the Alzheimer's Disease Society stated that research at a Newcastle hospital had shown that sage has similar affects on dementia to drugs such as Aricept. The same year, common sage (*S. officinalis*) was found to improve mood and cognitive performance following the administration of single doses to healthy young participants.

More recently, in 2008, a North Korean study has shown that dimthyl lithospermate (DML), a powerful antioxidant isolated from *S. miltiorrhiza*, is potentially capable of helping to protect the body against Alzheimer's and against conditions such as stroke, heart disease and atherosclerosis. Scientific portents for the future use of sage are looking good.

Cautions: *S. officinalis* is not commonly an allergenic food, and is generally regarded as safe as a natural seasoning and as a plant extract/essential oil. However, sage does interfere with the absorption of iron and other minerals when taken internally. For this reason, avoid excess consumption during pregnancy or while nursing, unless you are ready to stop breastfeeding. Individuals with seizure disorders should not use sage. The plant is toxic in excess or when taken for extended periods, but the toxic dose is very large.

Elder

Botanical name *Sambucus nigra*
Family Caprifoliaceae

Description: The common elder is an ornamental deciduous shrub or small tree, growing to 6 m (20 ft) tall, with a lifespan of 80–100 years. It is native to the northern hemisphere: across most of Europe and to north-west Africa, and also found in North America. It has arching branches and cork-like, brownish-grey bark, with creamy-white flowers in midsummer that are pollinated by flies. The fleshy fruit is a dark purplish-black berry produced in drooping clusters in autumn.

Parts used: Mainly flowering tops, berries (fruits); also bark, leaves, seed oil.

History: The elder is sometimes called the 'Judas tree', because it is thought to be the tree on which Judas Iscariot hanged himself. Folklore also held that it was unlucky to have elder in the garden. According to ancient pagan belief, a poem called the 'Wiccan Rede' states that if an elder tree is destroyed, a spirit known as the Elder Mother will be released and take her revenge.

In the past, the strong-smelling foliage was tied to a horse's mane to keep flies off while riding. And early Native American tribes used elder's hollow stems for arrows or bored holes into them to fashion flutes. Many types of wind instrument have been made from elder, including Pan's pipes, linking the tree to hunting, rustic music and fertility.

Main therapeutic properties: The herb is anti-inflammatory, aperient, cellular-regenerating, detoxicant, diaphoretic, digestive, diuretic, emetic, emollient, expectorant, galactogogue, gastrointestinal, haemostatic, immuno-stimulant, laxative, ophthalmic, purgative and a salve for sores.

Folkloric medicine employed the inner bark from young trees as a diuretic, an emetic and strong purgative for constipation and arthritic conditions, and the green inner bark as an emollient ointment. The leaves are a diaphoretic, diuretic, expectorant and haemostatic; their ointment is emollient and is used in the treatment of bruises, sprains, chilblains and wounds. The leaf extract, combined with St John's wort (*Hypericum perforatum*) and soapwort, inhibits both the influenza and *Herpes simplex* viruses.

Elderflower extract was traditionally used in the treatment of catarrh, to induce sweating in feverish chills and to aid breathing in bronchitis, colds, coughs and flu, and as a gargle for mouth ulcers and tonsillitis. It was also used for mild gastrointestinal complaints and as part of a detox programme for weight loss.

The fresh flowers are used in the distillation of 'elderflower water' (*aqua sambuci*), which is mildly astringent and a gentle stimulant, and was commonly used as a treatment for the complexion, for conditioning the skin and clearing it of freckles and sunburn, to calm skin eruptions and irritations and keep fair skin white and blemish-free. It is still used in cosmetics, chiefly as a vehicle for eye and skin lotions.

Elderflower water is an official preparation of the British Pharmacopoeia and the Pharmacopoeia of Switzerland. Elderflowers were at one time also part of the US Pharmacopoeia. The *British Herbal Compendium* lists its use for the common cold, feverish conditions and as a diuretic; the German Standard Licence for elderflower tea calls it a diaphoretic

medicine for the treatment of feverish common colds or catarrhal complaints; and the German Commission E approved internal use of elderflower for colds.

The flowers and berries are edible after cooking, and both can also be made into elderberry wine. Rich in Vitamin C and high in anthocyanin and bioflavonoid content, the elderberry is medicinally antibacterial, anti-inflammatory, antiviral, antioxidant and a mild laxative. The juice is used for rheumatism and neuralgia, and for colds, influenza, sinusitis and other related conditions. As an immuno-stimulant, the juice is beneficial to AIDS patients and others at risk of developing infections. Elderberry extract also reduces the damaging effects of LDL or 'bad' cholesterol.

Although there is no satisfactory medication to cure type-A and -B influenza, black elderberry extract was found in clinical studies to achieve a significant improvement of the symptoms (including fever) in 93.3 per cent of cases within two days and a complete cure was achieved within two to three days by nearly 90 per cent of the extract-treated group.

Most recently, elderberry in juice and tablet form (together with asparagus) has shown promise in the formation of a weight-reduction supplement. Elderberry-seed oil may also be massaged onto painful joints to relieve the pain of arthritis.

Cautions: Only those elder plants with purple/black berries are medicinal, while species with red berries are toxic. All green parts of *S. nigra* 'Black Lace' are poisonous: the leaves, stems, roots, berries and seeds should never be consumed as they contain a cyanide-producing glycoside; the bark contains toxic calcium oxalate crystals.

Elder taken as a laxative has resulted in some reports of dizziness and stupor. Rare ill effects are generally of mild gastrointestinal distress and allergic reactions, but high doses of berries can cause diarrhoea, nausea and vomiting. Its safety in infants, pregnancy, or severe liver or kidney diseases is unknown.

Juicy jet-black elderberries make a tempting wine, a traditional Pagan drink used to celebrate the Gaelic Lughnasadh Festival.

Saw palmetto

Botanical name *Serenoa repens*

Family Arecaceae

Description: Saw palmetto is a 'fan' palm tree that is mainly endemic to the south-eastern US's Atlantic seaboard and the Gulf coastal plains; it is also native to the West Indies. It is a small evergreen shrub growing to about 4 m (13 ft) in height, with leaves that grow from a crown to form a rounded fan of about 20 long leaflets, or 'palmettos', with sawtooth-edged spines. It has yellowish-white flowers and oblong berries, which may be eaten raw or cooked and have a strong vanilla-like aroma, but a soapy taste.

Parts used: Fruits (pulp and seeds).

History: Humans and animals alike have eaten the fruit of saw palmetto for millennia. Its medicinal use can be traced in the

Americas back to the Mayans, who used it as a tonic, while the Seminole tribe used the fruit as an expectorant and antiseptic. Medicine men used saw palmetto to treat atrophy of the testes, impotence, inflammation of the prostate, low libido in men and as a general tonic to nourish the body. American colonists found that regular consumption of it improved digestion and was useful to convalescents to boost weight-gain and bodily strength.

Saw palmetto was listed in the US Pharmacopoeia from 1906 to 1917, and in the National Formulary from 1926 to 1950. In the 1950s, when there was a revival of interest in natural medicine, major pharmaceutical companies reintroduced saw palmetto in a standardized form.

Main therapeutic properties: Saw palmetto is considered an antiseptic, aphrodisiac, diuretic, expectorant, sedative and a uterine and general tonic. It is still a 'tonic' herb used in the treatment of debility, and is one of the few Western herbs to be considered anabolic. It is also used for chronic pelvic pain, bladder disorders, male pattern hair loss and hormone imbalances. Although more research is required, promising new evidence suggests that androgenetic alopecia is caused by the same mechanism that causes enlarged prostate glands, making saw palmetto *the* herbal contender for this condition.

The fruit has a probable oestrogenic action and is used in the treatment of impotence, loss of libido and testicular atrophy in men, and to stimulate breast enlargement in women. However, saw palmetto is mainly used for urinary symptoms associated with an enlarged prostate gland. Several small studies suggest that it may be effective for treating urine flow and burning urination, and may help reduce the frequency of night-time urination.

Cautions: Saw palmetto is believed to be quite safe. Few allergic symptoms have been reported, although it may cause mild side-effects, including stomach/intestinal discomfort and headaches. However, it may increase the risk of bleeding when taken with anticoagulant drugs or ginkgo biloba and garlic.

Pregnant women or those who may become pregnant should not take saw palmetto. It may interact with birth-control pills and HRT in women and may also interfere with other hormone-related drugs. Some men have reported tender breasts and a decline in sexual desire.

Milk thistle

Botanical name *Silybum marianum*

Family Asteraceae

Description: Milk thistle is an annual to biennial herb that was originally discovered growing in the Kashmir region bordering India and Pakistan and is a native of southern Europe. The hermaphrodite flowers, which are pollinated by bees, are composed of red to purple tubular florets that produce long, blackish seeds with a tuft of white hair, which when ripe are a medicinal part of the plant.

Parts used: Whole plant, mainly flowerheads, seeds.

History: Milk thistle has been used for thousands of years as a herbal remedy and was originally believed to help nursing mothers produce milk – tradition holds that the distinctive white markings on the veins of the plant's leaves were caused by the Virgin Mary's milk.

Its use for liver problems can be traced back to ancient Greco-Roman times. Pliny the Elder (23–79 CE) referred to the milky juice of this plant as being excellent for 'carrying off bile'. And the English 16th-century herbalist John Gerard recommended it for 'expelling melancholy', a condition ascribed to liver disease in that era.

In 19th-century Germany doctors treated jaundice and other liver disease with milk-thistle seed extract. In 1949 confirmatory German research found that it seemed to protect animal livers that were exposed to high doses of a potent liver toxin. And in 1968 the active agent was located in its seeds and is now referred to as the flavonoid silymarin, which is currently used in Europe to treat all kinds of liver disorders.

Main therapeutic properties: Milk thistle is an astringent, a bitter, cholagogue, diaphoretic, diuretic, emetic, emmenagogue, hepatic, stimulant and tonic. Herbalists use it in cases of cirrhosis, jaundice and hepatitis, gallbladder disease, and against poisons. Today's science shows it to be most effective when treating the liver, spleen and kidneys. This has particular importance in the area of 'binge-drinking' among the very young.

Milk thistle may also lower cholesterol levels, reduce insulin resistance in those with type-2 diabetes who also have cirrhosis, and limit the growth of cancer cells in breast, cervical, prostate and other cancers. It can also aid psoriasis. Research continues into the use of milk thistle for chronic hepatitis C, and for liver diseases that occur in people who drink little or no alcohol.

Milk thistle is increasingly being investigated for its use as a supplementary treatment both during and after chemotherapy. It may also have applications in ameliorating the long-term liver and cardiovascular effects of cancer treatment and as a chemo-preventive agent, as well as to treat complications in HIV patients.

Cautions: The herb may produce reactions in those who are allergic to the daisy family. Rarely does milk thistle cause side-effects except for a mild laxative effect, although clinical trials have reported nausea, minor gastrointestinal upset, diarrhoea and/or headaches.

Pregnant or nursing women and those with hormone-dependent conditions should exercise caution in taking milk thistle, which may also interfere with oral contraceptives. Men with prostate cancer should not take it without professional consultation. Milk thistle could also decrease the insulin requirements of diabetics with alcoholic liver cirrhosis.

Pau d'Arco

Botanical name *Tabebuia impetiginosa*

Family Bignoniaceae

Description: Pau d'Arco is a broad-leafed evergreen tree that grows up to 38 m (125 ft) tall, and is native to the moist rainforest of Amazonia and other tropical parts of South and Latin America; it is also said to be indigenous to the West Indian islands of Trinidad and Tobago. It has flamboyant magenta flowers and capsules that contain numerous winged seeds.

Parts used: Wood, inner bark.

History: Pau d'Arco refers both to the tree and to the medicine made from its inner bark. This tree has a long history in herbal medicine around the world, but its use is particularly well documented by the indigenous peoples of the rainforest. The Guarani and Tupi Indians call it *tajy*, meaning 'to have strength and vigour'. Usually ingested as a decoction, the tree's powerful bark has been used to treat a variety of conditions, from malaria, sexually transmitted diseases and cancer to pustules and carbuncles.

During the 1960s the Pau d'Arco tree attracted considerable attention in Brazil and Argentina as a 'wonder drug'. In the 1980s it was said to improve quality of life for cancer and immuno-depressed patients. In recent decades, as a tea, in pill form or as a tincture, herbalists have used Pau d'Arco as a tonic and adaptogen. But its popularity and use have been controversial, chiefly due to lack of quality control, confusion regarding the parts used and method of preparation, and to other unrelated tree species being exported from South America as 'Pau d'Arco'.

Main therapeutic properties: Pau d'Arco is analgesic, anti-inflammatory, bactericidal, fungicidal, insecticidal, parasiticidal and virucidal. It has anticarcinogenic capabilities and is immuno-stimulatory. Traditionally it is also anti-allergy, anticoagulant, antidysenteric, antioxidant, antirheumatic, anti-ulcerous, antivenin, astringent, cardiotonic, diuretic, hepatotonic, mildly laxative and it dries secretions.

Its ethno-medicinal and traditional herbal uses vary depending on a country's medicinal needs and practices. But this 'cure-all' covers every aspect of bodily health, from upper-respiratory bacterial and viral infections to parasitic and sexually transmitted diseases, from hair follicles to foot fungi. Topically, it appears to have a broad spectrum of bactericidal, fungicidal, antiprotozoal and virucidal virtues, some of which are used for skin complaints, including dermatitis and psoriasis.

The herb's compounds are immuno-stimulatory, purifying and encourage the production of red blood cells to increase oxygenation of the blood, thus assisting the healing process. Further research needs to be carried out on the herb's usefulness as a short-term antimicrobial and disinfecting expectorant.

Nevertheless, in Taiwan, South Korea and Brazil, recent research shows the potential use of the herb's compound, beta-lapachone, for wound-healing and to block tumour growth; a water extract may be developed as a new remedy for various inflammatory diseases such as arthritis and atherosclerosis; and an extract of bark commonly used for the treatment of peptic ulcers in Brazil has a protective action against gastric lesions.

Cautions: Pau d'Arco appears to be generally safe, though in excessive amounts it may cause gastrointestinal upset or nausea. Use is inadvisable in pregnancy, as its safety in young children, pregnant or nursing women is unknown.

Feverfew

Botanical name *Tanacetum parthenium*

Family Asteraceae

Description: Feverfew is a strongly aromatic, perennial herb, which is native to Eurasia, specifically the Balkan peninsula, Anatolia and the Caucasus, but now grows in numerous continents around the world. Its medicinal part is the yellow-green leaves. It has numerous small, daisy-like flowerheads, with yellow centres and outer white rays arranged in clusters.

Parts used: Leaves.

History: *T. parthenium* is also known as *Pyrethrum parthenium*, *pyrethrum* being derived from the Greek word *pur* ('fire'), an allusion to the hot taste of the root. The ancients called it *parthenium* because, according to legend, the herb was used to save the life of someone who fell from the Parthenon, the temple of Athena in Athens.

The Greek physician Dioscorides praised its use for many complaints, including 'St Anthonies fire', which may be interpreted today as arthritis; and for 'all hot inflammations and hot swellings', as well as for phlegm and melancholy.

In Roman times, and thenceforward, feverfew was used for 'female conditions', to induce menstruation and aid expulsion of the placenta in childbirth.

Feverfew featured (as 'matricaria') in the 1791 Scottish edition of the *Edinburgh Dispensatory* for hysteria. In 1857, in Theophilus Redwood's Supplement to the British Pharmacopoeia, it was described as a tonic, stimulant and anti-hysteric.

Main therapeutic properties: Feverfew is anticoagulant, anti-ecchymotic, anti-inflammatory, antispasmodic, aperient, bitter, carminative, emmenagogue, sedative, stimulant, stomachic, vasodilator and a vermifuge.

Used for centuries for fevers, headaches, stomach aches, toothaches, insect bites, menstrual problems and childbirth, feverfew has also been used for psoriasis, allergies, asthma, tinnitus, dizziness, nausea and vomiting. Research also suggests that it could help those with milder symptoms of rheumatoid arthritis.

Feverfew is now chiefly used for migraine headaches, which research suggests it may be helpful in preventing. It is thought that by inhibiting the release of serotonin and prostaglandins – both of which are believed to provoke the onset of migraines – feverfew limits the inflammation of blood vessels in the head, thus stopping the spasm that is believed to contribute to migraine headaches.

In 2005, the active feverfew compound parthenolide was found to induce cell death in leukaemia stem cells. In 2007, California researchers found feverfew also induced cell death in high-risk pre-B leukaemia cells. Most recently, feverfew has been used in a commercial skin-care preparation to calm red and irritated skin.

Cautions: Those who are allergic to the daisy (Asteraceae) family should not take feverfew. No serious side-effects have been reported, but it may cause gastrointestinal upset or nervousness in some individuals; those who take feverfew for a long time and then cease may experience headaches, difficulty in sleeping, stiff muscles and joint pain. Feverfew may interact with existing prescription drugs. Do not take it in pregnancy or lactation. It should not be given to children under two years of age.

Red clover

Botanical name *Trifolium pratense*

Family Fabaceae

Description: Red clover is a herbaceous perennial plant that is native to North Atlantic regions and central Europe, the Mediterranean and north-west Africa, the Balkans, Asia Minor, Iran, India, the Himalayas, Russia, the Caucasus and the Far East. The sweet-tasting edible blossom comprises dark-pink to magenta 'pom-poms' with a honey-like fragrance.

Parts used: Flowering tops.

History: *Trifolium* means 'trefoil', or three-leaved, while *pratense* is Latin for 'found in meadows'. Red clover was one of the world's first agricultural crops. The plant was used to treat scrofula, a condition sometimes know as the 'King's evil', believed during the Middle Ages and later to be cured by the sovereign's touch.

Since the 1800s red clover has been promoted as a potential treatment for cancer, which is controversial, mainly because of the herb's high concentration of phyto-oestrogens. It is also used in the herbal disciplines of Russia and China to accelerate wound-healing and alleviate water retention. In Turkish folk medicine some *Trifolium* species are used for their analgesic, antiseptic, expectorant properties and to treat rheumatic aches.

Main therapeutic properties: Red clover is an alterative, antiscrophulatic, antispasmodic, aperient, detergent, diuretic, expectorant, sedative and tonic. The flowering tops are used to prepare extracts, tablets and capsules for supplements, as well as teas and liquids.

Russians recommend red clover to treat respiratory infections and congestion, especially bronchial asthma. The Chinese take the tea as an expectorant and to treat coughs. In the West, the herb is traditionally used to treat inflammation and infection, including sexually transmitted diseases and tuberculosis. It has been used for respiratory problems such as whooping cough, bronchitis and asthma.

Currently, red clover is used mainly for menopausal symptoms, and for breast pain associated with menstrual cycles, high cholesterol, osteoporosis and symptoms of prostate enlargement. Recent American research into the plant parts used for extraction suggests that all aerial parts combined may be more beneficial. Such research is important because several studies of red clover have had mixed results, with one large study declaring it to have no beneficial effects on menopausal symptoms.

However, in Singapore, recent research into supplementing isoflavones for the menopause has led to significant improvements in bone density, tissue integrity and so on, making red clover a viable alternative to conventional regimens using synthetic oestrogens. Austrian researchers have also found that red-clover extract could be simultaneously used for ameliorating metabolic syndrome. More research is required, but at least one study looks promising for male prostate conditions.

Cautions: Red clover appears to be safe for most adults when used for short periods of time. Its safety for women who are pregnant or breastfeeding, and for breast or other hormone-sensitive cancers, is unknown, so caution is advised. It may also interfere with combined oestrogens, and is contra-anticoagulants and anti-platelet inhibitors.

Slippery elm

Botanical name *Ulmus rubra*

Family Ulmaceae

Description: Slippery elm is a member of the elm family that is native to the eastern half of Canada and the US. It is a stately deciduous tree, typically reaching 15–18 m (50–60 ft), with spreading branches forming an open crown. The heartwood is a reddish-brown, giving the tree its other common name of 'red elm'. Its flowers appear before the leaves in spring and produce flat fruits, whose winged edges aid their airborne dispersal.

Parts used: Inner bark.

History: Slippery elm has been used as a herbal remedy in North America for centuries. Native Americans were the first to discover the medicinal properties of the tree's inner bark. English settlers keenly followed suit, using the herb to treat boils, sores and wounds. The use of slippery elm bark was developed by colonists to relieve sore throat, coughs and urinary-tract infections. In times of war the herb, made into a topical antiseptic cream, aided the dressing of gunshot wounds.

Historically, slippery elm was used as an abortifacient, the bark being first moistened and then inserted into the cervix. The practice became so widespread that it was regulated by Elm Stock Laws in a number of US states, which forbade the purchase of bark beyond a certain length. Selling whole slippery-elm bark is now banned in several countries, including the UK.

Main therapeutic properties: Slippery elm is demulcent, diuretic, emollient, expectorant and nutritive, with abortifacient potential. It is considered to be one of the most valuable remedies in herbal tradition. It aids digestion and helps cleanse the colon, neutralizes stomach acids, boosts the adrenal glands, draws out impurities and heals all parts of the body.

Gentle and effective, slippery elm soothes the mucous membranes of the respiratory tract, urinary tubules, stomach and intestines, and in particular bowel inflammations such as colitis, irritable bowel syndrome, diverticulitis and diverticulosis, relieving painful attacks often within a couple of hours. Prior to diagnosis of the cause for such illnesses, slippery elm is an excellent tool to aid symptoms and could contribute much to mainstream medicine, but is frequently underused.

Externally, slippery elm still helps to soothe, heal and reduce swelling and pain. It is used as a poultice for removing toxins, especially bacterial inflammations containing pus, such as abscesses, boils and spots, and for drawing out splinters. Topically, the herb relieves minor skin injuries such as burns, cold sores, shaver's rash, scrapes and sunburn.

Cautions: Slippery elm is considered a safe herb when taken as recommended. It mainly comprises mucilage and nutrients and is not technically a drug. It is deemed to be safe for use during pregnancy and lactation. Some individuals may develop an allergic rash when it is applied topically to the skin.

Stinging nettle

Botanical name *Urtica dioica*

Family Urticaceae

Description: The common stinging nettle is found in temperate regions throughout the world, including Europe and North America, South America, northern Mexico, much of Asia, northern Africa and Australia. It is a herbaceous flowering perennial, with edible soft green leaves and inconspicuous flowers. Both leaves and stems are covered in non-stinging and stinging hairs, whose tips break off when touched, causing an injection into the skin of several chemicals.

Parts used: Aerial parts, leaves and roots.

History: Although many gardeners consider the stinging nettle a wretched weed, it deserves respect, for it has been used since ancient times as a source of food, fibre and medicine. In Denmark burial shrouds made of nettle fabrics dating back to the Bronze Age (3000–2000 BCE) have been discovered. And from ancient Egypt come records of nettle infusion for the relief of arthritis and lumbago pains.

Nettle was one of the nine plants – including *stune* (lamb's cress), *wergulu* (crab apple), *fille* (thyme) and *finule* (fennel) – to be invoked in the pagan Anglo-Saxon 'Nine Herbs Charm', recorded in the 10th-century *Lacnunga* manuscript. With the prescribed incantations, the charm was intended for the treatment of poison and infection through the preparation of the nine herbs, which were crushed into a powder and mixed with old soap and apple juice to make a salve.

Roman soldiers are said to have brought their own stinging nettle to the British Isles to treat their legs – tired from long marches and painful in the inclement climate – with urtication (flogging with nettles); this was also standard practice among Canadian and American native tribes and Ecuadorean Indians. In Russia, Siberian men use urtication in their saunas, beating each other with stinging nettles for their restorative properties. The practice has to an extent received contemporary scientific validation for arthritic treatment: firstly, urtication stimulates the circulation and helps to remove toxins that cause rheumatics; secondly, the nettles' formic acid appears to have a beneficial effect on rheumatic joints.

Main therapeutic properties: Nettles feed, strengthen and support the whole body and its immune system, both as a first-rate medicinal herb and as a 'food medicine'. The herb is considered to be anti-asthmatic, anti-dandruff, astringent, diuretic, galactogogue, haemostatic, hypoglycaemic, hypotensive, pectoral, styptic, rubefacient and a tonic.

Down the ages, nettles have been used to staunch wounds and stem nosebleeds, but are also useful to relieve symptoms whenever there is a haemorrhage in the body. Their blood-purifying and strengthening properties are useful to pregnant women and those prone to anaemia. The young vitamin- and mineral-rich edible leaves are an excellent spring tonic and general detoxifying remedy. The list of vitamins and minerals that nettle contains is extensive and includes Vitamins A, C, D and K. It reputedly contains more chlorophyll than any other herb, which is indicative of high levels of iron (which promotes red blood-cell formation) and calcium (which is good for the bones, hair, skin and nails); potassium, phosphorus and sulphur are particularly abundant.

Freshly pressed nettle juice is good for nervous and physical exhaustion; it can also be used for gout, as research has shown that nettle increases uric-acid excretion by the kidneys.

A homoeopathic remedy made from the leaves is used to treat rheumatic gout, nettle rash and chickenpox, and is applied externally to bruises. Nettle extracts can be used to treat arthritis, anaemia, hay fever, kidney problems and pain; certain extracts are known to be used by body-builders.

The herb is also an anti-allergenic and aids the treatment of asthma, itchy skin and insect bites. Both Western and Chinese herbalists use *Hsieh-tzu-ts'ao* for childhood eczema and other variants of the skin condition, and it is especially beneficial for nervous eczema. *King's American Dispensatory* gives a specific indication of chronic diarrhoea and mucous colitis, as well as eczema.

Ayurvedic practitioners use nettles, combined with other herbs, as a hair-loss treatment, to massage the scalp and stimulate hair growth. Both they and traditional herbalists believe that nettle tea makes an excellent hair tonic and may restore natural hair colour.

In some cases of rheumatism and arthritis, nettles are extraordinarily successful. Nettle leaf has a long tradition of use as a supplementary remedy in the treatment of arthritis in Germany, and in 2002 German research on a stinging-nettle leaf extract was shown to be a promising potential remedy for inflammatory joint diseases.

There has also been research into nettle root to treat benign prostatic hyperplasia (BPH) in the US, Germany and Japan. New studies have revealed that root preparations relieve some of the

symptoms of BPH. Although it does not affect or decrease the enlargement of the prostate, nettle root may help relieve urinary difficulties associated with the condition's early stages.

Cautions: Excessive use may interact with treatment for diabetes and blood pressure, and with anti-inflammatory and sedative medications. Stinging nettle is contraindicated in cases of water retention caused by impaired cardiac or renal function. Rarely, allergic reactions have been observed, or nausea has

Although many gardeners consider the stinging nettle a weed, it has been used since ancient times as a source of food, fibre and medicine.

resulted, from the use of stinging nettles. Gastrointestinal irritation has been documented in a few cases.

Dried nettle or *Urtica* extract is widely used as a nourishing tonic for pregnant women, but fresh nettle has a uterine-stimulant action and may not be used in pregnancy. However, nettles may help to increase milk production in lactating women.

Valerian

Botanical name *Valeriana officinalis*
Family Valerianaceae

Description: Valerian is native to Europe and temperate Asia, including Japan. It is a hardy perennial with massive spindly, hairy roots and small pink or white, sweetly scented flowers. The fruit is a one-seeded nut. At two years old the roots and rhizomes are harvested for medicine.

Parts used: Roots and rhizomes, oil (in perfumery).

History: Valerian has been used in Indian Ayurvedic medicine and traditional Chinese medicine for millennia. Since the 1600s it has been one of the greatest sedative and restorative remedies for the nervous system. Italian nobleman and epileptic sufferer Fabio Colonna (b.1567), having discovered Galen's reference for valerian, used it to completely restore his health. This led to the medicinal evolution of the plant as a sedative, following which it was used to relieve spasms and as a sleep aid during the 17th to 18th centuries. Until the 20th century, valerian was used for nervous disorders, commonly referred to as hysteria or hypochrondirasis. Today, throughout Europe, North America, Australia and New Zealand, valerian is still used as a sedative and a restorative to treat nervous disorders. Formerly it was also used to treat diarrhoea, epilepsy, convulsions, vertigo, delirium, neuralgia, nervous cough, flatulence pains, stomach and muscle cramps, spasms, palpitations, croup and colic.

Valerian was an official remedy in the US Pharmacopoeia from 1820 to 1936, and a popular herb for insomnia in the US until after the Second World War and the advent of synthetic drugs. It is now listed as a sleep aid in more than 16 different pharmacopoeias of the world, and is also said to stimulate the appetite and relieve pain.

Main therapeutic properties: The herb has a long and proven record of efficacy and is considered an antispasmodic, carminative, diuretic, hypnotic, nervine, sedative and stimulant. In Europe more than 100 different valerian products are sold in pharmacies. Studies have shown that the fragrance alone has a powerful calming and profoundly relaxing effect.

Known as 'God's Valium', valerian is an established tranquillizer and is mainly used to encourage and improve sleep quality (it is unsuitable for acute insomnia because treatment may take several weeks to work) and to lower blood pressure, which is often heightened by stress and fatigue. It is also valuable for anxiety, nervous tension, panic attacks, emotional stress and other stress symptoms that may lead to a depressed state. In addition it is used as a muscle relaxant and for mild spasmodic affections, irritable bowel syndrome, premenstrual syndrome, menstrual cramps, irritability, nervous headaches and hypochondria.

Valerian has a history of exceptional safety, confirmed by clinical studies, and was approved by the German Commission E in 1985 as a sleep aid. Sold as a dietary supplement in the US, it is listed by the FDA as being generally safe.

Cautions: Valerian is not generally associated with addiction, but excessive use may cause headaches, giddiness, upset stomach, blurred vision, restlessness, nausea and morning wooziness. Do not combine it with other sedatives or alcohol, and practise caution with regard to driving or operating machinery. Valerian should not be taken by people with liver problems or during pregnancy or when lactating.

Chasteberry

Botanical name *Vitex agnus-castus*

Family Verbenaceae

Description:
Chasteberry is the fruit of the chaste tree, and is also commonly referred to as vitex. It is a small, deciduous, flowering shrub-like tree that grows to about 1–5 m (3–16 ft) tall. The plant is native to central Asia and can be found growing on river banks in southern Europe and throughout the Mediterranean region, and in tropical and sub-tropical regions throughout the world. It has a pleasing peppery, aromatic scent and taste and sprays of slender, beautiful flowers ranging from violet and lilac to blue and white in summer. The blooms develop into

red and then dark-brown or black peppercorn-sized berries that are used medicinally.

Parts used: Fruit (berries).

History: Chasteberry, which was known to the ancient Greeks and Romans and used by both Hippocrates and Dioscorides, has been employed medicinally for at least two millennia. Early on it was associated with the clergy, the name 'chaste' berry being thought to derive from a belief that the plant encouraged chastity: the ground-up seeds – literally 'monk's pepper' – were used in the Middle Ages in monasteries to suppress sexual desire. Chasteberry was also used by European nuns for women's hormonal problems.

A traditional plant in Africa, it has been suggested that chasteberry has the potential to improve nutrition, boost food security and play a role in rural development and sustainable land-care.

Main therapeutic properties: The plant is mostly used by women to ease menstrual problems and to stimulate breast milk. It is a diaphoretic, diuretic, febrifuge, galactogogue, libido-balancer (can act as both an anaphrodisiac and an aphrodisiac), sedative and stomachic.

Predominantly the leaves, then the flowers and berries (in descending order) are flavonoid-rich. Progesterone and testosterone both appear in the flowers and leaves.

Chasteberry is still used for various menstrual complaints, for conditions such as premenstrual syndrome and premenstrual breast tenderness, as well as for menopausal symptoms such as hot flushes, uterine fibroids, ovarian cysts and endometriosis. It is also used for infertility due to anovulation, hyperprolactinaemia, poor lactation and acne.

Cautions: Chasteberry has few side-effects (affecting just 1–2 per cent of patients in studies), although it may cause gastrointestinal problems, nausea, headaches and dizziness, increased menstrual flow, diarrhoea, acne or skin rash. It is contraindicated in pregnancy due to its hormonal effects and, for the same reason, should not be used by women with a hormone-sensitive condition, such as breast cancer. Chasteberry may interact with existing prescription drugs and with oral contraceptives. It may also affect the dopamine levels in the brain so should not be used by people taking dopamine-related medications.

Edible healing plants

Good food, great health

In recent years enormous advances have been made in our understanding of the relationship between food and health. We now appreciate the importance of such nutritional components as vitamins, minerals, antioxidants and fibre, and researchers have also concluded that the best source of many of these nutrients is plants.

Phytonutrients, or the nutrients derived specifically from plants, have now become a major focus of preventive healthcare (see pages 112–115). Researchers have concluded that plants are generally the best source of nutrients, without the added problems of high calories or fats that are often found in meat or dairy products. In fact, most of the so-called 'superfoods' – foods considered to be especially high in nutrients – are fruits, vegetables and grains.

Research based on ethnographic studies of the diets of populations around the world clearly shows that people who are major consumers of fruits and vegetables experience less cancer, heart disease, diabetes, high blood pressure and other chronic ills. People eating the traditional low-meat, high-vegetable diet of certain regions, including the Japanese

island of Okinawa, the Mediterranean area and the Hunza Valley in Pakistan, have demonstrably lower rates of chronic Western diseases and live longer.

The Stone Age diet

Researchers studying our Stone Age ancestors have been able to form conclusions regarding the content of their diet and their general health, through analysis of their skeletons and teeth. They have shown that Stone Age people ate lean meat when they could get it, or fish on coastal forays and from rivers, but mainly vegetables and/or vegetation and berries. They consumed up to 150 g (over 5 oz) of fibre a day, which is five times today's quota, and also consumed up to three times more of a far wider variety of fruits and vegetables than we do today, which – together with legumes, nuts and honey – provided 65 per cent of

their daily calories. The other 35 per cent was taken up with lean game, eggs, wild fowl, fish and shellfish.

Researchers have deduced that although Stone Age people may not have lived as long as we do today, with large numbers of them dying while hunting animals or from infection, those who did survive these challenges did not face cardiovascular disease, diabetes, hypertension or obesity at any age. Palaeolithic people also escaped the modern problem of osteoporosis, because their plant foods were so rich in calcium that their intake averaged 1,900 mg per day, whereas our current food content often offers less than the recommended daily allowance (RDA) of 1000 mg and

Serried ranks of vegetables and salad plants; which together form an army of healing and preventive medicine in our daily diets.

requires supplementation. Consuming large quantities of fibre daily in plant food prevented constipation, diverticulitis and possibly even colon cancer.

Today, many nutritionists are recommending a return to aspects of the Stone Age diet, including increased consumption of plant foods, to promote good health. In this part of the book (pages 120–247) you will find a guide to the edible fruits, vegetables, cereals, culinary herbs, nuts and seeds that can help protect you from disease and enhance your general health and well-being.

Phytonutrients

Researchers have identified the key phytonutrients that offer important health benefits. Interestingly, an easy way to identify many of these key plant nutrients is by the colour of the fruit or vegetable in question.

Colour-coding your choice of fruits and vegetables may not be an infallible system – a leafy vegetable that appears green overall may contain some of the same phytonutrient active compounds as another, different-coloured plant, for example – but it is a practical guide to what you can expect from your food.

Red-blue-purple foods

These foods contain anthocyanins, which belong to a group of plant compounds called flavonoids and are powerful pigment antioxidants, searching for and disabling the harmful 'free radicals' that deteriorate the internal structures of cells. It is this deterioration that causes various diseases, including heart disease and certain cancers. There is some evidence to suggest that the antioxidants contained in foods consumed in their natural state, such as fruit, are best.

Red foods

Red foods are high in lycopene, which is a carotenoid red pigment that imparts the colour to fruit and vegetables, especially tomatoes. It is a powerful antioxidant and may help to lower the risk of certain diseases, including heart disease; it is

Pomegranate is thought to provide natural antiviral, antifungal and bacterial benefits.

best known for lowering the risk of prostate cancer. Lycopene is oil-soluble and can be more easily absorbed if it is cooked or consumed with beneficial fats, such as olive oil.

Orange foods

These are rich in beta-carotene, an orange-coloured plant pigment that is known to be a precursor (inactive form) of Vitamin A and is used in the manufacture of Vitamin A in the liver. It belongs to the family of fat-soluble vitamins called carotenoids. Beta-carotene's antioxidant actions make it valuable in protecting against (and in some cases even reversing) pre-cancerous conditions affecting the breast, mucous membranes, throat, mouth, stomach, prostate, colon, cervix and bladder. Individuals with the highest levels of beta-carotene intake have lower risks of lung cancer, coronary artery disease, stroke and age-related eye disease and eye function. Beta-carotene is also important because Vitamin A is required for cell differentiation, bone growth, immunity (protection), tooth development, reproduction, and healthy skin and hair.

Orange-yellow foods

These all contain beta-cryptoxanthin, a natural carotenoid pigment and a potent cell and DNA-protecting antioxidant. It is converted to Vitamin A (retinol) and is therefore considered a 'pro-vitamin A'. Research suggests that cryptoxanthin could potentially act as a chemo-preventive agent against lung cancer.

Yellow-green foods

Yellow-green foods are sources of lutein and zeaxanthin, both of which fight cataracts and macular degeneration in the eye. Lutein is a yellow-orange carotenoid pigment found in many green vegetables, but it cannot be seen because it is overpowered by the green of the chlorophyll. Both lutein and zeaxanthin may be protective in eye disease because they absorb damaging blue light that enters the eye.

Green foods

Green foods are rich in detoxifying sulforaphane, isothiocyanates and indoles, which play a key role in stimulating cancer-fighting liver enzymes. Sulforaphane is an anticancer and antimicrobial compound that is present in cruciferous vegetables, or 'brassicas'. Isothiocyanates are a family of sulphur-containing organic compounds, which are largely responsible for the typical flavour of cruciferous vegetables and for the hotness of horseradish, radish and mustard. They also stimulate enzymes that may block steroid hormones, and their presence in the diet helps to prevent the promotion of breast and prostate cancers. Indoles are one of the major anticancer substances and are also found in cruciferous vegetables. They are a member of the class of sulphur-containing chemicals called glucosinolates and are formed whenever cruciferous vegetables are crushed or cooked.

White-green foods

Providing manifold health benefits, white-green foods such as garlic and onions are a rich source of the antibiotic, antifungal and antitumour compound known as allicin. However, there is no allicin without a helping human hand – only dry fibre cells and liquid acid cells. When you cut or crush garlic, the acid pours onto the fibre and allicin is the result of that chemical reaction. The phytochemicals (or flavonoids) of the white crimini mushroom (*Agaricus bisporus*) have inhibited the proliferation of breast-cancer cells in chemo-prevention in post-menopausal women.

Green salad leaves are anticarcinogenic contenders and as such can form a delicious detoxifying bastion against disease.

Healthy diets

The two experiments described below, one into the diet of our Stone Age ancestors and the other into the diet that is traditionally followed in the Mediterranean region, show in detail the benefits to be gained from healthy eating.

The Palaeolithic experiment

Recently an experiment with the Stone Age or Palaeolithic diet – eating like a caveman in the broader sense – was promoted by scientists as a means to reduce the risk of heart disease. The regime banned grains, cereals, pasta and bread (refined flour), as some research has linked grains to arthritis, gastrointestinal problems, headaches and depression. All dairy products were barred, as well as refined sugar (honey being used instead), because sugar drives up the blood levels of insulin, glucose and tryglycerides, which are known factors in diabetes and heart disease. Also excluded were processed vegetable oils and shortening (any processed fat or oil in any form, including a butter substitute such as a 'spread'), including hydrogenated and trans fats – the consumption of which promotes cancer, inflammation, high cholesterol and heart disease. Just three weeks on this diet of 'original' food was found to be enough to lower the chances of the participants suffering a heart attack or stroke.

Today, the Space-Agers of the West often eat an unwholesome diet of pre-prepared 'ready meals' that are high in sodium (salt), and assorted forms of processed foods that may contain preservatives, colourants (E numbers in the EU) and additives, as well as 'junk food'. Fruit and vegetables that offer optimum health benefits are not really fresh unless they are home-grown or organic and locally sourced, because foodstuffs start to lose their vitamin levels immediately after picking and are then transported by road, rail or air and taken in and out of different 'chill' temperatures to stop them rotting, on their way to the table. They also have sanctioned levels of pesticides, contaminants and so on thrown in for good measure.

Stone Age people's food supplies were not perfect as some plants were either unpalatable or toxic unless cooked. But 10,000 years ago an enormous advance was made, which changed human diets and the course of history for ever: people started cooking otherwise inedible foods to make them edible. At first humans knew what fire was, having witnessed it in natural events such as lightning, heath fires

Prehistoric African rock painting depicting men hunting the eland (antelope) for food energy, spiritual power and connectedness.

and volcanic eruptions, but they did not know how to kindle it. The day they discovered the art of cooking, they embraced the earth's source of light, heat and energy – creating a basis of civilization that separated humans from the animal kingdom. At the same time, a precious link was broken in the chain of human 'at-oneness' with nature.

The Mediterranean diet

The much-vaunted 'Mediterranean diet' has brought food values – and what food medicine can do for the public – to wider attention. Living longer may not be a goal in itself, but living a longer functional and enjoyable life, as free from disease as possible, may be the ultimate modern goal.

There is no one clear-cut Mediterranean diet, for what is eaten is predominantly seasonal and varies substantially from one Mediterranean country to another, and within a country from one region to another. Even so, there are shared features of what is usually referred to as the Mediterranean diet, which is traditionally followed in areas such as Greece, southern France and parts of Italy. Essentially this includes a high consumption of *fresh* fruits and vegetables, bread and other cereals, potatoes, beans, nuts and seeds, with olive oil as the main monounsaturated fat source instead of butter. Little red meat is eaten. Wine is consumed in low to moderate quantities, as are amounts of fish (including a variety of seafood), poultry and diary products; eggs are eaten up to four times weekly.

The diet is the mainstay of the multi-aspected so-called *French Paradox*: low incidence of deaths by heart disease and relative longevity are attributed to it.

Many studies – one of them involving almost 400,000 patients – indicate that a Mediterranean diet, if strictly followed, may play an important role in preventing premature mortality. It has been scientifically shown to help those who follow it avoid cancer and heart disease by improving the flexibility of the cell linings the blood-vessel walls, thus keeping the arteries and lungs healthy. It is also credited with helping to prevent pre-diabetes 'metabolic syndrome', which is also known as 'insulin-resistant syndrome'. The dominant underlying risk factors for this syndrome appear to be abdominal obesity and insulin resistance (as well as physical inactivity, ageing, hormonal imbalance and genetic disposition).

In the American study mentioned above, the diet of 380,296 patients aged 50–71 years was analyzed and their health tracked over the subsequent five years. Those whose diet conformed most closely to the Mediterranean model were found to suffer from significantly fewer deaths from causes such as cancer and heart disease than those who did not follow the diet. In other research, the Mediterranean diet helped to prevent asthma and respiratory allergies in children, and was shown to reduce the risk of Alzheimer's disease. Clearly, the evidence suggests that to lead healthier and longer lives, we must eat less meat and more plant-based foods.

Oranges are part of the Mediterranean diet, providing vitamin-rich juice, pulp for roughage, and flavoursome zesty oils from their rind.

Crimini mushroom

Botanical name *Agaricus bisporus*

Family Agaricaceae

Description: Crimini – known as the 'table mushroom', 'cultivated' or 'button' mushroom – is an edible 'higher fungus', which occurs naturally in grasslands, fields and meadows across Europe and North America. It has grown wild since prehistoric times, and early hunter-gatherers would have been familiar with it. It has a white cap, stalk, flesh and light mushroom-pink gills, turning red-brown to dark-brown.

Edible parts: Whole fungus, when cooked.

History: Cultivation of *A. bisporus* commenced in France, when the 17th-century agriculturist Oliver de Serres found that transplanting mushroom mycelia (the threadlike filaments) created more mushrooms. It is now one of the most cultivated mushrooms in the world.

The ancients conferred 'special powers' upon mysterious mushrooms.

The Egyptians believed they granted the gift of immortality, but because only the pharaohs were judged worthy of this gift, the *fellahin* or labourers were not even allowed to touch a mushroom. To Greek philosophers, mushrooms were created by lightning bolts and rain. Eating mushrooms was a common practice in ancient Rome, and dignitaries designated such fare *cibus diorum* or 'food of the gods'.

Love of fungi is particularly widespread in the Far East and South-East Asia, and among those mycophiles (mushroom devotees) of Europe, the Italians, French, Poles and Russians are notable.

Main therapeutic properties: The common mushroom contains a fantastic menu of health-giving components – complete Vitamin B-complex, Vitamin E and folate; the total RDA of selenium, followed by copper, tryptophan, potassium, phosphorus, zinc, manganese, magnesium, iron and calcium. All of this is geared to deliver well-being through antioxidants that bolster the immune system.

It has been discovered that a phytonutrient in mushrooms that promotes optimal health is a powerful amino-acid antioxidant called L-ergothioineine, and that mushrooms contain more of it than the prior top-scorers, chicken liver and wheatgerm. The most commonly consumed mushrooms, portobellos and criminis, contain the most L-ergothioineine. Better still, this amino-acid antioxidant is not destroyed by cooking. Fresh mushrooms are therefore a useful and low-calorie food than can be consumed without expanding the waistline. Furthermore, recent research suggests that mushrooms and their extracts may have a potent anti-cancer effect in breast and prostate cancers (studies were undertaken in Holland in 1998, in Spain and the US in 2006 and in Australia in 2009).

Cautions: Do not eat mushrooms if you are allergic to them. Do not eat crimini if you are susceptible to compounds known as 'purines', excessive intake of which may aggravate an existing condition such as gout or kidney problems. All mushrooms of the genus *Agaricus* contain the hydrazine agartine, a chemical compound that is a suspected carcinogen and occurs in commercially produced *A. bisporus* species. However, in 1995 Swiss research showed that it would take an average consumption of 4 g mushrooms a day to contribute to a lifetime cumulative cancer risk of about two cases per 100,000 lives.

Pineapple

Botanical name *Ananas cosmosus*

Family Bromeliaceae

Description: The pineapple is a herbaceous perennial that is native to South America, including Brazil, Uruguay and Paraguay, and is cultivated throughout the tropics for its fruit. Growing up to 1 m (3 ft) high, with a short sturdy stem, it has a large, cylindrical, thistle-type fruit resembling a pine cone (hence its name), with 30 or more stiff, serrated leaves. The fruit is juicy and sweet, with cream-coloured to orange flesh.

Edible parts: Flesh of fruit.

History: First discovered on the Caribbean island of Guadeloupe by Christopher Columbus in 1593, this perishable fruit was coveted by early American colonists and became a prestigious symbol of social status. In the 19th century the Spanish introduced it to the Philippines, Hawaii and Guam. In Europe, the fruit was grown under glass, either in pineapple pits or in hot-houses. The first commercial plantation was set up in 1886.

Pineapple has a distinctive odour that spells out the allure of its enticing taste. It was beloved by wealthy Britons in the nineteenth century, who created pineapple pits in their walled gardens to cultivate the fruit for the table. It is an old symbol of hospitality and is often portrayed in carved stone decorations in the architecture of grand houses.

Main therapeutic properties: Pineapple is anti-inflammatory, antiviral and mildly oestrogenic, and helps to dissolve blood clots and build bones. It is believed to help relieve catarrh, arthritis, bronchitis and indigestion. It also provides significant levels of pro-vitamin A, carotene and potassium.

Pineapple suppresses inflammation via its main constituent, bromelain, which is an antibacterial, anti-inflammatory enzyme. More than 200 scientific papers have been published on bromelain since it was first recognized as a health-boosting substance in 1957, most of which have focused on its anti-inflammatory effects. Bromelain is frequently prescribed in Germany for its anti-inflammatory action.

Due to its very high content of manganese (a trace mineral that is needed for the body to build bone and connective tissues), pineapple contributes to good bone health, helping to prevent osteoporosis and bone fractures. It also contains significant amounts of Vitamin C and B_1. The stems have also shown antitumour activity. Pineapple may also help to ease ailments and conditions such as colds and flu, osteoarthritis and rheumatoid arthritis, and may increase the effectiveness of some antibiotics.

Recently, scientists have suggested that a Brazilian cousin of the table pineapple, *A. ananassoides*, which is commonly used in that region against gastric pain, shows promise as a new anti-ulcerogenic drug.

Cautions: Pineapple should not be taken by those who are allergic to it or those suffering from protein deficiencies or disorders. It should also not be eaten by those with haemophilia and kidney or liver disease, because its anticoagulant property can pose a risk for those taking aspirin or blood-thinning drugs.

Asparagus

Botanical name *Asparagus officinalis*

Family Asparagaceae

Description: Asparagus is a slender-stemmed perennial that originated in the eastern Mediterranean region, but is native to most of Europe, northern Africa and western Asia. It has upright 'spears' (shoots from the underground crown) that can grow up to 2 m (6 ft) high. On 'going to seed', the bracts on the spear-heads branch out into stems with delicate fronds, which are nicknamed 'maidenhair fern' and are red-berried in the autumn.

Edible parts: Shoots, when cooked.

History: Discovered by the Greeks growing along the shores of the eastern Mediterranean, asparagus was being cultivated by the Romans by 200 BCE. However, there are ancient Egyptian tomb

drawings of asparagus from *c.* 4000 BCE, and indications that it was used for urinary conditions and for worming.

During the Renaissance asparagus was promoted as an aphrodisiac and was banned from the kitchens of most nunneries. In his *Complete Herbal* (1653) Nicholas Culpeper advised that it 'stirreth up bodily lust in man or woman, whatever some have written to the contrary'.

In the Arabic love manual *The Perfumed Garden* by Sheikh Nefzaoui (translated in 1880), it was written that he who ate every day of this dish would find it a stimulant for his amorous desires. Later, Theodoor Henrick van de Velde (1873–1937), a Dutch physician, gynaecologist and sexologist, also hailed asparagus as an aphrodisiac.

Main therapeutic properties: Asparagus has higher antioxidant levels than many other vegetables, even when canned. Antiviral and antifungal, it is used to treat urinary-tract infections, is a natural diuretic, detoxificant, cardiac tonic and laxative.

In the past asparagus was mainly used to treat cystitis, pyelitis, kidney disease, rheumatism and gout, some of which uses have recently been called into question. However, in 1996 promising American research found the plant's saponin compounds to inhibit the growth of leukaemia cells *in vitro*. They were also found to display inhibitory activities against colon cancer, melanoma and renal cancer. In addition, asparagus provides inulin, which facilitates gut-friendly bacteria.

Asparagus spears are a very special food that is low in calories but also highly nutritious. Asparagus is rich in folate (necessary to the unborn, and for some elderly to avoid chronic disease) and in Vitamins K, C and A, plus B-complex, and it contains a valuable amount of calcium and fibre. Its detoxifying, diuretic effects help expel waste products – such as uric crystals that have accumulated in the joints and excess water (bloating) – via the urine, and it is used to treat kidney and bladder stones. Asparagus also contains the phytochemical glutathione, which has antioxidant and anticarcinogenic properties.

Cautions: Some people, after eating asparagus, will notice a harmless, malodorous effect in their urine, which is engendered by a sulphur compound called methyl mercaptan, but the scent disappears when the vegetable is completely digested and absorbed. For now, asparagus is not recommended for arthritics, as researchers are unsure if it aggravates or reduces pain.

Beetroot

Botanical name *Beta vulgaris* var. *rubra*

Family Chenopodiaceae

Description: Beetroot is a dark red root vegetable. Its ancestry runs through prehistoric times in North Africa, and it grew along the Asian and European seashores and as far as India. Beetroot is also native to Russia and other cool areas of the world. It is a herbaceous biennial related to the swede, turnip and sugar beet, with nutritious red-veined leaves like Swiss chard, and wind-pollinated flowering spikes.

Edible parts: Leaves and root, either cooked or raw.

History: Evidence of the cultivation of beetroot has been found in the Neolithic site of Aartswoud in the Netherlands, dating its use to at least 8500 BCE. Remains were also excavated in the Saqqara pyramid at Thebes in Egypt (*c*. 2667–2648 BCE. And Hippocrates, the 'father of medicine', was using beetroot leaves as bandages in around 400 BCE.

Originally the highly nutritious beet leaves, and not the roots, were eaten.

The ancient Romans were one of the first civilizations to cultivate beets to use their roots as food, describing it as a panacea for all ills. Beetroot was used in ancient Greek and Roman cookery, and was a food that the ancients deemed worthy of offering to Apollo at Delphi. Today, the famous borscht beetroot soup is familiar to all Eastern Europeans.

Beetroot was reputedly an ancient aphrodisiac, owing some of its status to salacious scenes that were discovered on the walls of brothels in the town of Pompeii, which was destroyed in 79 CE by the eruption of Mount Vesuvius. In and around Pompeii, seeds and other traces of beetroot have been excavated.

Main therapeutic properties: Low in calories, beetroot is an excellent source of folate and iron, and is abundant in Vitamin C and potassium. The plant promotes optimal health by helping to keep cholesterol levels stable and protect the body against heart diseases, birth defects (DNA alterations) and certain cancers, especially colon cancer.

anthocyanins and beta-carotene, plus multi-nutrient compounds.

Modern advocacy for beetroot as an aphrodisiac is based on it being a rich source of the mineral boron, which plays a role in the production of the male sex hormone, testosterone. It has also been referred to as an aphrodisiac in contemporary Indian medicine.

Cautions: Some people who eat beetroot may experience beeturia, a red or pink colour in the urine or stool, which is a totally harmless, transient condition. Because

It is a good fortifying general tonic, suitable for pregnant women, and is a liver, kidney and gall-bladder purifying herb. Its juice and leaves are packed with powerful immuno-stimulatory high-octane antioxidants contained in its colouring pigments, including purple-red beetroot greens contain oxalate, those with kidney stones should avoid over-consumption of the vegetable, especially the leaves. As beetroot has a high level of natural sugar, raw beetroot rather than processed is more suitable for diabetics.

Chinese cabbage

Botanical name *Brassica campestris* subsp. *napus* var. *pekinensis*

Family Brassicaceae

Description: Chinese cabbage is a leaf vegetable related to the Western cabbage and is of the same species as the common turnip. The plant originated in China, near the Beijing region, and has been widely used in eastern Asia. It is a hardy biennial plant that is grown as an annual, and forms a large, cylindrical, compact head.

Edible parts: Leaves, either cooked, pickled (as *kimchi*) or raw.

History: Chinese cabbage has been cultivated in China for more than 6,000 years and was a common constituent of southern China's diet by the 5th century CE. Its seeds have been found in jars excavated at the Neolithic-period settlement of Banpo, part of the Yangshao culture in China (5000–4000 BCE). During the Ming Dynasty the physician and pharmacologist Li Shizhen (1518–93), author of the *Compendium of Materia Medica*, studied the medicinal virtues of Chinese cabbage and used it with amaranth to treat ulcers.

Historically, Chinese cabbage was first introduced into Korea as a type of pickled (salted) vegetable (*kimchi*) in the 7th century CE. The highly infection-preventive *kimchi* dish came to the attention of commentators during the SARS epidemic in China in 2003.

Main therapeutic properties: Chinese cabbage comprises 45 per cent Vitamin C and almost no fat, and is mainly used as a depurative (purifying the blood). *Kimchi* is a wholesome, therapeutic herbal-food amalgamation. It is fermented through lactic acid at low temperatures to ensure proper ripening and preservation, and seasoned with a herbal bactericidal, antiviral and antifungal mix, mainly of red pepper (chilli powder), garlic, ginger, green onion (spring onions) and radish (and mustard greens in *kimchi* soup).

The US magazine *Health* named *kimchi* in its list of top five 'world's healthiest foods' for being rich in vitamins, aiding digestion and potentially retarding cancer growth. The dish contains numerous antioxidants, cancer-preventing compounds, and each of its herbs brings its own valuable collection of enriching Vitamins A, B_1, B_2, C and carotenes, the minerals calcium and iron, as well as other significant curative compounds, with a high content of dietary fibre and very little fat.

There are several research papers documenting the medicinal properties of *kimchi* and reports of its past reputation in aiding people with SARS, bringing to attention to its potential to assist against Avian flu (H5N1), which in 2008 transferred from one human to another in China. This is particularly important as a report in *Nature*, the international weekly science journal, found that common mutations of the H5N1 avian-flu virus that have emerged in human influenza are resistant to some current antiviral treatment. It may also have potential to assist against swine flu (SIV) strains including H1N1, H1N2, H3N1, H3N2, and H2N3.

Cautions: Some research focusing on high-sodium dietary dependence found over-consumption of *kimchi* and soybean paste to be a risk factor in gastric cancer. However, *kimchi* recipes vary by region; one oncological study found one type of *kimchi* to be protective against gastric cancer and two others to contain such high sodium as to be risk factors.

Cabbage

Botanical name *Brassica oleracea* var. *capitata*

Family Brassicaceae

Description: The cabbage is a herbaceous, biennial flowering plant with leaves forming a characteristic layered, compact cluster. It is not known precisely where the cabbage originated, but it first spread across northern Europe into Germany, Poland and Russia. Cabbage grows in late autumn and, before forming a head, is called 'colewort' when it is similar to 'kale', a hardy cabbage with coarse curly leaves that does not form a head.

Edible parts: Leaves (head), either cooked or raw.

History: From medicinal reference to it we know that the cabbage, which was held in high esteem for its broad spectrum of healing powers, was grown in ancient Greece and Rome and, it is thought, was brought to Europe in around 600 BCE by roving groups of Celts. Cato the Elder (234–149 BCE) praised cabbage for its medicinal properties, declaring it to be 'the first of all the vegetables'. And cabbage is widely, if anecdotally, documented as a wound-healing plant, because Roman soldiers used it to allay infections and encourage healing of their injuries.

Sauerkraut (German for 'sour cabbage') is made from fermented cabbage. In his 1772 *Treatise on Scurvy* James Lind, the British pioneer of naval hygiene in the Royal Navy, found its consumption by Dutch sailors to be the defining factor that prevented them getting scurvy on long sea voyages; five years later this finding was used to allay scurvy in British crews.

Main therapeutic properties: This 'superfood' is anti-inflammatory, antioxidant, detoxificant and anti-carcinogenic, especially for prostate, colorectal, stomach, bladder, lung, breast and ovarian cancers. According to research, cabbage consumption also provides significant benefits for cardiovascular health.

Cabbage's medicinal phytonutrients and vitamins chiefly comprise Vitamin K (a blood coagulant) and antioxidant

cure for colds, flu and headaches, especially hangovers.

In European folk medicine, and no doubt further afield, observations of cabbage use over the centuries has been shown in modern times to be based upon accurate scientific deliberations. For example, raw cabbage juice is a well-known domestic remedy for upset stomachs; research now suggests that its success in effectively treating and healing peptic ulcers is due to its anti-inflammatory glutamine (amino-acid) content.

Reports of other anti-inflammatory remedies abound. For example, to reduce the discomfort of acute inflammation, place a paste of raw cabbage in a cabbage leaf and wrap it around the affected area. This remedy is also acclaimed in alleviating the pain of mastitis in breastfeeding women.

Vitamin C, as well as Vitamin B-complex, folate and other mineral trace elements. In addition, its cancer-fighting properties are thought to result from high levels of glucosinolates, which are bodily metabolized into potent anti-carcinogens called isothiocyanates.

There is a long history of cures by cabbage for many different diseases, including both simple and complicated injuries, rheumatic pains, facial neuralgia, headaches, leg ulcers, anthrax, and so on. Cabbage-water has been used as a

Cautions: At the time of writing, allergy to brassicas in general is very rare, but it can present with other plant food and pollen allergies and is said to be on the increase. In 2009, researchers in Greece found the IgE-mediated allergy pertains to raw cabbage but not to cooked.

Broccoli

Botanical name *Brassica oleracea*

Family Brassicaceae

Description: Calabrese broccoli is an annual or biennial vegetable that is a relative of wild cabbage. It originated along the northern and western coasts of the Mediterranean. The sprouting plant has multi-flower heads that are usually blue-green to dark green, but can be purple, at the branch-like ends of its stalks, which are picked and eaten before the flower blooms. While Calabrese broccoli is green and single-headed and resembles a cauliflower, Chinese broccoli (also known as kale or kai-lan), another member of the *B. oleracea* family, is a loose-leafed, slightly bitter-tasting vegetable.

Edible parts: Flowering parts and stalks, cooked or raw.

History: Whatever broccoli's exact origin, Pliny the Elder (23–79 CE), the Roman historian and naturalist, wrote about a vegetable that fitted its description. And some devotees of the cookbook of the ancient Romans' 'celebrity chef' Apicius declare that they recognize broccoli in his works, which indicates that the Italians were probably growing the vegetable in the 1st century CE. Later, Italian immigrants brought broccoli to North America.

Main therapeutic properties: Broccoli is truly a health-giving 'superfood', offering a portmanteau of nutritional and pharmaceutical benefits. An unadulterated natural neutraceutical, it contains glucosinolates, phytochemicals that break down compounds, and the carotenoid known as lutein. The plant is an excellent source of Vitamins K, C and A, B_6 and E, as well as folate and fibre, with a sound complement of minerals, especially phosphorus, potassium and magnesium.

Like other cruciferous vegetables with an arsenal of phytonutrient anti-cancer weapons, broccoli helps to prevent tumour growth. In particular Indole-3-carbinol has been shown to suppress not only breast-tumour cell growth, but also the spread of cancerous cells from the original site to other parts of the body.

Research also shows that kaempferol-rich broccoli is protective against ovarian cancer, and can also help to prevent bladder cancer and lower the risk of certain aggressive prostate cancers (it is especially effective for the latter when combined with tomatoes). Most recently science suggests that a topical broccoli extract could offer better protection against skin cancer than a conventional sunscreen.

Apart from its anti-cancer and cardio-protective roles, broccoli's carotenoids may assist in the prevention of cataract formation. All in all, broccoli is a marvellous edible health support, especially the purple-sprouting variety.

Cautions: People suffering from thyroid problems should avoid excessive intake of cabbage and broccoli (cruciferous vegetables), because they contain a natural substance called goitrogen, which may hinder the proper functioning of the thyroid glands. Those taking anticoagulants should avoid kale and other cruciferous vegetables that are high in Vitamin K content.

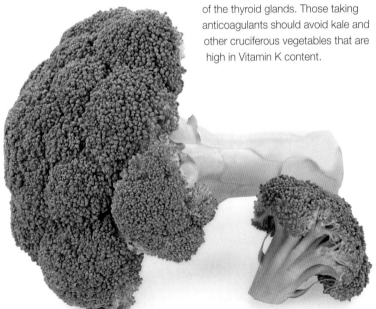

Orange

Botanical name *Citrus aurantium*

Family Rutaceae

Description: The orange is a flowering tree growing to about 7.5 m (25 ft) tall. The exact location of its origin has not been clearly identified, although most researchers place it in South-East Asia, from where it is believed to have spread to north-eastern India, Burma and China, eventually finding its way to Africa, Arabia

and the Holy Land, and thence to the Mediterranean. It has delicate, perfumed white flowers and orange fruit; the peel contains volatile oil glands in pits. The bergamot (*C. aurantium* subsp. *bergamia*) is a hybrid cross between the bitter (Seville) orange and the small-fruited 'true' or Key lime. It is a small, almost pear-shaped citrus fruit with an aromatic bitter peel that becomes bright reddish-orange on maturity.

Edible parts: Flesh and juice of fruit. Peel used in small quantities as flavouring.

History: The word 'orange' is believed to come from the Sanskrit. By the end of the 12th century it was being cultivated in Seville, in Spain, giving the bitter orange its common name of Seville orange.

The origin of bergamot is obscure, one theory being that Columbus brought the plant back from the Antilles or the Canaries to Spain, and it then reached Calabria from the town of Berga, near Barcelona, whence it took its name.

Main therapeutic properties: Bitter-orange peel is an appetite-stimulant, and orange-peel tea is good for digestive disorders and gastric-juice deficiency, for gastrointestinal disorders and the prevention of abnormal growths. The German Commission E also lists orange peel for treating poor digestion due to hypo-acidity.

Oranges are a first-rate source of Vitamin C as well as a good source of B vitamins, Vitamin A, folate and dietary fibre, and of calcium and potassium. Oranges' high content of Vitamin C, which is the primary water-soluble antioxidant in the body, helps to prevent internal and external damage to the body and also aids the proper functioning of a healthy immune system.

The tasty bitterness of Seville orange marmalade is attributed to its triterpenes and flavonoids. The triterpene limonene in orange's essential oil provides its characteristic citrus fragrance and taste, which acts through scent alone to encourage appetite. The water-soluble flavonoids of an orange's zest are highly antioxidant and immuno-protective.

Cautions: Sweet oranges and their juice are considered safe for unrestricted consumption. However, bitter orange contains synephrine (or oxedrine), a stimulant drug, similar to ephedrine, that is extracted from the peel and used to encourage fat loss. Consumption should not be abused as synephrine may increase blood pressure and can, among other cardio-effects, cause arrhythmias.

Lemon and lime

Botanical names *Citrus* x *limon, C.* x *latifolia, C. aurantifolia*

Family Rutaceae

Description: The true lemon (*C.* x *limon*) is a small hybrid tree cultivated from wild plants 3–6 m (10–20 ft) in height. It has mildly fragrant white flowers that produce ovoid fruits with an acidic yellow pulp; the peel is usually light yellow and is dotted with aromatic oil glands. The Key lime tree (*C. aurantifolia*) and Persian lime trees (*Citrus* x *latifolia*) are similar, but the fruits have a greenish pulp and green peel that becomes yellow when mature.

Edible parts: Juice of fruit. Peel used in small quantities as flavouring.

History: As with other fruiting citrus trees the exact origins of the lemon and the lime remain a mystery, although the lemon has been linked with north-western India. Lemon trees allegedly entered Europe via southern Italy in 200 CE, and were cultivated in Iraq and Egypt by 700 CE, reaching Sicily and China and then being distributed by the Arabs throughout the Mediterranean region.

The Persian lime (*C. latifolia*) was introduced to Europe during the Crusades. The fruit known in English as a lime derived its name from the Persian term *limu*. The Key lime is native to the Indo-Malayan region. It is assumed it was carried to North Africa and the Middle East by Arabs and taken by Crusaders from Palestine to Mediterranean Europe. Well-known and cultivated in Italy by the mid-13th century, doubtless it was later conveyed to the Caribbean islands by the Spaniards. It was reportedly commonly grown in Haiti in 1520 and became naturalized in America. There is no record of the lime's arrival in Florida, although the 'Key' name comes from its association with the Florida Keys.

Main therapeutic properties: The lemon is a highly antioxidant food, as well as a bitter aromatic 'cooling' herb with diuretic, anti-inflammatory and anti-infection properties. Nutritionally, lemon juice is very high in antioxidant Vitamin C, as well as in A vitamins, with carotenoid and small amounts of Vitamin B_1, B_2 and B_3. It is very high in potassium, with good amounts of folate and calcium, as well as trace elements of sodium, zinc, copper and iron.

Because of its high Vitamin C content, lemon juice is an excellent tonic for the gastrointestinal tract and digestion, liver disorders, infections and boosting the immune system. Lemon juice is widely known as a diuretic, antiscorbutic, astringent and febrifuge. Lemon's citro-flavonoids are chiefly used internally in vascular disorders where venous insufficiency results in haemorrhoids and varicose veins. Lemon is excellent for sore throats and minor fevers attending colds.

Renowned as an antiscorbutic and highly antioxidant, the lime fruit's antioxidant value has been proven by science to increase with its ripeness. It has a high content of Vitamins C and A and folate. It is also high in potassium and is calcium-rich, with phosphorus, magnesium and iron, plus trace amounts of selenium, zinc, manganese and copper. Concentrated extract of lime juice has also shown potential anti-cancer properties against the proliferation of human breast and lymph cancers.

Cautions: At the time of writing, no contraindications for use of lemons as food have been identified. However, lemon may reduce the effects of malaria chloroquine plasma concentrations. Overuse of lime peel could interfere with anticoagulant drugs. Citrus juice is often implicated in the worsening of gastroesophageal reflux symptoms. Conventionally grown fruits are likely to have pesticide residues on their skin.

Grapefruit

Botanical name *Citrus* x *paradisi*

Family Rutaceae

Description: Grapefruit is a sub-tropical evergreen citrus tree grown for its fruit. It is not known in its wild state, but is thought to have been developed as a hybrid in the Caribbean, whence the plant spread to America. It grows to around 5–6 m (16–20 ft) tall, with dark-green, glossy leaves, white flowers and sphere-shaped fruits with yellow-orange or pinkish-red skins. The flesh is acidic and segmented, the colour varying according to the cultivars, including white, pink and red pulps.

Edible parts: Flesh of fruit, juice.

History: The name 'grapefruit' was coined in Jamaica in 1814, although it is also claimed to be one of the 'Seven Wonders of Barbados'. Prior to the fruit becoming popular from the late 19th century, it was grown as an ornamental plant.

Main therapeutic properties: Whether eaten fresh, canned or juiced, grapefruit pulp, though consisting mainly of water and fibre with cholesterol-lowering pectin, is a rich source of potassium and Vitamins B, E and especially C, and of folate, iron, calcium and other minerals. The pink and red grapefruit varieties are rich in antioxidant Vitamin A. Grapefruit also contains lycopene, which contributes towards the prevention of prostate and other cancers, aids the prevention of heart and kidney disease and even helps to improve sperm count.

Grapefruit's antioxidant flavonoids have recently been under the microscope of American and Chinese researchers. It is reported that one specific flavonoid, called *narignenin*, helps to repair damaged DNA in human prostate cells. Grapefruit also contains phytonutrients called limonoids, which inhibit tumour formation and are potent anticarcinogens that may prevent cancerous cells from proliferating.

Grapefruit juice significantly increases the production and activity of liver detoxification and helps to protect against lung and colon cancer. Its compounds not only increase the death of cancer cells, but also the production of normal colon cells.

Grapefruit-seed extract is a natural preservative with stated antiviral, antibacterial, antiparasitic and antifungal properties for various ailments. Most recently, in 2008, Nigerian research in animals has supported grapefruit seeds' traditional use in the management of type-I diabetic patients. However, grapefruit seed extract has also aroused serious controversy for its contamination with biocidal drugs added to commercial branded grapefruit seed products.

Cautions: The compounds in grapefruit juice slow the normal detoxification processes in the intestines and liver and are known to increase the circulating levels of several prescription drugs. It is therefore advisable not to drink grapefruit juice while taking prescribed drugs.

Globe artichoke

Botanical name *Cynara cardunculus*

Family Asteraceae

Description: The globe artichoke is a giant cultivated perennial thistle with downy, grey-green, deeply serrated leaves. Native to the Mediterranean basin, it is said to have originated in Ethiopia and to have travelled to southern Europe via Egypt. It produces huge flower heads with individual purple florettes that are inedible and are known as the 'choke'.

Edible parts: The lower portions of the bud's numerous triangular fleshy scales and the base known as the 'heart'.

History: The artichoke is one of the oldest cultivated and medicinal plants. Its image is found on ancient Egyptian tablets and sacrificial altars, and Persian tablets dating from *c*. 4000 BCE also indicate that it was among the legendary panoply of foods and spices consumed by the Persian royalty of Mesopotamia. The ancient Greeks and Romans considered the artichoke a 'noble' vegetable, meant to be eaten by royals and the rich. In the 15th century it made its debut in wider

Europe and spread to England, and thence in the 16th century to America.

Main therapeutic properties: This bitter and salty, detoxifying herb is predominantly used for indigestion and dyspepsia, to protect the liver and stimulate its function by increasing bile production. The Greeks and Romans traditionally used artichoke as a remedy for indigestion following a meal that was high in fat, although its consumption was reserved for the elite. Today, science has shown this use to be correct, because the plant contains cynarin, an active constituent that is derived from the dried or fresh leaves and/or stems of the plant, and which causes an increase in bile flow, thus aiding digestion.

In Vietnam, artichoke tea (*tra itso*) made from the flowers and leaves claims all the plant's virtues in one, that is to act as a diuretic and liver tonic, guard the liver against toxins and infections and lower blood cholesterol. According to recent studies, it also plays an essential role in fat and alcohol metabolism. In addition it

helps to reduce nausea, abdominal pain, constipation and flatulence.

Cautions: Do not handle artichokes if you are allergic to them or the Asteraceae family generally. Do not eat artichoke if you suffer from a bile-duct blockage. Use it with caution if you suffer from gallstones, as it could cause you to have painful spasms.

Wild strawberry

Botanical name *Fragaria vesca*

Family Rosaceae

Description: The wild strawberry is a delicate, perennial, low-growing plant, which spreads by means of 'runners'. There are still wild strawberries in some parts of Europe and in the temperate regions of Asia and North and South America. They have white flowers and small scarlet, cone-shaped fruits studded with tiny brown 'seeds'.

Edible parts: Fruits.

History: From a few tiny seeds discovered by archeologists in Mesolithic sites in

Denmark, Neolithic sites in Switzerland and Iron Age sites in England, we know that prehistoric humans ate their share of wild strawberries. In England, the earliest recorded mention of 'stroeberrie' comes in an Anglo-Saxon plant list.

Sporadic efforts at cultivation of the wild variety began in the 1300's in home gardens. In Europe, hybridizing began to take root early in the 18th century. There is a record of the French King Louis XV being presented with a pot of Chilean wild strawberries (*Fragaria chiloensis*) in 1764.

Fragaria comes from the Latin *fragum*, meaning fragrant, while *vesca* means 'little'. It is suggested that they got their name 'straw'-berries because they were both mulched and packed for transport in straw.

Native North Americans have a mythological tale of the fruit's origin in which it is named the 'heartberry', because it is shaped like a heart and symbolizes the love of the First Man and the First Woman. The Native Americans ate wild strawberries for colds and used the juice, mixed with water, to bathe reddened eyes.

According to the philosophical Doctrine of Signatures, the shape and colour of the fruit, resembling a heart, also meant that is was good for heart disease. A traditional use for a limited amount of fruit is to steep them in wine to make a remedy for 'reviving the spirits and making the hart merrie'!

Main therapeutic properties: Wild strawberries are high in carbohydrates and contain fibre, Vitamins B, C and E, folic acid and carotene, as well as the minerals iron, magnesium and calcium, among others, and phenols, tannins, mucilage, sugars, fruit acids and salicylates. The leaves contain flavonoids, tannins and volatile oil.

The wild strawberry plant is hardly used medicinally today, but its leaves are mildly astringent and diuretic and treat diarrhoea and dysentery, as well as being used as a gargle for sore throats and in a lotion for minor scrapes and burns. Europeans consider the fruit to have cooling and diuretic properties, and it has been prescribed as part of a diet in cases of TB, gout, arthritis and rheumatism. The Chinese also categorize the juice as *yin* and 'cool'. The fruits are judged to be a liver tonic and are laxative. In Ayurvedic medicine, strawberry leaves are a cooling, astringent diuretic.

Cautions: Do not consume strawberries if you are allergic to them. The leaves may also cause allergic reactions in people hypersensitive to strawberries.

Shiitake mushroom

Botanical name *Lentinula edodes*

Family Marasmiaceae

Description: This brown, rubbery-looking edible fungus is known in the English-speaking world by its Japanese name 'shiitake', and is the second most commonly cultivated edible mushroom. Its origins were in China, but its name, *shii* meaning 'mushroom' derives directly from the Japanese evergreen Chinquapin tree, native to southern Japan and southern Korea, which provided the logs on which it is typically cultivated.

Edible parts: Whole fungus (fruiting body).

History: The first written record of the shiitake's husbandry was by Wu Sang Kwuan during the Song Dynasty (960–1127 CE). However, the wild mushroom is documented as being eaten as early as 199 CE. A Ming Dynasty (1368–1644) physician, Wu Juei, recommended it in writing for upper respiratory diseases, poor blood circulation, liver trouble, exhaustion and weakness, and to boost *qi* (life energy). It was also used to prevent premature ageing and promote longevity.

Before 1982 the Japanese variety of shiitake could only be grown in traditional locations using ancient methods. But in the late 1970s Gary F. Leatham, a researcher and prolific author, made commercialization of the Japanese variety possible worldwide. It is now cultivated in many Asian countries, as well as being dried and exported, and is a feature of Chinese, Japanese, Korean and Thai cuisine.

Main therapeutic properties: The shiitake mushroom (especially sun-dried) is one of the few known natural sources of Vitamin D. Fresh shiitake's macronutrients are mainly Vitamin C, sodium, iron, folate and dietary fibre; when dried, it shows high levels of potassium, phosphorus and magnesium, and lesser levels of selenium, calcium and iron. It contains excellent micronutrients, with a compliment of 18 amino acids, especially glutamic acid. It also has more than 50 different enzymes, including pepsin (which aids digestion) and asparaginase (a substance that has been used to treat childhood leukaemia).

These days, shiitake extracts – and sometimes the whole dried mushroom – are used in herbal remedies. Shiitake is used in traditional Chinese medicine to fight cancer and AIDS by boosting the body's immune system. It also helps infections such as hepatitis by producing interferon, which stops viruses from multiplying.

Recently, the focus has been on shiitake's powerful antitumour polysaccharide, called lentinan, which is an important component of traditional Chinese medicine and one of the most common anti-cancer drugs in Japan.

Lentinan is found in several mushroom, yeasts and other foods, and is combined with chemotherapies to treat a variety of cancers. It is effective against cancer recurrence and in prolonging the lifespan of patients. Further research into the anti-cancer properties of lentinan is in progress.

Cautions: Shiitake mushrooms and their extracts are generally considered safe, although there are reports of diarrhoea or bloating. Some people who have developed allergic reactions affecting the skin, nose, throat or lungs should avoid exposure to this fungus.

Goji berry

Botanical name *Lycium barbarum*

Family Solanaceae

Description: Goji berry, or Chinese wolfberry, is a woody perennial. The berries are gathered wild from the hills in the Ningxia region of China, and in remote areas of central China near inner Mongolia. The plant grows 1–3m (3–10 ft) high, with lavender-purple flowers in groups of one to three growing along stems that produce bright orange-red berries.

Edible parts: Only ripe fruits (raw, dried or cooked), young shoots and leaves (root bark, medicinally).

History: Chinese physicians have used and studied the goji berry for thousands of years. An early medical work, *Shen Nung Ben Tsao* (475–221 BCE), noted that its benefits ranged from replenishing vital essences to reinforcing and restoring major organs. Another mention occurred in the 7th-century Tang Dynasty treatise *Yao Xing Lun*. The berries were also used in traditional Tibetan and Mongolian as well as Korean and Japanese medicine systems, to nourish the *yin* and improve the functioning of the 'water element'. The ability of the goji berry to inflame passions is reflected in the implied aphrodisiac aspect of the old Chinese proverb 'He who travels one thousand kilometres from home should not eat goji'.

In China, dried goji berries, which are traditionally cooked before consumption, are used in tonic soups or boiled as a herbal tea, or drunk as a combined grape and goji-berry wine. The young shoots and leaves are also grown commercially as a leaf vegetable. In the West, dried goji berries are mainly used as a snack and in raw food diets, and are sometimes used in stir-frys and other Asian dishes.

Main therapeutic properties: In herbal medicine the plant's roots and berries are used for myriad ailments and conditions. The goji berry is a powerful antioxidant with anti-ageing properties. It has been used in traditional Chinese medicine for treatments ranging from strengthening the eyes, liver and kidneys to fortifying the *qi* or life force, and to boost the immune system and sperm count and improve circulation.

Goji berries contain more beta-carotene than carrots, and 500 times more Vitamin C than oranges. They also contain many nutrients and phytochemicals, among them high amounts of Vitamins B_1, B_6 and E. This powerful berry may be eaten raw, consumed as juice or wine, brewed into a herbal tea or prepared as a tincture.

Several studies have been published in China showing good medicinal results, especially in relation to goji berry's antioxidant properties, which include potential benefits against cardiovascular and inflammatory diseases and vision-related diseases, such as age-related macular degeneration and glaucoma. It also looks to have promising neuro-protective and anticarcinogenic properties as well. Currently, in the West, none of this research has been scientifically verified, confirmed in clinical studies or accepted by the regulatory authorities. However, scientific interest and research are ongoing.

Cautions: No contraindications are known, but only ripe berries may be used; these can loosen the bowels when taken in very large quantities.

Tomato

Botanical name *Lycopersicum esculentum*

Family Solanaceae

Description: The tomato plant is a perennial, often grown outdoors in temperate climates as an annual. It is native to Central, South and southern North America, and is now grown across the world. It has a hairy, slightly woody stem and its small yellow flowers bloom in groups of three to 12; they are best pollinated by bees, but many varieties will also self-pollinate if shaken by the wind.

Edible parts: Fruits.

History: The tomato is a member of the same family as deadly nightshade and tobacco, and is a

close cousin of chilli peppers, aubergines and potatoes.

It derives its name from the Aztec Nahuatl word *tomatl*. Its botanical origins may lie in Mexico, where one of two oldest wild plants were found, but historically it may have dispersed from Peru. It was first introduced into Europe during the Elizabethan era, when tomatoes were thought to have aphrodisiac properties and were known as 'love apples'.

Tomatoes are fruits in the botanical sense, and can be red, yellow, orange, green, purple or brown in colour. They have fleshy internal segments filled with slippery pulp-covered seeds. Their subtle sweetness is complemented by a slightly acidic flavour. Yellow tomatoes are higher in sugar content than red ones.

Main therapeutic properties: Today, the tomato's main strengths lie in its phytonutrient antioxidant powers, especially (but not exclusively) in the cancer-preventive carotenoid lycopene, which is found in tomatoes and all its derivatives. Lycopene has been extensively researched and its anticarcinogenic effects are now known to span an array of cancers, including breast, colorectal, endometrial, lung, pancreatic and, notoriously, prostate cancer. The antioxidant function of lycopene also protects DNA and accordingly helps to prevent heart disease.

A low-calorie yet nutritious powerhouse, the tomato is high in carotenoids, potassium and Vitamins C and K, with a good range of Vitamins B and E, plus many useful minerals to promote the immune system and support wellness. Tomatoes aid digestion by assimilating fats, oils and fried foods. They are both a laxative and a diuretic. In traditional Chinese medicine, it is believed that tomatoes are an effective detoxificant, reduce blood pressure and help to prevent cancers and ageing.

In addition to its importance in scientific research, the tomato has great versatility and features in a wide variety of folk remedies, both old and new. For example, acids and sugars in slices of raw tomato soothe sunburn or cleanse the pores of greasy skin. Tomato juice is a restorative sports drink, while tomato leaves steeped in boiling water make a good organic insect spray.

Cautions: Tomatoes are a relatively common cause of allergies. They contain small quantities of solanine, which may trigger headaches in susceptible people. Tomatoes and tomato-based products can also cause acid reflux.

Apple

Botanical name *Malus domestica*

Family Rosaceae

Description: Today the apple is the fruit most commonly grown across the world. The wild ancestor of *M. domestica* is *M. sirversii*, a tree still found in the wild in the mountains of central Asia. The domestic apple tree has now spread to most temperate regions of the world. It is a small deciduous tree reaching 5–12 m (16–40 ft) tall, with a broad, often densely twiggy crown. The blossoms are five-petalled and white with a pink tinge that gradually fades. Apples must be cross-pollinated to develop fruit, which matures in the autumn; the centre of the fruit contains one to three seeds (pips) in a five-point star arrangement. Apples themselves are crisp, white-fleshed fruits with red, yellow or green skin. They range in taste from moderately sweet to tart, depending on the variety.

Edible parts: Fruits.

History: Archaeologists have found evidence that humans have been enjoying apples since at least 6500 BCE. The apple was probably the earliest tree to be cultivated, but it was the discovery of the grafting technique by the Greeks that led to the development of more than 7,500 known cultivars of apples. The wild apple (*M. sirversii*), which has no 'common name', has importance for the future of apple cultivation as it resists many diseases and pests that affect domestic apples, and research on it continues to develop new disease-resistant strains of apple.

Winter apples, picked in late autumn, have been an important food in Asia and Europe for millennia, and in the New World since the arrival of Europeans there. The alcoholic beverage of cider dates back at least 2,000 years and was commonly quaffed at the time of the Roman invasion of England in 55 BCE. In the 1800s in the US, Johnny Appleseed – the alter ego of John Chapman – walked barefoot across an area of 260,000 sq km (100,000 square miles), planting apple trees that provided food and a livelihood for generations of settlers. A resurgence of interest in past-era apples had led to their revival.

Main therapeutic properties: Apple is an excellent foodstuff and a highly curative, cleansing and detoxifying fruit. Apart from its sugars, which help to stabilize blood-sugar levels, and important dietary fibre, apples contains Vitamins C, B_1, B_2, B_3, B_5, B_6 and B_9 and A, E and K. They are very high in potassium and phosphorus, with calcium and magnesium and small amounts of iron, zinc, manganese, copper and selenium.

The fruit is extremely versatile and may be taken as a food medicine to eat, as a pulp poultice or as a juice (cloudy is

best). Apple juice is a mixture of sugars (mainly fructose, glucose and sucrose), starch, malic, quinic and citromalic acids, tannins, nitrogenous compounds, soluble pectin, Vitamin C, minerals and a diverse range of esters, which give the juice its typical apple-like aroma.

Apple is useful against demineralization and good for anaemia, aiding the absorption of iron. Apple acids, such as malic and tartaric acids, are easily digested in the body and may assist the digestion of other foods. Apple fibre helps constipation, the elimination of body waste, lowering cholesterol and reducing the risk of cancer. Certain varieties of apple peel contain phenols that may provide UV-B protection against sunburn.

Some varieties of apple are cultivated for cider production. When imbibed in moderate amounts, cider is a healthy drink, for recent research revealed that it may be as rich in antioxidants as red wine; both contain phenolics that have been found to be protective against cancer, heart disease and stroke.

Red-fleshed apples, which are rich in flavonols, can be hard to source, but they are expected to be available in supermarkets within the next five to ten years. In Montreal, Canada, an exclusive 'red' cider known as *Cidre de glace rosé*

Classic oil painting on panel of Adam and Eve (1528) beneath the apple tree by German artist Lucas Cranach the Elder 1472–1553.

(ice ruby cider), which uses a little-known dry, red-fleshed, Geneva apple, is already on the market.

Research has found there is tremendous healing value in apple pulp, which is high in pectin (soluble fibre) and can also be used in powder form. The apple's insoluble fibre works like bran, latching on to LDL or 'bad' cholesterol in the digestive tract and removing it from the body, while apple's soluble fibre (pectin) reduces the amount of LDL cholesterol produced in the liver. Pectin helps to relieve diarrhoea, soothing the intestines and acting against several types of bacteria that cause diarrhoea. It is also cleansing and detoxifying, helping to eliminate heavy metals, such as lead and mercury, from the body. This makes the proverbial 'apple a day' a sound habit for those living in heavily polluted urban environments.

Apple's phytonutrients, flavonoids, phenolics and other compounds have been shown to offer protection to asthmatics and reduce the risk of colon, prostate and lung cancer, as well as helping with heart disease, weight loss and controlling cholesterol. Recently it was discovered that a flavonoid found only in apples, called phloridzin, may help prevent the bone loss associated with the menopause. Furthermore, regular apple consumption helps to build up antioxidant protection against a tissue-damaging process associated with Alzheimer's disease and other neuro-degenerative disorders.

Most recently, a rare ancient breed of English apple called 'Evesse' (which has its origins in the hawthorn apple dating back to 1650) was found to have unique health-boosting properties. It is a rich source of polyphenols that help to increase blood flow and relax the arteries. One glass of Evesse juice provides the equivalent nutritional value to eating 30 raw, red-fleshed apples, and regular drinking of the juice is said to bring the arteries to a condition 10 years younger than their actual age.

Cautions: Avoid eating unripe fruit, as it causes stomach ache. It is best to eat home-grown or organic apples or those with a known pedigree, otherwise they may contain pesticides that were used in their production, which will have a negative impact on health.

Apples are a highly curative, cleansing and detoxifying fruit.

Black mulberry

Botanical name *Morus nigra*

Family Moraceae

Description: The common or black mulberry grows wild in Asia Minor and is native to south-western Asia, including Iran. The trees are fast-growing when young, but soon slow in growth and usually reach 6–9m (20–30 ft) in height. They are a handsome deciduous tree, reaching a very old age and bearing fruit for hundreds of years. Mulberries were very popular in the Elizabethan era. The mulberry tree has a rugged, bushy-headed appearance, with small, cylindrical catkins or spikes. The scentless deep-red to purplish-black berries are exceedingly juicy, having a subtly acidic and contrasting sweet taste.

Edible parts: Fruits.

History: The black mulberry has been grown for its fruits in Europe since before Roman times. The name is derived from the Latin *mora*, meaning 'delay', and the tree is so called because of the tardy expansion of its buds.

In Greek myth, Pyramus, thinking his lover Thisbe is dead, stabs himself in the heart beneath a white mulberry tree. His blood sinks into the roots of the tree, turning the white mulberry black.

The Azerbaijanis have used mulberries in their folk medicine since the Middle Ages. Azerbaijanis still enjoy mulberry-syrup concentrates, which are also used as a medicine.

In recent years mulberry fruit juice has been commercially produced as a health beverage, and has become very popular in China, Japan and Korea. Without adding preservatives, the original juice of the mulberry fruit remains fresh under cold storage for three months, while the bottled beverage remains fresh at room temperature for 12 months.

Main therapeutic properties: The main contents of fresh, ripe mulberry fruit are water; carbohydrates; sugars: mainly glucose and fructose, producing the sweet taste; protein; fat: fatty acids in the seeds; free acids (mainly malic acid, producing the sharp taste) and fibre.

Black mulberry's fruit and juice are the subject of scientific excitement. The fruit contains many excellent antioxidants. It is carotene-rich, with Vitamins C, B_1 and B_2, as well as small amounts of calcium, iron, magnesium and potassium. In addition it contains some of the most powerful and effective antioxidant phytochemicals – water-soluble phenolic flavonoids called anthocyanins. These are edible pigments that have potential use as dietary 'free-radical scavengers', providing health benefits against a variety of diseases. They are also in demand by the food industry as natural food-colourant additives, instead of synthetics. Research revealed five anthocyanins present in *M. nigra*, all of which contribute to the mulberry's ability to boost blood circulation and the immune system.

Mulberry fruit also contains the phytochemical known as resveratrol, which has a variety of effects, including protecting against heart-muscle injury and stopping the blood-vessel formation that usually accompanies the growth of malignant tissue. Resveratrols are being researched extensively for their anti-ageing abilities and are present in mulberry juice.

Cautions: At the time of writing there are no known cautions.

Yumberry

Botanical name *Myrica rubra*

Family Myricaceae

Description: *M. rubra* is an evergreen tree that is chiefly native to China, where it has been grown for at least 2,000 years, but also probably to Japan and South-East Asia. It has pale silvery bark and grows up to 10 m (32 ft) high in temperate environments. The sweet fruit (drupe) is round, knobbly and crimson to purple-red, slightly larger than a cherry, with similarities to a strawberry in flavour and texture, but with stringier pulp and a central small pit.

Edible parts: Fruits.

History: According to archeological findings, wild *yangmei*, as yumberry is known there, was eaten south of the Yangtze River in around 5000 BCE. In Japan, this is the prefectural flower of Kôchi and the prefectural tree of Tokushima, Shikoku island; the plant's name also appears in many old Japanese poems.

Yumberry as a medication was first recorded in the *Shi Liao Ben Cao*, a herbal by Meng Xian in the Tang Dynasty (618–907 CE), and again in the 16th-century *Materia Medica* of Li Shi Zhen. Among other effects, it was described as being able to stop vomiting, boost the digestion, cleanse the stomach and intestines, cure diarrhoea, quench thirst and clear a muddled head.

Yumberry's modern name was coined by Charles Stenftenagel, an American garden importer from Indiana, in about 2003 when visiting a friend in Shanghai who owned a company that bottled the juice. There are more than 100 varieties of the plant, including white, pink, red and purple, though the purple yumberry is reputed to have the most flavoursome taste. The juice, which keeps for longer than the highly perishable fruit, has become the preferred mode of distribution for the plant. The delicate fruit is an expensive import as it needs to be refrigerated and cannot be stored for more than one week.

Main therapeutic properties: The fruit's sugar-acid flesh contains multiple organic acids and is high in nutritional value. It is rich in Vitamins C, B_1 (the vitamin that maintains appetite and growth), B_2 and carotene; calcium, magnesium, potassium, iron and copper are also present.

Yumberry's purplish pulp and sweet-tart juice (like a lighter version of pomegranate or mulberry) has red pigmentation denoting the presence of highly antioxidant phenolics. In Taiwan, research found that yumberry extract's anthocyanidin delphinidin induced an increased rate of cell death in human breast tumours. Yumberry is also unusually rich in OPC's (Oligomeric Proanthocyanidins), the most powerful class of free-radical-scavenging antioxidants, which are believed to support every metabolic system in the body. More health benefits are expected to emerge from research into yumberry in the near future.

Cautions: At the time of writing there are no known cautions.

Olive

Botanical name *Olea europaea*

Family Oleaceae

Description: The olive tree is an evergreen species of tree, which is considered native to countries within and around the Mediterranean basin, although whether the plant stems from this region or is native to central Asia is debatable. It rarely exceeds 9–10 m (30 ft) in height, and has a rough, gnarled and twisted grey trunk, with small leathery leaves and clusters of small greenish-white flowers. The fruits can be harvested at the green stage or left to ripen to a rich purple black colour.

Edible parts: Fruits.

History: Cultivation of the olive tree is known to have taken place in the eastern Mediterranean for five millennia. The olive is one of the most-cited plants in recorded literature, multi-referenced in the Bible, in mythology and in ancient Greek and Roman texts: the Greek poet Homer wrote of it in his *Odyssey* and called olive oil 'liquid gold', and the Roman poet Horace made mention of it in his own diet. The olive has been seen as the symbol of peace, wisdom, glory, abundance, power and purity and has been used to anoint kings and crown victors of games and wars in Ancient Greece. Olive branches were once used in rituals as offerings to the gods and are still used in some religious ceremonies today.

Main therapeutic properties: Olives are a good source of nutrition, mainly of monounsaturated fat and of Vitamins A and E, iron, valuable copper and calcium. They also contain lesser amounts of Vitamins C, B_6, potassium, zinc and magnesium, and dietary fibre.

The nutrients in olives support gastrointestinal health and help to protect the heart. Low in calories, with no cholesterol, olives are easily absorbed by the body. Their Vitamin E content offers protection at a cellular level, helps to strengthen the immune system and acts against premature ageing. In addition, olives contain a variety of active phytonutrient compounds with significant anti-inflammatory properties, which may help to reduce the severity of asthma, osteoarthritis and rheumatoid arthritis.

Although olive oil may be most important in terms of health benefits, olives themselves are a scientifically recognized part of the 'Mediterranean diet' (see pages 118–119). Science shows that the consumption of olives may protect against a variety of cancers, including lung cancer. The famous Provençal olive recipe 'Tapenade' can enhance the diet.

Olive-leaf extract is said to lower blood pressure and reduce blood sugar, enhance the immune system, increase energy, cleanse internally and act as an antibacterial, antifungal, antiparasitic and antiviral medication.

Cautions: Olives are believed to be safe. However, olive-leaf extract may generate detoxification symptoms in the infirm and it should not be taken with antibiotics produced from yeast or fungus, or with amino acids other than those that occur naturally in the diet, for they may cancel each other out. Pregnant and nursing women should consult their healthcare provider before taking olive-leaf extract.

Avocado

Botanical name *Persea americana*

Family Lauraceae

Description: Related to the magnolia and bay-laurel trees, the avocado pear is not in fact a pear, but a 'drupe' with a large central stone or seed and inconspicuous greenish-yellow flowers. Avocado originates from tropical and sub-tropical areas of the Americas (Mexico, Florida and California). Some varieties can reach 20 m (65 ft) in height. The flesh of the avocado is not like any other fruit: buttery but not sweet, somewhat nutty and oily in flavour, firm enough to be sliced or diced, yet pliable enough to be mashed into a paste or purée that can be served straight to a baby or a convalescent.

Edible parts: Flesh of the fruit.

History: The romance of avocado as a food medicine is part of its long history of cultivation in South and Central America, including Mexico, where it has been a staple food since 500 BCE. 'Avocado' comes from the Nahuatl word *achuacatl* (meaning 'testicle') after the fruit's shape and its reputation as an aphrodisiac. It was prized by the Aztecs, and was discovered growing in swamplands in the Americas by Spanish conquistadors in the 15th century and was subsequently introduced to Europe. It acquired its nickname, 'alligator pear', due to its habitat, shape and the fruit's coarse, wrinkly skin.

The earliest-known written account of the avocado in Europe is that of Martín Fernández de Enciso (*c.* 1470– *c.* 1528), or 'El Bachiller Enciso', in 1519 in his book *Suma de Geografía que Trata de Todas las Partidas y Provincias del Mundo*. In the 16th century the Franciscan missionary Torbio de Montolinia recorded the use of avocado in Mexico. The plant was introduced to Indonesia by 1750, to Brazil in 1809, the Levant in 1908 and South Africa and Australia in the late 19th century. It was not until the early 1900s that the *achuacatl* was grown commercially in the US. By 1914 there was great demand for the fruit from the West Coast hotel industry, which firmly established it on the menu and brought about its change of name.

An Amerindian matron in ceremonial dress pictured with Avocados 'the fertility fruit' used for hair and face masks.

In the West, the avocado pear is best known in the form of the Mexican-Spanish dip guacamole, which has numerous variations, its original Aztec recipe being prepared with added tomatoes and salt. The avocado is also used in Japanese cuisine as a filling for several kinds of sushi. In Brazil and Vietnam, it is considered a sweet fruit and is used for milkshakes and may be added to ice-cream and other desserts. In Brazil, Colombia, Vietnam, the Philippines and Indonesia, a dessert drink is made from puréed avocado. Heated avocado can be bitter, so add avocado purée to dishes when they have cooled.

Main therapeutic properties: Seldom can one plant offer up so many solutions for both human health and beauty. Avocado fruit is a highly nutritious food and is also renowned for its beneficial oil, both being exceedingly remedial as anti-cancerous and palliative for various diseases and conditions.

Avocado is one of the few fruits to contain a lot of fats, two-thirds of which are heart-healthy monounsaturated fat, which can reduce LDL or 'bad' cholesterol and boost HDL or 'good' cholesterol. It has more potassium than bananas, and the highest fibre content of any fruit. It is rich in Vitamins K, B_6, C, A and E, folate and copper. In addition to containing phytonutrient combatants for oral cancer and potentially prostate cancer, it has the highest content of lutein among commonly eaten fruits.

Avocado promotes heart health, increases the absorption of antioxidant carotenoids from vegetables, and may give protection against atherosclerosis and be helpful to those suffering from osteoarthritis. Its unbleached 'green' oil

is in itself a magnum of vitamins and minerals, containing Vitamins A, B_1, B_2 and D, potassium, phosphorus, magnesium, sulphur, calcium, sodium and copper.

Unlike some beauty remedies that are only skin-deep, avocado – when taken internally as fruit pulp or capsules – seems to trigger DNA into producing soluble collagen, which promotes skin strength and resilience, guarding it against degeneration and ageing. A recently researched avocado oil and vitamin B_{12} cream showed the potential to aid the difficult skin disease psoriasis. Overall, science suggests that the avocado provides a complete dietary strategy for total good health, both inside and out.

Cautions: The poisoning of cattle, horses, goats, rabbits, canaries and fish by the avocado's leaves, fruit, bark and seeds has been reported. Bear in mind that avocado is highly calorific and rich in vaso-active amines, which may trigger headaches and migraine. The bleached oil should not be used therapeutically.

The versatile and creamy flesh of avocados particularly captured public taste buds and European imagination in the late 20th century.

Pomegranate

Botanical name *Punica granatum*

Family Lythraceae

Description: A deciduous shrub or tree, renowned for its longevity, the pomegranate is native to a region stretching from Afghanistan, Pakistan and Iran to the Himalayas in northern India. It has spiny-tipped branches, bright-scarlet flowers and leathery, reddish-yellow fruit about the size of an orange, containing many sweet pulp-encapsulated seeds (arils) intersected with bitter white pith. One single fruit or 'apple' may contain up to 800 seeds.

Edible parts: Seed pulp.

History: The pomegranate has a long history as food medicine and was among 2.7 kg (6 lb) of food and beverage remains found in 1957 in the tomb of King Mita (or Midas, who reigned in the 8th century BCE) at the ancient Phrygian capital in Turkey. The pomegranate's roots, bark, leaves, flowers, fruit, rind and seeds have all been used for their medicinal properties from the time of the ancient Egyptians, Greeks and Romans onwards. The plant has been cultivated over the entire Mediterranean region, the Caucasus and tropical Africa since Classical times.

In 1769 pomegranate cultivation was introduced into Latin and North America by Spanish settlers for juice production.

Main therapeutic properties: Pomegranate provides minerals to the liver and aids the assimilation of Vitamin A. It boosts the immune system against disease, relieves hypertension and is a heart tonic. The juice is good for digestive disorders, and the powdered form for diarrhoea and nosebleeds. The leaves may be used on cuts and lesions, and the rind for toothpaste or gum powder. Pomegranate is thought to provide natural antifungal, antiviral and bactericidal benefits.

Pomegranate juice is very antioxidant due to its polyphenolic activity, which is higher when extracted from whole pomegranates than when obtained solely from the luscious red arils; one glass of its juice is said to contain as many antioxidants as two glasses of red wine or ten cups of green tea. The juice is packed with Vitamins A, C and E and folate. It is a good source of Vitamin B_5 and potassium, as well as tannins and oxalic acid.

Currently the juice's anticarcinogenic values have elevated the pomegranate to the ranks of a 'superfruit'. Importantly, its compounds may prevent or delay prostate cancer and reduce the risk of breast cancer. Pomegranate has also been reported to reduce inflammation in cartilage cells, which could make it useful to arthritis. What is more, pomegranate-seed oil has shown definite potential as a safe and effective chemo-preventive against skin cancer.

Science tells us that antioxidant-rich pomegranate can help prevent LDL or 'bad' cholesterol damage and, in turn, atherosclerosis, and that it is also anticoagulant. Drinking 250 ml (8 fl oz) of juice daily can improve oxygen supply to the heart muscle, aiding those with coronary disease. Long-term use of the juice may also help combat erectile dysfunction, backing up ancient aphrodisiac claims.

Cautions: The available studies on pomegranate juice and drug interactions are very limited. The juice may interact with existing prescription drugs and should not be used by pregnant and nursing women. Overuse may cause cramps, vomiting and diarrhoea. Some people may be allergic to pomegranate.

Blackberry

Botanical name *Rubus fruticosus*

Family Rosaceae

Description: *Rubus* is one of the most diverse genera of flowering plants in the world and includes both raspberries and blackberries. It is a perennial, semi-deciduous, prickly shrub, with entangling stems arising from a woody crown, and forms thickets up to several metres high. The flowers are white or pinkish, and the fruit changes colour from green to red to shiny black as it ripens; like the raspberry, each berry comprises many single-seeded segments (drupelets).

Edible parts: Fruits, leaves, roots (medicinal).

History: Claiming its origins in ancient and Classical times, the blackberry is a delicious fruit that even finds reference in the Bible. The Greek dramatist Aeschylus (*c.* 525–456 BCE) and the 'father of medicine' Hippocrates (*c.* 460–377 BCE) both made mention of the blackberry. In the 1st century CE, the Greek physician Dioscorides first recorded a ripe-blackberry gargle for sore throats. Called 'gout berry' in Europe, the blackberry

was also used by the Greeks to treat gout, and by the Romans for sore throats and inflammation of the bowel.

It is known from the discovery in Denmark of the Iron Age remains of Haraldskaer Woman (500 BCE) that blackberries have been part of the human diet for some 2,500 years, and it is presumed that they were eaten some thousands of years prior to that date, for 'the bramble' is a very pushy plant and an evolutionary survivor. It remained a food harvested only from the wild until the 19th century. Going 'blackberrying' is still a family outing with rich rewards.

Main therapeutic properties: The blackberry is known to contain poly-phenolic antioxidants, naturally occurring phytochemicals that can boost certain beneficial metabolic processes. Among its many health-giving constituents, blackberry contains Vitamins A, C and E, folate and dietary fibre. It is very high in potassium, calcium, phosphorus and magnesium, with good amounts of manganese, selenium, iron and zinc, and a trace amount of copper. Additionally it has tannins, flavonoids and gallic acid, as well as anthocyanins, pectin and fruit acids.

Blackberries bestow a number of health and nutritional benefits on their consumers and are one of nature's 'superfoods' gifted from the wild. They have increasingly appeared fresh in grocers and supermarkets, mostly in season, although available out of season in the form of jams, juices, syrups, desserts and wine. However, it is the fresh fruit (or frozen if necessary) that is so antioxidant-rich and helps the body destroy free radicals in order to avoid various types of cancer. Following research using blackberries for protection against oesophageal cancer in animals, which found that they could inhibit progression and even initiation of tumours, cancer-prevention trials in humans have now commenced.

The pectin found in blackberry is an old-fashioned anodyne remedy for painful arthritis. Studies have shown that pectin could be a useful anticarcinogenic treatment, as pectin added to human prostate-cancer cells induces programmed cell death, while cell death does not occur in the non-cancerous cells. How to kill malignant cells and at the same time preserve healthy ones has always been a concern in conquering cancer and pectin may turn out to be an important anti-cancer phyto-treatment. Additionally, blackberries' main phenolic compounds, anthocyanins, flavonols, tannins and so on, make them – along with black raspberries and strawberries – one of the most effective remedies against several cancer cell lines to be studied recently.

The tissue-tightening antiseptic properties of blackberries, deriving from their high tannin content, boost healing, and are also beneficial for treating

Blackberries are a superfood. The fresh fruit is antioxidant-rich and helps the body destroy free radicals that can cause various types of cancer.

Until the 19th century blackberries were a wild food and were not cultivated. They still grow wild today and blackberrying is a fun pastime.

diarrhoea and intestinal inflammation, as well as mild infections of the throat and mouth. Blackberries' anti-bacterial properties are also said to be blood-cleansing. Blackberry root is sometimes used in herbal medicine as a treatment for diarrhoea and dysentery. Blackberry leaves were chewed to treat bleeding gums and mouth sores and it has been found that blackberry-leaf extract is active as a multi-functional anti-ageing treatment; further research in that direction can be expected. All in all,

blackberry is an impressive healer for an ancient plant that was considered to be an invasive species and a noxious weed.

Cautions: Blackberry leaf should not be used for an extended period (of more than one week at a time), because its high astringency may cause constipation or diarrhoea or inhibit menstrual bleeding. Do not eat blackberries that are growing close to busy roads as they will have accumulated polluting toxins from the traffic. Avoid eating blackberries and/ or using the leaves if you have an existing or untreated kidney or gall-bladder problem.

Raspberry

Botanical name *Rubus idaeus*

Family Rosaceae

Description: Belonging to the rose family, the raspberry is part of a widespread and well-known group of several hundred species that are native to Asia, Europe, North and South America and are found all around the northern hemisphere. The European red raspberry is a deciduous shrub whose origin was reportedly at Mount Ida, in the Caucasus Mountains of Asia Minor, where it is indigenous. A closely related plant (*R. strigosus*) is also native to North America, but the rarer black raspberry (*R. occidentalis*) is a species of its own. The fruits are fragrantly sweet with a subtly tart overtone. Although the most common type of raspberry is red-pink in colour, raspberries come in a range of colours, including black, purple, orange, yellow and white.

Edible parts: Fruits; leaves when infused (medicinal).

History: Raspberries were foraged by the Trojans and people in the foothills around Mount Ida about the time of Christ. Records of domestication were found in the 4th-century CE writing of Palladius, a Roman agriculturist, and seeds were discovered at Roman forts in Britain, which indicates that the Romans probably spread their cultivation throughout Europe. The British popularized and improved the plant throughout the Middle Ages, and had exported it to New York by 1771.

The black raspberry, which is indigenous only to eastern and central North America, was not domesticated until the 1800s. It was used as a purple to dull-blue dye by Native Americans, who also cooked the new shoot stems like rhubarb. Medicinally, black raspberry was used as an astringent, cathartic, ophthalmic, pectoral and salve. The whole plant was used to treat various conditions – for example, a decoction of the roots, stems and leaves was used to treat whooping cough; the root has been chewed in the treatment of coughs and toothache; and an infusion of astringent root bark was used to treat diarrhoea and dysentery. By 1880 there were at least 17 named black raspberry cultivars and several thousand acres under cultivation in New York. Today there is little commercial production of the black raspberry compared to that of blackberries or red raspberries, but all that is likely to change soon, for the black raspberry is powerful medicine.

Main therapeutic properties: Raspberry leaves contain polypeptides, antioxidant flavonoids and tannins. Raspberry fruits contain significant amounts of polyphenol antioxidants, such as anthocyanin

pigments, which may provide protection against several human diseases. Anthocyanins are found in fresh and frozen berries, but not in processed foods. Yellow raspberries and others with pale-coloured fruits are lower in anthocyanins.

High in dietary fibre and low in fats, with no cholesterol, the raspberry is high in manganese and Vitamin C, as well as being a good source of Vitamin B_2, folate, potassium magnesium, Vitamins B_3, A, E and copper, as well as pectin, fruit sugars and fruit acids. Additionally, the fruits contain significant amounts of the anti-cancer phytochemical ellagic acid, plus polyphenolic antioxidants with promising health benefits that are subject to ongoing research.

Herbalists use raspberry leaf in decoctions to relieve diarrhoea and as a tea or in tablet form in the last trimester of pregnancy to facilitate easy labour during childbirth. The leaves' astringent property is also used externally in an eyewash for conjunctivitis, a mouthwash and gargle, and as a lotion for ulcers, wounds and excessive vaginal discharge. Preliminary medical research shows the likely benefits of eating raspberry fruit in aiding inflammation, pain, cancer, cardiovascular disease, diabetes, allergies, age-related cognitive decline and degeneration of eyesight.

Raspberries are rich in antioxidants, high in dietary fibre and low in fat so are not only tasty but healthy, too.

Recent studies have highlighted the tremendous health benefits associated with eating black raspberries, which contain Vitamins A, C, E and folic acid, as well as calcium, selenium and a range of anthocyanins, and possess one of the highest amounts of antioxidants of all fruits and vegetables. One study has shown that the natural chemo-preventive properties in black raspberry's antioxidants can prevent (in animals) oesophageal cancer up to 60 per cent. In another experiment, a diet containing freeze-dried black raspberries reduced the incidence of colon cancer by up to 80 per cent. In addition, black raspberries can inhibit cancer of the oral cavity. And this is just the beginning.

The Chinese raspberry (*R. chingii*) is a sub-species of *R. idaeus* that is native to China. It is similar in appearance to the traditional raspberry plant, but the fruits are small, cone-shaped and hard in texture, ranging from reddish-yellow to pale brown in colour. They contain a variety of organic acids and plant sterols and are high in Vitamin C. In traditional Chinese medicine, Chinese raspberries are considered to have sweet and warm properties and are associated with the liver and kidney meridians. They are astringent, tonic and mildly diuretic, and their function is to tonify and stabilize the kidneys to preserve vital energy. They are primarily used to treat liver and kidney deficiency and control seminal emission; and to promote visual acuity, clear blurred vision and treat a variety of urogenital conditions, all of which may derive from kidney and liver malfunction.

Cautions: Do not take red raspberry leaves in the early stages of pregnancy. Avoid eating raspberries if there is an existing and/or untreated kidney or gall-bladder problem.

*Botanical coloured drawing of Red Raspberry (*R. idaeus*) by Franz Eugen Köhler from Koehler's Medicinal-Plants 1887.*

Potato

Botanical name *Solanum tuberosum*

Family Solanaceae

Description: Potato belongs to the same family as deadly nightshade, the aubergine and the tomato. Research botanists agree that it originated in the area of modern-day Peru some 4,000–7,000 years ago. It is a perennial plant with white or purple flowers with yellow stamens, green berry-like fruits and swollen tubers (potatoes).

Description: Root, when cooked.

History: A seasoned traveller, the potato has had many name changes and inhabited many countries on its journey to our plates. The first European description of it was in Pedro Cieza de León's *Crónica del Perú* (1533) and it was introduced to Spain for cultivation under its Quechua name *papa*. Potatoes found their way to France in around 1540, and were cultivated under the name *truffole*. In 1585 they came to England, where popular history credits Sir Walter Raleigh with their introduction.

In the 18th century the potato was grown and eaten as a food in northern Italy, Spain, Germany, Poland, Russia and Britain, but the French considered it animal feed until a public-spirited nutritionist called Antoine-Augustin Parmentier (1737–1813) got it promoted to the kitchen. In the 19th century the terrible Irish potato famine (1845–52) reduced the Irish population by 20–25 per cent. Today, the potato is established as one of the most popular vegetables throughout the world.

Main therapeutic properties: The potato is one of the most important food medicines in the world, and is high in Vitamin C and folate, with good amounts of Vitamins K and B_3 and smaller amounts of B_6, B_1, B_2 and E. Potatoes are mineral-rich, with a large amount of potassium and phosphorus, followed by calcium, sodium, iron and selenium. They also contain some copper, manganese and zinc, plus dietary fibre.

Nutritionally, potatoes are best known for their carbohydrate content, starch being its predominant form. A certain amount of 'resistant starch' remains intact in the stomach and is estimated to have similar health benefits to fibre, acting as bulk and protection against colon cancer, improving glucose tolerance and insulin sensitivity, lowering plasma cholesterol, increasing satiety and possibly reducing fat storage. Although potatoes' high-carb reputation has knocked them off many a weight-watcher's list, they are an important 'one-stop' source of vitamins and minerals. And, in these days of anxiety about chemical crop-spraying, the idea that all of the potato's nutrients are found in the skin is, thankfully, a myth, for more than half are found in the potato itself.

According to research, 60 different kinds of phytochemicals and vitamins are found in the skins and flesh of 100 wild and commercially grown varieties. Analysis of red and Norkotah potatoes revealed that their phenolic content rivals that of broccoli, spinach and Brussels sprouts and includes flavonoids with protective activity against cardiovascular disease, respiratory problems and certain cancers. Kukoamines, with the potential to lower blood pressure, were also identified.

Cautions: Never eat green potatoes, as they are toxic.

Blueberry

Botanical name *Vaccinium corymbosum*

Family Ericaceae

Description: The blueberry is a deciduous shrub, belonging to the heather family, and is native to eastern North America, although other species may be found in Asia, Europe and South America. It grows up to 4 m (13 ft) high, with dark-green glossy leaves and white bell-shaped flowers, and is often found in dense thickets.

Edible parts: Fruits, juice, leaves, roots (medicine).

History: Legend has it that, having emerged after the Ice Age 13,000 years ago, blueberries are (or are related to) the oldest plant now living in North America. It is recorded that the ancient Roman poet Virgil and the naturalist Pliny recognized blueberries, and described them under the name that continues to identify the blueberry plant: *vaccinium*.

The English had whortleberries, the Danes bilberries, the Swedes *blåbär*, the Germans *Bickberren* and *Blauberren*. It was the Scottish wild blaeberry that was turned into blaeberry jam at the court of

James V, who became King of the Scots in 1513. His French wife, Madeleine de Valois, had brought her own cooks to Scotland and devised the delicacy to delight Scottish palates.

In 1615 the explorer Samuel de Champlain viewed Native Americans along Lake Huron collecting wild blueberries, which they then dried, beat to a pulp and combined with ground cornmeal, honey and water to make a pudding named *sautauthig*, which was loved by the early settlers. Blueberries were also pounded into meat, which was then smoked and dried; some natives smoked the berries to preserve them for the winter. The wild blueberry was held in high esteem by Native Americans because the blossom of each blueberry flower forms a five-pointed star and they believed that their Great Spirit sent the star-berries to relieve the hunger of children during a famine.

Blueberries were used in traditional Native American medicine for a wide spectrum of ailments. Blueberry tea was used as an antispasmodic for cramps,

hiccoughs, colic, severe gastroenteritis, epilepsy and hysterics. Blueberry juice was used for 'old coughs', and tea made from wild blueberry leaves as a tonic to purify the blood. A strong aromatic tea made from the root acted as a relaxant during childbirth; early medical books indicate that this remedy was also used by the wives of settlers during labour. Berries were eaten to treat scurvy, diarrhoea, dropsy and bilious fevers, while the Chippewa people dried the berries, placed them

on hot stones and inhaled the fumes to drive out madness. The Native Americans' belief in the blueberry was not misplaced, for it is a powerhouse of nutrients.

Main therapeutic properties: Today, blueberries are accepted to have a laxative effect, to cleanse the blood and improve circulation and visual acuity. According to research, they exert a similar effect on urinary-tract health as cranberries, and may protect against cataracts and glaucoma. Recently it was found that blueberries may aid post-menopausal osteoporosis and may have antitumour and anticarcinogenic properties. Introductory studies have also shown blueberries to be effective in the treatment of varicose veins, haemorrhoids and peptic ulcers. The leaves of the plant are used to help regulate blood sugar in borderline diabetes and hypoglycaemia.

Strong in carbohydrates, the blueberry is a wonderful source of antioxidant Vitamin C, and E, with high levels of iron and dietary fibre and a diverse range of micronutrients. The edible berries offer many therapeutic

Indulging in blueberry tartlets is a delicious way to reap the health benefits these berries offer.

Due to the shape of their flowers, blueberries were believed by Native Americans to be sent by their Great Spirit to feed children during a famine.

increasing communication between them and stimulating the regeneration of brain cells. They may thus alleviate the cognitive decline that occurs in Alzheimer's disease and other ageing conditions, as well as conserving eye health and protecting DNA integrity.

properties. Blueberries are rich in anthocyanins, compounds that provide pigmentation to fruits and serve as natural antioxidants, which have demonstrated a broad spectrum of biomedical functions. These include helping cardiovascular disorders, age-induced stress, inflammatory responses and degenerative diseases. Berry anthocyanins also improve neuronal and cognitive brain functions; reports have revealed that the flavonoids in blueberries (and similar fruits, including cranberries) interact with nerve cells,

Cautions: There are no known safety issues or interactions associated with blueberries at this time. Fresh (but not dried) berries tend to be laxative and should be avoided in cases of diarrhoea. However, blueberry extract may interfere with the effectiveness of insulin, oral drugs for diabetes, and herbal products that affect blood-sugar levels. Blueberries contain small amounts of tannins, which in large doses have been associated with liver and kidney damage. Consumption of high-tannin supplements can also lead to oesophageal or mouth cancer.

American cranberry

Botanical name *Vaccinium macrocarpon*

Family Ericaceae

Description: Cranberries are a group of evergreen, creeping dwarf shrubs or trailing vines with slender wiry stems and small leaves. They grow in acidic bogs throughout the cooler parts of the northern hemisphere and are one of only three commercially important fruits native to North America (the other two being the blueberry and the Concord blue grape). The flowers are dark pink and the astringent fruit is initially white, turning to a deep red when fully ripe.

Edible parts: Fruits.

History: The Native Americans, who called the red berries *sassamanash*, were the first to use the American cranberry as food, dye and medicine. They already knew about the berries' natural preservative power and mixed them into *pemmican*, a type of cake made with dried meat pounded to a paste and mixed with animal fat and grain. It is said that they also smoked the leaves as an inebriant. They introduced the American cranberry to English Pilgrim settlers in 1620 and by 1683 the settlers were making juice. Henry Hall is credited as being the first to farm cranberries in Dennis town, Cape Cod, Massachusetts, in around 1816, and by the 1820s cranberries were an exported crop.

In 1840, American cranberries accidentally became established in the damp dune valleys on the small island of Terschelling, one of the West Frisian Islands in the northern Netherlands. An escapee barrel of the cranberries that sailors ate to prevent scurvy was washed ashore from an American ship and took root on a massive scale. Cranberries have been grown there ever since.

Elsewhere, other common cranberry species (*V. oxycoccus*) are native and have been in use since the Iron Age. It is said that cranberries have been eaten by Arctic peoples for millennia, and they remain a popular fruit for foraging in Russia and the Nordic countries. The Romans recognized cranberries' medicinal use while they were in England. Noted horticulturist Henry Lyte documented the plant's healing effects in his 16th-century botanical volume *Niewe Herball*, which was published in 1578. From the Elizabethan era onwards, cranberries were popular in Britain as a folk remedy. Traditionally they were used to treat stomach ailments, urinary-tract infections, gall-bladder problems and fevers.

Cranberry sauce is an accessory to the turkey for traditional American and Canadian Thanksgiving menus, and likewise for European festive winter fare, such as Christmas dinner.

Main therapeutic properties: Cranberries are considered a 'superfruit' in the commercial food industry, because of their popular nutritious and antioxidant qualities. Cranberry is one of the top natural antioxidant foods, and the riper the fruit, the higher its score in this area. It contains moderate levels of Vitamin C, B-complex vitamins, dietary fibre, manganese and Vitamin K, as well as a balanced profile of essential multi-micronutrients.

Research has shown that the cranberry still offers some protection against urinary-tract infections and helps to prevent bladder infections, while the juice is effective as a urinary deodorant in bedridden patients with high levels of white blood cells and bacteria in the urine. It can also reinforce the effects of antibiotics, but is not a proven alternative to them. However, cranberry has highly potent antiviral strength and activity – for instance, a phytonutrient isolated from it tested effective against the *Herpes simplex* virus, the cause of genital herpes. Cranberry juice has also successfully neutralized E. coli, among other bacteria that can cause severe illness or death.

This probiotic berry is also useful for fighting yeast infections, such as *Candida albicans*, which causes thrush, as well as gastrointestinal infections – for example, it boosts the effectiveness of drugs against the *Helicobacter pylori* bacterium. It may also help prevent kidney-stone formation and has beneficial effects on cholesterol, its antioxidants lessening the oxidation of 'bad' LDL cholesterol and boosting cardioprotective HDL cholesterol, aiding the prevention of heart disease.

Cranberries are also a source of polyphenol antioxidants, which are under active research for possible benefits to the cardiovascular system, immune system and as anti-cancer agents.

Dried cranberries in muffins, muesli, salads and in stuffing for festive poultry add flavour and also offer many health benefits.

American laboratory studies in 2002 indicated that the antioxidants may prevent the formation of fat deposits that can block arteries and may relax blood vessels, protecting even those with atherosclerosis against cardiac events. Further research in 2007 suggested that polyphenols, including those found in cranberries, may contribute to reducing the risk of cardiovascular disease by increasing the resistance of LDL cholesterol to oxidation, inhibiting platelet aggregation and reducing blood pressure. Cranberry also helps to keep cancer cells from spreading; its phytonutrients help to shut down human breast-cancer cells. The fruit can also help protect against age-related macular degeneration. Most recently it has been found to aid dental

The Cranberry Harvest, Island of Nantucket, 1880, by Eastman Johnson (1824–1906).

hygiene, its antioxidants battling against dental plaque.

Cautions: Cranberry is safe to use during pregnancy, when breastfeeding and for young children. Do not use cranberry as a substitute for antibiotics. If you are taking drugs for urinary or kidney problems, do not take medicinal doses of cranberry concentrate, for the oxalates present may cause some types of kidney stone. Fresh (but not dried) berries tend to be laxative. Diabetics should be aware that commercial cranberry products contain high amounts of sugar. Cranberries may alter the effects of anticoagulant drugs, including Warfarin.

Bilberry

Botanical name *Vaccinium myrtillus*

Family Ericaceae

Description: The bilberry is a small deciduous shrub that grows chiefly on moorlands, heaths and in undergrowth in forested and mountainous regions. It is native to Europe and North America, and is also found in Siberia and across all of northern Asia and Barbary (Morocco, Algeria, Tunisia, and Libya). Its ornamental, leathery leaves are at first rosy-coloured, then turn yellowish-green and finally red in autumn. The pink or white waxy flowers bloom in spring, while the summer fruits are globular black berries, which when ripe are dusted with a delicate silvery-grey bloom, giving them a blueish hue.

Edible parts: Fruits; leaves when infused (medicine).

History: Although there is a variety with white fruits, the name bilberry is derived from the Danish *bollebar*, meaning 'dark berry'. It is a name given to several species of low-growing shrubs in the *Vaccinium* genus that bear fruits, but it should not be confused with the blueberry (see page 176–179).

Bilberries have been used for nearly 1,000 years in traditional European medicine and other parts of the world. Europeans chiefly used the fruit to treat diarrhoea and scurvy. Before the Second World War, large quantities of bilberries were imported to Britain annually from Holland, Germany and Scandinavia. Bilberries remain one of the most popular berries in Russia, where traditionally people travel out of the cities and into the forests to collect them on summer weekend outings, bringing them home by the bucketful to make preserves for the winter.

Main therapeutic properties: Bilberries contain a number of healthy vitamins and minerals, including Vitamins A, C and B_1, chromium, iron and copper. The herb is antidiarrhoeal, an anodyne, astringent, disinfectant, diuretic, haemostatic, stomachic, vermicidal and vulnerary. The fruits' active agents are anthocyanin pigments.

In Russia, herbalists traditionally prescribe infused bilberry leaves for intestinal-tract disorders, including low

problems, varicose veins, venous insufficiency (poor blood flow to the heart) and other circulatory problems. The leaf is used to treat diabetes.

As part of a six-berry extract (including wild blueberry, cranberry, elderberry, raspberry seeds and strawberry), bilberry has shown anti-angiogenic (anti-tumour), antioxidant and anticarcinogenic potential. Research in 2009 shows the high antioxidant level of bilberry's anthocyanins to have great healing potential, for example in reducing stress-induced damage to the liver and in developing colorectal cancer chemopreventive agents.

acidity, inflammation and diarrhoea; bilberry is also prescribed for the kidneys and liver and to reduce high blood pressure. In both Russia and the UK the fruit is claimed to aid night vision, but this has not yet been scientifically validated. However, dietary supplementation of bilberry extract has been shown to be effective in the prevention of macular degeneration and cataracts in animals.

Today in the West the fruit is used to treat diarrhoea, menstrual cramps, eye

Cautions: Bilberry fruit is generally considered safe. However, high doses of bilberry leaf or bilberry-leaf extract and long-term use or consumption of the leaves have been known to produce symptoms of poisoning and are considered unsafe. Before use, check out the current cautions with a healthcare professional.

Grape

Botanical name *Vitis vinifera*

Family Vitaceae

Description: The grape vine is a perennial, deciduous woody climber that is native to the Mediterranean region, central Europe and south-western Asia. It bears bunches of fruit (grapes) that vary from green to black in colour.

Edible parts: Fruits, leaves.

History: Since humans first trod grapes to make wine, this alcoholic drink has been used in religious ceremonies and in festivities that are common to many cultures globally. The oldest archeological evidence for wine production comes from about 8,500 years ago, from sites in Georgia, Iran and, later, Macedonia (Greece). The Greek god Dionysus and the Roman god Bacchus represented wine, which was used in their pagan rites and ceremonies, as well as in those of Christianity and Judaism and by other cultures and peoples, such as the ancient Egyptians.

The grape is famously versatile, being used to make wine and grappa (Italian grape brandy), eaten as a fruit, raw or dried, and also used in products ranging from jam to grape-seed oil (which is odourless and does not feel greasy) to the syrup (*arrope*) used in ancient Roman cuisine. This dark-coloured, delicious pure grape syrup was cited by St Isidore as *defrutum* or cooked must (reduced boiled wine), described by Varro, Pliny and Columella by the 1st century CE and is still made traditionally today by sherry-makers in Cádiz, Spain.

Main therapeutic properties: Grapes as fruit, and particularly as wine, are part of the healthy 'Mediterranean diet' (see page 118), which may explain the 'French paradox' – that is, how the French have great heart health despite eating a high-fat diet. Grapes are good sources of Vitamins B_6, B_1 and C, with some manganese, potassium and antioxidant flavonoids. In their various forms grapes are highly antioxidant, anticarcinogenic and zealous supporters of heart health.

Apart from the general benefits of alcohol taken in moderation – including increased blood flow and reduced blood clotting against thrombosis – research has found that red wine in particular can also provide protection against strokes, help to lower cholesterol, prevent pancreatic cancer and even stave off potentially fatal food-poisoning bugs such as E. coli, salmonella and listeria.

Special compounds of the grape skin and grape-seed extracts, or polyphenols, are highly protective and beneficial to health. Among other benefits, polyphenols have the potential to lower the risk of Alzheimer's disease. Other arrows in red wine's powerful cardio-protective quiver are procyanidins and saponins, which help to reduce blood pressure and protect against hardening of the arteries. And the latest research suggests that the grape's resveratrols aid longevity.

Cautions: Avoid alcohol if you are pregnant or breastfeeding. Limit consumption of red wine to no more than one glass daily, unless your doctor advises abstinence for any reason.

Oats

Botanical name *Avena sativa*

Family Poaceae

Description: A hardy cereal grain, oats have spread in cultivation throughout various temperate zones worldwide. Genetic evidence shows that the ancestral forms of the wild red oat *A. sterilis* grew in the 'Fertile Crescent' of the Levant and Mesopotamia. Oats are an annual grass growing up to 1 m (3 ft) high, with straight hollow stems, razor-edged leaves and inflorescences that turn into sharp spikes containing seeds.

Edible parts: Seeds, raw or cooked; straw when infused.

History: Oats were the last of the major cereal grains to be cultivated. Initially dismissed as a weed, they were considered inferior to wheat for much of their 3,000-year history. From the Bronze Age, wild oats were found in Eurasia and North Africa and reached some northern parts during the Iron Age. The Romans regarded oats as horse fodder, and 'oat eaters' was the dismissive term used to describe the Barbarians who eventually destroyed their empire. In the late Middle Ages in Europe, it was believed that a man could lose his *membrum virile* through magical attacks by witches, who, according to research, used oats and corn to nourish penises that were stolen by them.

In Scotland, oats became the subsistence crop. The 18th-century writer Dr Samuel Johnson cynically defined the oat as 'A grain, which in England is generally given to horses, but in Scotland supports the people.' But had he felt less disdain for oats and for the Scots' habit of eating porridge daily, he might not have had circulatory problems, suffered a stroke and died of congestive heart failure.

In the early 17th century Scottish settlers brought oats to North America, and ever since they have been a dietary staple there. Oats have been an important commercial crop for many countries.

Oats are not in themselves considered an aphrodisiac, but being oat-fit and well fortifies sexual expression. The comparison to the friskiness of horses that are fed oats might better relate to

drinks like athel brose, an ancient and effective oat whisky-cream liqueur that is drunk on special occasions such as Burns' Night in Scotland, causing a loss of inhibition resulting in wild behaviour.

Main therapeutic properties: Oats have many uses, from being a superb human food and animal fodder crop to their modern application in cosmetics and chemicals, but their primary strength is their use in medicine and health, both internal and external. Oats are valuable both for the nutrition of infants and for the sustenance of adults; they are an all-round therapeutic food. Full of soluble and insoluble fibre, they are extremely rich in minerals, chiefly manganese, selenium, phosphorus and magnesium, and multi-vitamins, especially Vitamin B_1. For some years, heart health has been the main focus of oats as a breakfast cereal. In particular, antioxidant compounds that are unique to oats, known as avenanthramides, help to prevent free radicals, which in turn reduces the risk of heart disease.

Oats lay a sound physical foundation against general and seasonal ailments, ranging from digestive problems (they are eaten raw to avoid constipation) to boosting the immune system against infection and preventing colon cancer.

Oats contain b-sitosterol, an anti-cancer compound. Oats, oat bran and oatmeal all help to lower cholesterol levels via their dietary-fibre content, which also helps to prevent mutations, tumours and cancer. Because they stabilize blood-sugar levels, cooked oats (porridge) eaten daily help to guard against heart disease and diabetes, relieve fatigue and balance the hormones, combating the over-production of prostaglandins (hormones that act on the blood vessels and other organs of the body) and improving stamina. Furthermore, oats are a important source of energy in a healthy diet as they are cholesterol-free and contain complex carbohydrates that provide a slow release of energy over the morning period, reducing the desire to snack on quick energy-release, sugar-based foods.

The selenium content of oats is also involved in DNA repair associated with a reduced risk of cancer, and its antioxidant action within the body is important in helping to decrease asthma symptoms. Although the avoidance of gluten (which is found in wheat, rye, barley and oats) has been *de rigueur* for those suffering from coeliac disease, recent research suggests that the small amount of gluten present in oats is usually well tolerated.

Oats also have a high level of tryptophan, an essential amino acid in the human diet. Clinical research is inclined to confirm its effectiveness as a sleep aid, which helps to explain the role of oats in alleviating fatigue. Oats' tryptophan may also be instrumental in other areas, such as reducing depression, stress and other nervous disorders. Tryptophan appears to be typically associated with low serotonin levels or activity in the brain, and has been showing significant potential as an antidepressant or 'augmenter' of antidepressant drugs, but further research is required.

In traditional Ayurvedic medicine, an extract of oats has been used to treat opium addiction, and in a case report six out of ten opium addicts successfully gave up the drug using a decoction of green oats.

Oat straw is not just for bedding down horses or cattle, but is used in various forms in traditional herbal medicine, including liquid extracts, tinctures, powders and teas, the last-named being the most popular, mainly to treat arthritis and rheumatism. As a diuretic, women take oat-straw tea to counter fluid retention. This source of silicon dioxide is important in developing healthy skin, hair, nails and bones. Anecdotally, European herbalists used oat-straw extracts and tinctures as nerve tonics, and as a general physical and emotional tonic for fatigues and insomnia; today it is largely used as a topical remedy for irritated and inflamed dry skin.

Cautions: Adverse side-effects are not usually associated with the use of oats as a food. However, ingestion of oats may precipitate the symptoms of coeliac disease or *Dermatitis herpetiformis* in sensitive individuals. Oat bran, which increases the bulk of stools and frequency of defecation, may result in abdominal distension, flatulence and possible perineal irritation. Oats are potentially contraindicated for use with morphine.

A peasant scything oats *by Aldebrando de Firenze from a Medieval Treatise 1356.*

191

Rice

Botanical name *Oryza sativa*

Family Poaceae

Description: Currently, out of hundreds of rice species, domesticated rice comprises just two species in the 'true grass' Poaceae family, *O. sativa* and *O. glaberrima*. These plants are native to tropical and subtropical southern Asia and south-eastern Africa. Rice is grown as an annual plant, although in tropical areas it can survive as a perennial. It is not known where the domestication of rice took place, but new archeological evidence points to an area along the Yangtze River in central China. The lower part of the plant floats in water or prostrate. The small wind-pollinated flowers are produced in a branched inflorescence and the resulting edible seed is a grain 'caryopsis'. The husked seeds, commonly called 'paddy', are either a round shape (for soft rice, puddings and so on) or flat (which keeps its shape, as in the Patna rice used for curries). The flour derived from the seeds is known as rice flour, commonly called 'ground rice'.

So-called 'wild rice' usually indicates the species of a different, but related genus (*Zizania*), which is both wild and domesticated, although it may be used for primitive or uncultivated varieties of *Oryza*.

Edible parts: Seeds, when processed and/or cooked.

History: Rice is the cereal foodstuff and crop that constitutes the dietary bulk of almost two-thirds of the world's population and provides one-fifth of the calories consumed by humans globally. It is believed that the domestication of rice dates back 11,000 years. However, it was not until the development of 'puddling' and 'transplanting' that the spread of rice as an agricultural crop really began. This method was practised in the wetlands of China, then adopted by South-East Asia in around 2000 BCE, after which the technique migrated to Indonesia, then Japan. Rice was also an important early crop in India and Sri Lanka, dating back to 2500 and 1000 BCE respectively. The Parable of the Tares in the Bible also tells us that rice's wild relative *Zizania*, otherwise known as 'darnel' or 'tares', was growing in Mediterranean Israel some time before 33 CE.

Controversially, German and Swiss researchers have now genetically engineered rice to produce beta-carotene, with the intention of using it to treat Vitamin A deficiency. Additionally, efforts are being made to improve the yield and quality of other nutrients in what is known as 'golden rice'. In 2008 there was a world rice shortage, caused by adverse weather, high fuel prices and other factors, which led to increased prices across the board and resulted in hardship for many, given rice's position as a vital staple of global diets.

Main therapeutic properties: The starch of rice in its semi-processed brown state is a good provider of fast energy that is easily digested. The grain's central 'germ' is full of phytonutrients: fats, proteins and dietary fibre, with magnesium, potassium, iron, calcium, phosphorus, zinc and manganese, as well as Vitamins B_3, B_2 and folic acid (B_9). It is also an important source of water-soluble, antioxidant Vitamin B_1. In 1911 Casimir Funk, a Polish researcher working in London, isolated and concentrated a substance from rice polishings (bran) that cured beriberi in a pigeon, which was used to prevent and cure that human disease in the Philippines. The substance was an 'amine', essential to a healthy life, so Funk called it a 'vitamine'. Since then the 'e' has been dropped, but the chemical was subsequently named thiamine or water-soluble Vitamin B_1 and is vital to the processes that make energy available in the body and to maintaining a healthy nervous system. Indisputably, 'brown' rice is the healthiest to eat, because the nutrient-rich outer layers

of bran are stripped away in the process of refining polished white rice.

The benefits of rice are not solely dietary. Brown rice bran protects against alcoholism, is good for depression, stress and anxiety, improves mental ability and helps indigestion and heart function. It is good for bowel health, and is thought to be of benefit in the prevention of colorectal cancers.

Rice germ is used to treat children with persistent diarrhoea (dysentery). Its compounds and products have been detected in the treatment of diseases, including hyperlipidaemia, fatty liver, kidney stones and heart disease. It also provides a thickened feed to alleviate swallowing dysfunction. As a diuretic, rice grain is useful for urinary dysfunction and excessive lactation, and rice sprouts are used for poor appetite, indigestion and abdominal problems such as bloating.

Authentic brown-rice vinegar, known as 'Japan's liquid treasure', boasts 22 amino acids and 16 organic acids that are used medicinally to counteract lactic acid in the blood, which may cause fatigue, sore muscles and irritability. It also helps to prevent the formation of toxic fat peroxides, which contribute to cholesterol formation on blood-vessel walls and to ageing. In the East the

plant's rhizomes are also used to treat night sweats associated with pneumonia and tuberculosis. Mirin, a sweet rice wine, forms the base of the ritual medicinal tonic called *o-toso*, used to salute the Japanese New Year.

Long before scientific validation or official recognition in the Pharmacopoeia of India, decocted rice water was used there to assuage stomach irritations. This home-made cooling drink, also used to reduce fevered body temperature and to help soothe inflammatory diseases, is still in common use. Rice water is also used

Manual labourers set rows of young plants in a lowland irrigated rice paddy in China.

in India in an ointment to counteract inflamed skin. In Malayan medicine boiled rice 'greens' can be used as an eye lotion and for acute inflammation of the inner body tissue. It is also recommended to apply a mixture of dried, powdered rice on certain skin ailments.

Cautions: It is advisable not to eat solely white rice if it is the staple carbohydrate of the diet, but to eat brown rice instead.

Rye

Botanical name *Secale cereale*

Family Poaceae

Description: Cereal rye is an erect, tufted annual grass that is thought to be native to the mountains of south-western Asia. It has flat blue-green blades (leaves) and dense spikes. The grain colour varies from yellowish-brown to greyish-green. Its wide-ranging fibrous root system enables it to be drought-tolerant and among the best green manures for improving soil structure.

Edible parts: Seeds, either raw or cooked.

History: Rye cereal should not be confused with rye grass (*Lolium perenne*), which is used for lawns and in permanent pasture and hay for livestock. A member of the wheat tribe, rye cereal is grown extensively as a grain and forage crop and is available in the form of whole or cracked grain kernels or as flour or flakes.

Rye cereal has been found at a number of Neolithic sites in Turkey, including Can Hasan III, dated *c.* 6500 BCE. It is then absent from the archeological record until the Bronze Age of central Europe, but seems not to have been cultivated until around 400 BCE.

After the ancient Greek and Roman eras, as Western nations became more affluent, rye was downgraded in status to a food for the poor, except among Scandinavian and Eastern European countries, where its nutritional benefits and characteristic taste were appreciated. In the 10th century rye was a staple in Ireland, used in the distilling of spirits for medicines.

Ergot of rye is a parasitic plant disease caused by the purplish fungus *Claviceps purpurea*. It is a poison whose misunderstood effects famously began the 'witch-hunt' for the 1692 Witchcraft Trials in Salem, Massachusetts. However, medicinal drugs are extracted from rye's ergot to treat headaches and migraine, control post-partum haemorrhage and cause contraction of the uterus.

Main therapeutic properties: Rye's component phytochemicals are outstanding, supplying a variety of nutrients for the body to use as building blocks. Rye contains starch, 'free sugars', dietary fibre and protein, as well as Vitamins B_3, B_1, B_6, B_2, E, and folate. It also contains the minerals phosphorus, potassium, magnesium, selenium, calcium, iron, zinc, manganese and trace copper, as well as omega-6 and omega-3 fatty acids.

So-called 'black' bread (including pumpernickel) is made from rye flour, which has a low gluten content and a good quantity of soluble fibre. The combination of a wholegrain and fruit diet can assist the menopause and help protect against breast cancer, as rye contains a type of lignan that balances a lack or excess of human oestrogens through plant oestrogens. Whole grains are also good for the heart.

A Swedish rye-pollen extract is used to treat hyperlipidaemia and benign prostatic hyperplasia. Australian proprietary liquid herbal-extract products include drops claimed to boost the immune system's response to allergens, irritants, viruses and bacteria that trigger asthma attacks, bronchitis, hay fever, rhinitis and sinusitis; and a wound-healing spray and cream that are analgesic, antibacterial, antifungal, anti-inflammatory, and antiviral .

Cautions: When buying rye or any other such products read the label carefully, as coeliacs or those with high gluten intolerance or allergy should avoid consumption.

Wheat

Botanical name *Triticum aestivum*

Family Poaceae

Description: Wheat is an annual or biennial cultivated grass that is not frost-tender. It is a worldwide crop that originated in the Levant area of the Middle East at the beginning of agriculture. It has erect flower spikes and light-brown grains. After maize (corn), wheat is the second most-produced cereal food in the world.

Edible parts: Seeds, either raw or cooked.

History: Wheat has been consumed as a food for more than 12,000 years. Its cultivation began to spread beyond the 'Fertile Crescent' of the Levant and Mesopotamia during the Neolithic period, reaching first Ethiopia, India and Spain and thence travelling to England and Ireland 5,000 years ago, arriving in China a millennium later.

Wheat is a great multi-tasker: the grain is a staple used to make flour for breads, pasta and noodles, eaten raw, for example in muesli, and fermented to make beers, alcohol and vodka, or biofuel (ethanol). It is also planted as a forage crop to provide feed for livestock.

Main therapeutic properties: Wheat has great nutritional value. Wheatgerm is the embryo of the wheat kernel, which is separated from wheat that is being milled for flour. It is sodium- and cholesterol-free and very rich in magnesium, Vitamins E, B complex, including B_6, B_5, B_1, phosphorus and zinc. The kernel also yields 2.5 per cent wheat-germ oil containing octacosanol, which has been studied as an exercise-enhancing agent. The oil has the highest content of Vitamin E of any natural unprocessed food.

Mainly used in the bread and cereal-foods industries, wheatgerm's phytonutrient content points to its main benefits. Its antioxidant Vitamin E protects the immune system; its magnesium helps maintain heart, bone, muscle and circulatory system health; its phosphorus builds bones and teeth and aids metabolism; its Vitamin B_5 helps the body process food and metabolize cholesterol and fatty acids; its zinc is an antioxidant essential for proper growth, immune-system function and hormone production.

Wheat bran, a bulk laxative, not only prevents constipation and improves digestion, but has been shown to reduce the stool's concentration of bile acids and bacterial enzymes that are believed to promote colon cancer; it may also alleviate the symptoms of diverticular disease.

Traditionally wheat has many other herbal uses, being antibilious, antihydrotic, antipyretic, antivinous, sedative, dermatic, a stomachic and anticarcinogenic. The seed is said to contain sex hormones and has been used in China to help combat infertility. Today, wheatgerm continues to be seen as a good nutritional source of folate and vitamin B_6, as a support to conception.

The light grain is used as an antihydrotic for the treatment of night sweats and spontaneous sweating, and seed sprouts are used in the treatment of malaise, sore throat, thirst, abdominal coldness and spasmic pain, constipation and cough in China. In Western systems, the grain is antipyretic and sedative, and young stems and seed spouts are used in the treatment of biliousness and intoxication.

Cautions: Most allergenic compounds in wheat are present in the seed, germ or bran, gluten being the most notable, but trace amounts may also be present in the unrefined wheatgerm oil.

Garlic

Botanical name *Allium sativum*

Family Alliaceae

arranged around a central stem-base. The flowers atop the triangular stems and shiny green leaves may be white, pink or reddish, intermixed with small bulbs.

Edible part: Bulb, when peeled.

History: From earliest times garlic has been used as a food. It was part of the diet of the Israelites and

Description: Garlic is a perennial belonging to the lily family. Believed initially to have descended from *A. longicuspis* in south-western Asia, it was introduced to the Mediterranean region and is now cultivated worldwide. The bulb consists of individual cloves covered in a white papery skin and labourers employed to construct pyramids by Khufu, a pharaoh of the Old Kingdom who reigned *c.* 2589–2566 BCE. Virgil records in his *Ecologues* that garlic was consumed by ancient Greek and Roman soldiers, sailors and rural classes. According to Pliny the Elder, in his *Naturalis Historia*, it was eaten by African peasantry. Dioscorides wrote of garlic's ability to clear the arteries, and Galen gave it as the 'rustic's theriac' (panacea).

Garlic's medicinal use is at least 5,000 years old and it is one of the few herbs that continues to be used in all three great healing systems of the world: Ayurveda, traditional Chinese Medicine and traditional European medicine. The Egyptian, Chinese and ancient Greek cultures used garlic for infections, high blood pressure and digestive complaints. Traditional Chinese Medicine used it for fevers, dysentery and intestinal parasites.

Louis Pasteur confirmed garlic's bactericidal properties in 1858. When crushed, raw garlic cloves release allicin, which has been shown to be a more potent antibiotic than penicillin and tetracycline. Small wonder that garlic poultices were used to prevent wound infections from Roman times through to the First World War. During the Second World War, garlic was called 'Russian penicillin' and was used when medics ran out of antibiotics.

Main therapeutic properties: Modern research has found garlic to be anti-inflammatory, antimicrobial, bactericidal, antiparasitic, with fungicidal actions, as well as having the ability to reduce cholesterol and triglycerides in the blood. It lowers blood pressure, improves circulation and helps to prevent yeast infections as well as bronchial and lung infections such as colds and flu.

Garlic is also anticoagulant, immuno-stimulatory and has potential anticancer chemo-preventive effects, especially against gastrointestinal-tract cancers for those who consume it regularly. It also enhances the production of insulin, making it a useful remedy to lower blood-sugar levels in diabetics. At its very simplest, garlic improves the digestion, relieves wind and bloating and enhances the assimilation of food.

Cautions: Some people are allergic to garlic; stomach upsets are a possible side-effect. As a food, garlic seems to be safe in pregnancy and lactation, but garlic found in breast-milk could cause stomach upsets in sensitive infants. When pregnant, garlic supplements should be discontinued several weeks before delivery to prevent excessive bleeding, and medicinal uses should be discontinued at least two weeks prior to surgery or dental extraction. Garlic should be used cautiously with other anticoagulant herbs and medications. It should not be taken with anticoagulant prescription drugs such as Warfarin.

Gotu kola

Botanical name *Centella asiatica*
Family Mackinlayaceae

Description: Gotu kola, with its green
kidney-shaped leaf, is also referred to
as 'Indian pennywort' because it is about
the size of an old penny coin. It is a small
herbaceous, evergreen, perennial plant
that is native to Sri Lanka, India, northern
Australia, Indonesia, Iran, Malaysia,
Melanesia, New Guinea and other parts
of Asia. The flowers are pale violet to
pinkish-red, and each umbel bears two
to five fruits. The slightly aromatic,
succulent herb has a mildly bitter taste.
The crop matures in three months and
the whole plant, including the roots, is
harvested manually.

Edible parts: Leaves, raw, cooked or
infused.

History: Gotu kola featured prominently
in the *Shen Nong* herbal, which was
compiled more than 2,000 years ago,
as one of the 'miracle elixirs of life'.
As either a food or medicine, it is a
legendary leaf known for its powers of
fortification. In Sri Lankan folklore, the
10th-century King Aruna claimed that

gotu kola provided him with the energy and stamina to satisfy his 50-women harem.

The herb was also part of the myth of the T'ai Chi master Li Ching-Yun (d.1933), who allegedly lived to be 256 as a result of using gotu kola and other traditional Chinese herbs; although this claim is disputed, it is said to be certain that he lived for at least 197 years!

Today, gotu kola is sometimes served as a salad or cooked vegetable in Indian cuisine. It is mostly used as a leafy green in Sri Lankan cuisine and prepared as *mallung*, a traditional accompaniment to rice and curry. The leaves are also used in sweet 'pennywort drink'. Gotu kola leaves are also eaten in Thai cooking, and for centuries the Thais have drunk Gotu kola juice as a health drink for general well-being, and as a remedy for healing internal injuries. These days the drink is made by blending the fresh leaves with water.

Main therapeutic properties: Gotu kola is antioxidant, an adaptogen, a physical rejuvenator and cerebral tonic, a dermatic regenerator, anti-inflammatory, anti-ulcerogenic, a circulatory stimulant, a diuretic, nervine and vulnerary. Ayurvedic practitioners have held *Centella* in high regard for centuries, as they still do, particularly as an adaptogen for its revitalizing and rejuvenation properties that help alleviate stress and fatigue.

Gotu kola has been used medicinally to treat myriad conditions, including dysentery, leucorrhoea and excessive secretion of gastric juices, urethritis, arthritis and rheumatism, and liver, kidney and respiratory ailments. The extract has a good chemo-preventive anti-tumour effect to protect the colon, and gotu kola is still used to treat everything from varicose veins to psoriasis.

Gotu kola is also rich in terpenoids, which are known to provide dermatological benefits, such as facilitating the burn wound healing (in animals). Studies show that taking gotu kola tea along with foods that are rich in Vitamin C stimulates collagen synthesis, a key element of skin repair. Gotu kola extracts also aid scar management as they reduce inflammation and further stimulate the production of collagen. In addition it aids the regeneration of new cells, giving gotu kola a 'wow' factor for future botanical cosmeceutical applications targeting youthfulness.

Its healing potential is also of interest for varicose ulcers and cardiac repair. Gotu kola also purifies the blood and is said to have a direct action in lowering blood pressure and treating circulatory problems of the lower limbs, including chronic venous insufficiency, water retention in the ankles, foot swelling and varicose veins.

As well as being a physical tonic, gotu kola has a centuries-old folk reputation as a memory-enhancer. It is used to revitalize the brain and nervous system and increase attention span and concentration. In recent years some natural substances and standardized plant extracts, such as gotu kola, have been scientifically proven to be neuro-protective in the treatment of dementia and Alzheimer's disease. This is desirable because plant preparations produce fewer side-effects than mainstream pharmaceutical therapy and can have the same effectiveness.

Gotu kola is a good source of natural antioxidants. The leaf is rich in beta-carotene, sterols, sapponins, alkaloids, flavonols, saccharides, and amino and fatty acids. It contains manganese, sodium, calcium, magnesium, selenium and zinc, and Vitamins B_1, B_2, B_3, C and K. It does *not* contain cola or caffeine, as its name might suggest.

Cautions: Gotu kola needs to come from a reliable source because the plant is aquatic and vulnerable to water pollution. It is contraindicated during pregnancy, and excessive use should be avoided while breastfeeding. Extracts should only be taken on a long-term basis under professional supervision. Continued, repeated topical application is not recommended. Diabetic patients, high cholesterol sufferers, and epileptic and photosensitive individuals should consult a healthcare professional before taking gotu kola internally.

The leaves and stems of Gotu kola, a swamp plant, are dried in the sun for use in teas and herbal remedies.

Coriander

Botanical name *Coriandrum sativum*

Family Apiaceae

Description: Coriander is a pungently aromatic annual herb that is native from south-western Asia to North Africa, and in the Mediterranean and Middle Eastern regions. It has finely cut, tender upper leaves, with branching clusters of pinkish to white small flowers arranged in umbrella-like clusters.

Edible parts: Fresh leaves and dried seeds most commonly used, but all parts of plant are edible

History: Coriander (from the Greek *koris*, meaning 'bug') is named after what used to be considered the unpleasant bug-like odour of its flowers and may refer to either the seeds of the plant (used as a spice) or to the leaves (used as a herb and known as 'cilantro' in North America). Coriander was cultivated as a medicinal herb by the ancient Egyptians, Chinese, Indians and Greeks, and was introduced to Europe by the Romans.

A biblical herb, coriander is used in Jewish Passover food. It was also used from early on in Muslim cuisine and was cultivated in the traditional Islamic garden system, in which different gardens have different purposes. Coriander was grown in the *rawdah* or vegetable garden of his palace by Khumarawayh, the Tuluid ruler of Egypt (884–96 CE).

Today, coriander seeds and leaves are used worldwide. Usually dried, although they can be eaten green, the seeds have a nutty, spicy taste. They are eaten as a snack and used to flavour curries in Indian cooking, in Germany and South Africa they are a spice for sausages; in central Europe they are an alternative to caraway in rye bread. Coriander leaves and stems are similar to parsley but juicier, with citrus overtones. Both leaves and stems are important in South-east Asian foods, Asian chutneys and Mexican salsas. Coriander roots are used in a variety of Asian cuisines, especially Thai dishes.

Main therapeutic properties: Coriander is used as a diuretic in Indian medicine. Western herbalists use coriander-seed tea to prevent hormonal imbalances and treat menstrual difficulties in young women,

and for bloating and griping. The seeds are also chewed as a breath-sweetener after meals, especially after eating garlic.

Currently, coriander seed is listed by the German Commission E for alleviating digestive complaints and stimulating the appetite. The German Pharmacopoeia has also recognized coriander seed's essential oils, which can effectively treat mild stomach cramps, flatulence and colicky symptoms. The essential oil is considered to be spasmolytic, stomachic and carminative with antibacterial and antifungal activity. Coriander has also been reported to have strong lipid-lowering effects.

Coriander is a very good source of dietary fibre and of iron, magnesium and manganese. The herb is exceptionally well endowed with phytonutrients, mainly due to the healing properties of its active essential-oil components. It is also flavonoid-rich and has active phenolic-acid compounds that slow the release of glucose (sugar) into the bloodstream after a meal.

Cautions: Allergic reactions may occur in susceptible individuals. The plant and seed extracts are photo-sensitive and should not be used internally or externally before high UV levels or sunshine exposure. Prolonged high dosage of coriander seeds (above the culinary levels used in Indian cooking) may cause liver damage. Coriander may also interfere with hypo- or hyperglycaemic therapies and diabetic drugs.

Turmeric root

Botanical name *Curcuma longa*

Family Zingiberaceae

Description: Turmeric is a rhizomatous, herbaceous, perennial plant that is native to India and tropical southern Asia. Its oblong roots or tubers have deep-orange flesh inside, and the spiked and sheathing flower stems bear dull yellow flowers. Turmeric is a member of the ginger family, with a peculiar fragrant odour and a slightly acrid taste. The rhizome is boiled, dried in an oven and ground to produce the yellow spice powder.

Edible parts: Processed root. Fresh leaves are used as flavouring in some regions of Indonesia.

History: Because of ancient trade, the origin of turmeric (or Indian saffron) cannot be pinpointed, but is likely to have been in western India. It reached China by 700 CE, East Africa by 800 and West Africa by 1200, and was introduced to Jamaica in the 18th century. India produces nearly the whole world's crop and uses 80 per cent of it. Sangli, a town in the state of Maharashtra, is the largest and most important trading centre for turmeric (*halad*) in Asia and perhaps the world.

Turmeric's chronology of use dates back almost 4,000 years, to the Vedic culture in India, where it was the principal spice and of religious significance. It is used in some Hindu rituals, its colour symbolizing the sun. In many languages across the world, the name for turmeric means 'yellow root'.

Turmeric's long history of medicinal use in southern Asia is cited in Sanskrit medical treatises, and it was widely used in the Ayurvedic and Unani systems.

Main therapeutic properties: One of the most common food flavourings and colourings in Asian cuisine, turmeric has also had numerous medicinal uses in China, India and Indonesia, and is still one of nature's most powerful healers of the modern world. Its active constituents are the flavonoid curcumin, which comprises 0.3–5.4 per cent of raw turmeric, and volatile oils; other constituents include sugars, proteins and resins.

Turmeric is, within the various disciplines, used as an alterative, analgesic, anti-allergic, antibacterial, anticarcinogenic, anti-inflammatory, antioxidant, antiseptic, antispasmodic, antitumour, an appetizer, astringent, cardiovascular, carminative, cholagogue, digestive, stimulant and vulnerary.

Multiple studies suggest that curcumin has enormous potential in the prevention and therapy of cancers, through its potential to suppress tumour initiation and promotion and even metastasis (the spread of cancer). It is highly anti-inflammatory and works as well as many anti-inflammatory drugs, but without the side-effects, and is useful to those suffering from arthritis, rheumatoid arthritis and, when combined with frankincense, osteoarthritis.

Turmeric also has a positive effect on gall-bladder function and can aid in lowering cholesterol; it may also aid fat metabolism and weight management, as well as the treatment of psoriasis and other inflammatory skin conditions. It can help prevent bacterial infection in wounds. The German Commission E approves turmeric for treating dyspepsia, and notes that the choleretic (bile-stimulating) and anti-inflammatory action of curcumin is well documented.

In traditional Chinese medicine and the Ayurvedic medicine system, turmeric has been used to aid digestion and liver function, relieve arthritis pain and regulate menstruation. It is currently used for conditions such as heartburn, stomach ulcers and gallstones. It is also used to reduce inflammation, as well as to prevent and treat cancer. Susruta's Ayurvedic *Compendium*, of 250 BCE, recommends an ointment containing turmeric to relieve the effects of poisoned food, and it has been shown (in studies on animals) that curcumin does indeed have that potential effect, and may also aid hepatic fibrosis.

Most importantly, research studies in the US and Hong Kong from 2001 show that curcumin-rich dishes have the ability to reduce the effects of Alzheimer's disease. Statistics show that India has one of the lowest Alzheimer's rates in the world, estimated at 1 per cent of individuals over 65, whereas 10 per cent of Americans over 65 develop Alzheimer's and in Europe the rate is around 5 per cent.

Cautions: Turmeric is considered safe as a food ingredient or when taken medicinally in the recommended doses. However, do not use it without professional advice if gall stones are present or if the bile passages are obstructed. Excessive amounts of turmeric may cause stomach upsets, and in extreme cases ulcers. Used medicinally, turmeric's safety in young children, pregnant or nursing women and those with severe liver or kidney disease is not known.

*Crowds dance drenched with liquid turmeric at the Jain Festival of the head anointing ceremony (*Mahamastakabhisheka*) of Bahubali.*

Peppermint

Botanical name *Mentha* x *piperita* var. *piperita*

Family Lamiaceae

Description: A hybrid between spearmint (*M. spicata*) and watermint (*M. aquatica*), peppermint was originally native to Asia and Mediterranean Europe. It is a herbaceous perennial plant, with dark-green pointed leaves and purple flowers in summer, produced in whorls around the stem.

Edible parts: Leaves (raw, cooked or infused) and essential oil.

History: Peppermint is called 'the world's oldest medicine', with archeological trace evidence placing its use pre-history, *c.* 8000 BCE, long before any provenance for its use in Egyptian tombs that dates back to 1000 BCE. Mint was named by the Greeks after the mythical naiad Minthe. According to Pliny, both Greeks and Romans crowned themselves with peppermint leaves during feasts and used it as a culinary flavouring, as did the ancient Egyptians in their food and wine.

A biblical herb, the Pharisees collected mint, along with dill and cumin, as tithes, and peppermint was used to decorate the synagogues of the Hebrews. Its Arabic name is *na'ana* or *nana*, and the famous Baghdad doctor, Al-Kindi (*c.* 800–870 CE), used peppermint in a strong poultice for the spleen.

Peppermint was brought to Britain by the Romans and was grown in medieval monasteries and convent gardens. Powdered mint leaves were used during the Middle Ages to whiten teeth. The herb is also mentioned in 13th-century Icelandic pharmacopoeias. A potential 'garden thug', its prolific growth meant it quickly became established when introduced into the domestic gardens of Asia, Europe and North America.

Mint has great versatility and has been used as a perfume, a medicinal and culinary herb and in household products. Perfume and medicine were synonymous when Egyptian mint was an ingredient of *kyphi*, an Egyptian incense. Peppermint oil still plays an important role in the perfumes, toiletries and cosmetics of today.

The 17th-century English herbalist Nicholas Culpeper recorded that peppermint was most useful for 'complaints of the stomach, such as wind and vomiting, for which there are few remedies of greater efficiency'. However, it was not in general medical use in western Europe until the mid-18th century, and was then first used in England. It was incorporated in the London Pharmacopoeia in 1721 as *M. piperitis sapore* for its medicinal value. The American physician Samuel Stearns described it in *The American Herbal or Materia Medica* in 1801 as a stimulant that restores the stomach, promotes digestion, prevents vomiting and cures complaints such as the hiccups, colic and hysterical depressions.

Main therapeutic properties: Peppermint is high in Vitamin C and A and in manganese, with trace amounts of various other nutrients such as iron, calcium, folate, potassium, tryptophan, magnesium, omega-3 fatty acids, riboflavin and copper. The traditional therapeutic uses of peppermint are legion, and many continue today almost unchanged (some of them with scientific backing). Peppermint leaf is no longer much used medicinally compared with its oil, but its leaves still make an extremely popular and reliable digestif tea.

Peppermint oil, which is carminative, has been used for a variety of health conditions, including nausea, indigestion and cold symptoms, and for stomach and bowel conditions, such as irritable bowel syndrome (administered in capsule form). Several scientific studies have proven the support peppermint oil gives to those with IBS. The German Commission E recognizes peppermint for treating gall-bladder disorders and bile deficiency (it significantly increases bile secretion).

Peppermint extract has demonstrated strong antimicrobial effects against viral, bacterial and fungal infections, both internally and externally. As an analgesic, the oil is used against pain in cases of toothache, aching feet, rheumatism, neuralgia, muscle and nerve pains, and painful periods. Often peppermint oil is useful as a coolant to relieve skin irritation and itchiness and to reduce inflammation. Its cooling action has been used for dermatitis, acne, ringworm, scabies and pruritus.

Peppermint's other forte is in treatments for the respiratory tract, as an inhalant, for dry coughs, sinus congestion, asthma and bronchitis. Its fresh, sharp, refreshing menthol smell is also used in aromatherapy for mental fatigue and to stimulate mental agility. It

is used for apathy, shock, headache, migraine and nervous stress.

A 5th-century BCE fresco of a funeral banquet, Tomb of the Leopards, Tarquinia, Lazio, Italy. The guests wear herbal wreaths on their heads.

Cautions: Peppermint oil appears to be safe when used correctly, although possible side-effects include allergic reactions and heartburn. Peppermint leaf can also aggravate the symptoms of acid reflux, causing heartburn. Used as an inhalant, peppermint oil should not be used for more than a few weeks. As an oil or in a cream, peppermint should not be applied to grazes or broken skin.

Infants should not be given products containing menthol as it can cause throat swelling, inflammation and death. Due to insufficient research, as a precaution pregnant and breastfeeding women should avoid peppermint or menthol herbal remedies and essential oil. Peppermint should also not be used in conjunction with homeopathic treatment.

Moringa

Botanical name *Moringa oleifera*

Family Moringaceae

Description: The 'drumstick tree', or moringa, is a fast-growing, drought-resistant tree that reaches about 10 m (30 ft) in height. Its origins lie in the Indian states of Tamil Nadu and Kerala, and it is native to the foothills of the Himalayas, Arabia and possibly Africa and the East Indies. It has drooping branches, with fragrant white or creamy-white flowers borne in sprays. The fruit is a pendulous brown pod that contains about 20 angled seeds embedded in the pith.

Edible parts: Pods, seeds, flowers and leaves, when cooked.

History: Interest is growing in the use of moringa to help prevent famine and promote health and healing in the Developing World. Almost every part of it can be used for food or has some other beneficial property. For example, the leaves feed people as well as animals; the seeds contain compounds that clarify turbid water and cause traces of silt and clay to settle out and could potentially be used to make water safer.

Moringa's immature long pods, called 'drumsticks', have the appearance of giant green beans and taste like asparagus; the seeds may be eaten like peas or roasted like nuts. The flowers are edible when cooked and are added to curries. The roots are shredded and used as a condiment, but they contain a potentially fatal nerve-paralysing agent, and this practice is not recommended. The masses of small leaflets are boiled and eaten like spinach. They sun-dry quickly and can be stored against seasons when dietary vitamins and minerals are in short supply.

Main therapeutic properties: Moringa provides over 90 natural nutrients. The nourishing leaves are a significant source of beta-carotene and of Vitamins C, B_1, B_2, B_3, B_6, B_7, D, E and K. Moringa is also mineral-abundant, being a good source of iron, potassium and calcium, plus copper, magnesium, manganese and zinc. It contains 17 times more calcium than milk, 25 times more iron than spinach and 15 times more potassium than bananas.

Moringa is one of the most powerful sources of natural antioxidants. Also part of its armoury are phytonutrients, which help the herb to rejuvenate the body at cellular level – a popular extra for those with HIV/AIDs. The bark, sap, roots, leaves, seeds, oil and flowers are used in traditional medicine in several countries. According to a 2006 Botswanan report, the plant increases breast milk in lactating mothers, leads to improved health in babies and can treat diseases such as tuberculosis, diabetes, heart problems, low blood-sugar levels, eye and ear infections.

Extracts of moringa also appear to enhance recovery from liver damage after anti-tubercular drugs, and have been shown to have a possible chemo-preventive potential against chemically induced cancer (in animals). Moringa is traditionally used as a cardiotonic in Thailand, and research in 2008 confirmed its potential for the therapeutic prevention of cardiovascular diseases.

Cautions: At the time of writing, no adverse effects or contraindications are known. However, unregulated excessive use of moringa could in theory cause paralysis of the nervous system, and an overdose could impair the function of the cardiac and smooth-muscle system. Caution should be exercised about consuming raw mature seeds.

Watercress

Botanical name *Nasturtium officinale*

Family Brassicaceae

Description: Watercress is a creeping perennial that is native to Europe and temperate Asia and naturalized and cultivated in North and South America and the West Indies. It has compound leaves, spikes of white four-petalled flowers and small sickle-shaped pods. It grows wild in wetlands and is cultivated in or alongside water in temperate regions throughout the world. Characteristically, it contains a volatile mustard oil with a burning taste. It is cultivated as a salad herb in beds, some of which grow through the winter and yield ten crops a year.

Edible parts: Leaves and young stems.

History: Xenophon (430–354 BCE), the Greek general, is said to have considered watercress as both food and medicine, and ordered the soldiers under his command to take the herb as a tonic. Hippocrates (c. 460–377 BCE) also promoted the medicinal powers of watercress, being perhaps the first doctor to use watercress as an expectorant. He may even have located his first hospital by a stream in order to gather the fresh herb. During the Roman era, Pliny the Younger (61– c. 113 CE) called watercress *nasus tortus* or 'writhing nose', referring to the effect produced by its sharp, mustardy taste and nose-wrinkling smell.

While the ancient Greeks, who called watercress *kardamon*, believed it could boost their mental powers, the Romans and Anglo-Saxons ate watercress in order to purify the blood. In more than one region watercress is considered to have aphrodisiac qualities. For example, recipes for watercress aphrodisiacs are handed down from one generation to the next within Cretan families. And in Egypt,

it was not even thought necessary to consume watercress to take advantage of its aphrodisiac powers. Instead, a bunch of the strong-smelling herb under the bed was considered enough to increase masculine vigour. Legend has it that during the 1970s an Egyptian prince had large quantities of watercress flown in from the UK in order to help him meet his duties to his harem. These traditions may stem from the reputation of watercress as a blood-cleansing detoxificant.

Main therapeutic properties: As a food medicine, watercress is nutritious and is considered a blood-purifying antioxidant, antipyretic, antiscorbutic, antiseptic, cellular regenerator, detoxificant, diuretic, expectorant, hypoglycaemic, laxative, metabolic stimulant and aphrodisiac. The medicinal repertoire of watercress – including both traditional and modern uses – is huge, but today it is primarily considered useful for breathing problems and for release from respiratory congestion and bronchitis, and as an expectorant for coughs and colds. It is approved by the German Commission E for catarrh and other respiratory-tract problems. Watercress is also used for digestive and gastrointestinal disorders, and as an aid to heal bones and joints and help treat anaemia.

Illustration (c.1390–1400 BCE): Harvesting argula *(rocket)* and watercress, *from the* Tacuinum sanitas, *by Luisa Cogliati Arano.*

Outstandingly nutritious, watercress is a 'superfood' that contains more Vitamin C than oranges, more calcium than milk and more iron than spinach. (The calcium in watercress as almost as absorbable as that in milk.) It contains high levels of beta-carotene and Vitamin A equivalents, which are helpful for the skin and eyes, and Vitamins E and B-complex, as well as iodine for thyroid function, and folic acid, which is necessary in pregnancy. Watercress also contains calcium, iron, magnesium, phosphorus, potassium, sodium, zinc, copper, manganese, selenium, sulphur, iodine, and manganese, as well as fatty and amino acids.

Watercress has a serious role in coming to the rescue of smokers who are at risk of lung cancer. It is the richest natural source of a compound called phenylethylisothiocynate (PEITC), which is released by the plant's tissues when they are damaged in the process of chewing. Research has shown that PEITC is not solely a potent inhibitor of cancer development, but also has the ability to kill cancer cells and prevent cancer-causing agents being metabolized into carcinogens. Smokers eating 56 g (2 oz) of watercress with each meal were found to be protected from a key carcinogen (NKK) associated

Just a handful of anticarcinogenic watercress sprigs a day can help allay lung cancer.

with tobacco and implicated in lung cancer. Research has indicated that watercress may help guard against prostate cancer, and shows antimycobacterial activity against multidrug-resistant TB.

Cautions: In rare cases, peppery watercress may cause gastrointestinal upsets. The herb is contraindicated in cases of gastrointestinal ulcers and inflammatory disorders of the kidneys. It is also contraindicated as a medicine for children under four years of age.

Parsley

Botanical name *Petroselinum crispum* and *P. c. neapolitanum*

Family Apiaceae

Description: Parsley is a biennial, but is frequently grown in colder climates as an annual. It is native to Europe and the eastern Mediterranean. The leaves of French parsley (*P. crispum*) are curly, while those of Italian parsley (*P. c. neapolitanum*) are flat. The plant has an erect stem with bright-green compound leaves and small white flowers growing in clusters, with ribbed seeds.

Edible parts: Leaves, roots, seeds and oil.

History: Cultivated for more than 2,000 years, parsley was first used medicinally, prior to being consumed as a food. Its name is derived from the Greek word meaning 'rock celery', and it is indeed related to the celery family (Apiaceae). Known to the Egyptians and held in high esteem by the ancient Greeks, parsley was used to crown victors at the Isthmian Games and in funerary rites. Both the Greeks and Romans wore parsley because

they believed it absorbed the fumes of wine and prevented inebriation.

Medieval and Renaissance herbalists used parsley to treat kidney and stomach problems, insect bites and to avoid infections. But its curative assets have been largely ignored in favour of its conventional role as a garnish.

Main therapeutic properties: Parsley owes its bright-green colour to its chlorophyll content, which is responsible for eliminating breath odours. Chinese and German herbalists recommend parsley tea to help control high blood pressure. Tea made from the root is used to treat kidney stones and bladder infection, and to promote digestion, settle the stomach after a meal and reduce flatulence. Others use it to treat congestion caused by flu and colds, to lessen asthma attacks, for kidney and liver obstructions and anaemia. The herb is also used in poultices for tired and irritated eyes, and to speed the healing of bruises. The leaves, if crushed to extract the juice, relieve itches and stings from insects, making a superb mosquito repellent, and the seeds can be used as a diuretic.

Parsley is a highly nutritious food and an excellent source of Vitamins A, C and K, the last of which is particularly important. Recent evidence suggests that it may be instrumental in bone formation, preventing osteoporosis and keeping the circulatory and nervous systems healthy. Parsley is also a good source of folate.

Parsley's contribution of flavonoids to the antioxidant defence system is thought to be substantial – especially its luteolin, which (in animal studies) has been shown to increase the antioxidant capacity of the blood, prevent inflammation and modulate the immune system. Some studies have also shown that parsley contains a substance that prevents the multiplication of tumour cells. Its volatile essential-oil components play a significant role in the 'scavenging' of free radicals and are said to qualify it as a chemo-protective food.

Cautions: People with known allergy or hypersensitivity to members of the Apiaceae plant family should avoid parsley. It is high in oxalic acid (a compound involved in the formation of kidney stones) and may irritate kidney tissues, so those with kidney stones and nutrient deficiencies should avoid it. Parsley should not be consumed as a drug or supplement by pregnant women as these could lead to uterine stimulation and pre-term labour. Parsley essential oil can be toxic in high doses.

Dandelion

Botanical name *Taraxacum officinale*

Family Asteraceae

Description: Dandelions are tap-rooted biennial or perennial herbaceous plants, native to temperate areas of the northern hemisphere. The flower is a bright sunshine-yellow and the long leaves have deep-cut serrated edges like a saw's teeth, giving the English dandelion its name, from the French *dent de lion*, meaning 'lion's tooth'. The flower heads that make up the dandelion 'clock' are composed of florets that form a seed with fluffy 'parachutes', so that it can easily be wind-scattered.

Edible parts: Leaf and root, when cooked, flowers for wine, whole plant for beer.

History: Dandelions evolved about 30 million years ago in Eurasia. The Latin name *Taraxacum* comes initially from the Arabic *tarakhshaqun*, meaning 'wild chicory' and referring to the culinary use of the plant's blanched leaves, and from the Greek *taraxos* (disorder) and *achos* (remedy). The root and leaf are used in herbal medicine, and the roasted root is also used as a coffee substitute.

Dandelion is a 'famine food' that once sustained the inhabitants of Menorca. Canadians and British alike enjoy its beer, the Belgians a Wallonian pale ale called *Fantôme Pissenlit*, and the strength of potent home-made dandelion wine is appreciated by many.

Historically, the root and leaf have been used to treat breast diseases, water retention, digestive problems, joint pain, fever and skin diseases. *King's American Dispensatory* reports dandelion's long use as a digestive bitter and cholagogue in the treatment of liver and gall-bladder ailments, while the leaf's strong diuretic action was used for water-retentive oedema, loss of appetite and for its mild laxative effect in constipation.

In the Second World War, with no rubber available, thousands of hectares of dandelions were grown for the latex that oozes out of the plant, to make tyres for war vehicles to help the Russian army.

Main therapeutic properties: Dandelion is a highly nutritious and antioxidant food: its leaves contain high levels of potassium salts (up to 5 per cent), its Vitamin-A content is higher than that found in carrots, and it also has Vitamin B-complex, Vitamin C and Vitamin D, along with calcium and one-and-half times more iron than spinach.

The German Commission E has suggested that dandelion leaf be used for loss of appetite and dyspepsia. Research has confirmed that dandelion root has significant cleansing action on the liver and works well to stimulate bile production, and that its leaves are an excellent diuretic because it can stabilize the amount of potassium the body needs.

When young and tender, dandelion leaves make an excellent tonic, as well as a tasty spring green. They are recommended as a food supplement for pregnant and post-menopausal women. They also reduce serum cholesterol levels.

Cautions: Dandelion is generally regarded as safe, but fresh dandelion-leaf latex may cause contact dermatitis. The root may cause hyperacidity in some individuals and should be used with caution to avoid the over-production of stomach acid. Dandelion may also interact with prescription drugs. Dandelion products should only be used under a physician's supervision in cases of gallstones; if there is an obstruction of the bile ducts, it should be avoided altogether.

Thyme

Botanical name *Thymus vulgaris*

Family Lamiaceae

Description: Thyme is an aromatic perennial that is indigenous to the Mediterranean region, North Africa and Asia. It has a fresh, medicinal perfume, small evergreen greenish-grey leaves with white undersides, and white, pink and purple flowers in dense terminal heads. It is a cultivated variety of wild thyme (*T. serypyllum*) and an important nectar source for honey-bees.

Edible parts: Whole plant, leaves, flowering tops and oil.

History: Used by the ancient Egyptians for embalming, thyme has a long history in medicine. Knowledge of its powerful aromatic and antiseptic properties was spread throughout Europe by the Romans. In the 4th century CE, the people in Caucasian Albania (now northern Azerbaijan) used the herb as both a tonic and aphrodisiac. It is known in Russia as 'our Lady's herb' and was added to sacrificial holy fires by Slavic tribes before the advent of Christianity.

Thyme means 'courage', and Roman soldiers used it when bathing for strength and vitality. In the Middle Ages it was given to jousting knights, and a decoction of thyme in baths was used in early Azerbaijani folk medicine as an analgesic for joint pains. The Romans also used thyme to purify their rooms and to ward off diseases in courtrooms.

In the past century a handful of wild thyme in the daily diet was suspected to be the main contributor to longevity among Caucus mountain-dwelling men. Liberal use of thyme is also credited with being an important factor in the excellent heart health of Mediterranean peoples.

Main therapeutic properties: The herb provides a useful amount of Vitamin K and is an excellent source of iron and manganese, plus a good supply of calcium. Thyme and thyme-oil's actions are powerfully antioxidant and antiseptic, as borne out by science; analgesic, highly antibacterial and antimicrobial, astringent, carminative, expectorant, fungicidal and a tonic.

Thyme is used medicinally in connection with respiratory-tract problems, including coughs, bronchitis, whooping cough and catarrh. The most important constituent in its volatile essential oil is phenolic thymol. In experiments, thyme oil has been shown to lower arterial pressure, increase heart rhythms and respiratory volume, and lower blood pressure

Thyme is also used as an antiseptic against tooth decay and dental pain, as well as urinary-tract infection. It is good for colic, flatulence, sore throats and colds. The German Commission E lists thyme leaves and oil for treating poor digestion. Topically, thyme destroys fungal infections such as athlete's foot and skin parasites such as crabs and lice. It is used in anti-rheumatic preparations and in mouthwashes and toothpastes. Thyme can be taken as a tea, tincture, tisane and syrup or used as a salve or by steam inhalation.

Cautions: Excessive internal use of thyme may over-stimulate the thyroid gland and lead to symptoms of poisoning. Do not use thyme as a herbal remedy or use the oil in pregnancy or with high blood pressure. The oil may cause irritation in some people.

Fenugreek

Botanical name *Trigonella foenum-graecum*

Family Fabaceae

Description: Fenugreek is a strongly aromatic annual that has been grown in India, the Mediterranean and North Africa for many centuries. It is conjectured that its cultivation began with the wild seeds distributed over the eastern Mediterranean basin and Near East. Its flowers are yellowish-white, pea-like and develop into long, sickle-shaped green pods. The mature brown pods contain 20 small yellow seeds.

Edible parts: Leaves and seeds.

History: Fenugreek seeds have been recovered from archeological sites, such as Tell Halaf in Iraq (where charred seeds were carbon-dated to 4000 BCE), the Early Bronze Age site Lachish in Israel and the Iron Age site Dier Alla in Jordan. The Roman Cato the Elder listed fenugreek with clover and vetch as cattle crops in his essay *De Agri Cultura* (160 BCE).

Fenugreek leaves and (mainly) seeds were held in high repute among the ancient Egyptians, Greeks and Romans for help in treating diverse health conditions, including menopausal symptoms and digestive problems. It was also used for inducing childbirth, as well as for culinary purposes. The first recorded use of fenugreek is found on the ancient Egyptian *Ebers Papyrus* (1550 BCE), for treating fever.

Fenugreek is used in a variety of ways in different cuisines. The seeds, whole or ground, are frequently used in Indian cuisine in pickles, curry powders and pastes. The leaves are eaten as greens, and the fresh or dried leaves add flavour to other dishes. The dried leaves (called *kasuri methi*) have a bitter taste and a strong smell. The seeds are also used in spice blends, teas and even sweet dishes all over the Middle East, in both Islamic and Jewish cuisine (especially in the Gemora Omen foods customarily eaten during Rosh Hashanah or the Jewish New Year).

Main therapeutic properties: Highly antioxidant and anticarcinogenic, fenugreek seeds contain iron, vitamins A, B_1 and C, phosphates, flavonoids, steroidal saponins, mucilage, bitter fixed oil, volatile oil and alkaloids. Fenugreek is hypotensive, anti-inflammatory and tonic. It also has laxative, expectorant, anti-parasitic and anti-tumour effects. In Ayurvedic medicine, fenugreek is regarded as being rejuvenative and restorative.

The herb is used to stimulate milk production in breastfeeding women, as a uterine stimulant, febrifuge, digestive, demulcent and vulnerary. It helps lower blood sugar for diabetics, is used for loss of appetite and in cases of anorexia, and is applied to the skin to treat inflammation.

Cautions: Possible side-effects of fenugreek include gas, bloating and diarrhoea. It can also cause irritation when applied to the skin. Do not take fenugreek as a herbal remedy or use the oil during pregnancy as this stimulates uterine contractions, and avoid while contemplating pregnancy. Do not take it medicinally for diabetes without the supervision of your primary health-carer. Avoid fenugreek if there is any history of peanut or chickpea allergy, or if it is a migraine trigger. Do not use fenugreek powder if you are asthmatic or in cases of high blood pressure. Use it with caution if there is a history of an abnormal menstrual cycle.

Nasturtium

Botanical name *Tropaeolum majus*

Family Tropaeolaceae

Description: There are two forms of the annual nasturtium plant: compact and trailing/climbing. This flamboyant, flowering ornamental plant is native to the Andes in Peru and its leaves and flowers provide a festive salad herb. Nasturtium has orange to yellow blousy, trumpet-shaped flowers with an elegant long spur forming a 'helmet' above its leaf 'shields'.

Edible parts: Leaves, buds, flowers; seedpods when pickled.

History: The name 'Nasturtium' means 'nose-twister' and its botanical name, *Tropaeolum*, comes from the Greek *tropaion*, meaning 'trophy'. It belongs to the Tropaeolaceae family, and should not be confused with the watercress of the *Nasturtium* genus that belongs to the mustard family.

During the 16th century the plant was introduced to Europe from Peru by the Spanish conquistadors and was called *Nasturtium indicum*, or 'Indian cress', due to its peppery, watercress-type taste, although this particular species is now seldom seen. Peruvian Indians used the plant's leaves to treat coughs, colds and flu, as well as menstrual problems. The leaves were also used as a poultice for minor cuts and abrasions.

During the Second World War, when black pepper was unobtainable, dried, ground nasturtium seeds were used as a substitute.

All parts of the plant are edible, the exotic flowers, leaves and buds being used especially as ornamental salad ingredients or garnishes, for their slightly piquant flavour. They are also a popular addition to stir-fries. The green, unripe, crinkly-ball-like seedpods can be pickled with vinegar as a condiment and used like capers to go with fish. They are also good in martinis!

Nasturtium is a useful companion plant, defending brassica plants, especially broccoli and cauliflower, as well as beans, tomatoes and apples by attracting predatory insects and repelling aphids, cabbage looper, squash bug, white fly and cucumber beetles.

Main therapeutic properties: In Ayurvedic medicine the leaves are rubbed onto the gums to stimulate and cleanse them, which is not surprising because *T. majus* is high in sulphur content and has a glycoside that combines with water to make an antibiotic that is used as a disinfectant and to heal wounds. Reputed to retard baldness, nasturtium's sulphur content is a component of two essential amino acids that are present in every cell. It is also used to resist the formation of phlegm, or to clear and expectorate catarrh. Eaten raw, the whole nasturtium plant is antiseptic and a diuretic tonic, helping to fight fungal and bacterial infections.

Cautions: Nasturtium contains benzyl mustard oil and should not be used for infants and small children. It may cause an allergy in some individuals, and used in excess can irritate the mucous membranes and skin. If used as an internal herbal remedy, gastrointestinal disorders may occur.

Ginger

Botanical name *Zingiber officinale*
Family Zingiberaceae

Description: Ginger is a tropical herbaceous perennial that is native to Asia. It produces clusters of buds that bloom into yellow-green-purple flowers. Its aromatic underground rhizome is commonly used as a cooking spice throughout the world.

Edible parts: Root.

History: Ginger has been cultivated for millennia in both China and India, spreading through South-East Asia, West Africa and the Caribbean, and reaching the West at least 2,000 years ago. It was recorded in early Sanskrit and Chinese texts and in ancient Greek, Roman and Arabic medical literature. Its rhizomes owe their popularity as much to their medicinal virtues as to their food uses. For more than 5,000 years people have valued ginger's hot and warming qualities, from traditional *gan jiang* remedies for the 'internal cold' to a modern

Whisky Mac in inclement winter weather and to ward off the common cold.

Ginger has very varied culinary uses, being used fresh in Asian dishes, pickled in vinegar or sherry as a snack, or crystallized in desserts. There are also ginger liqueurs, green ginger wine and traditional ginger 'beer'; plus dried ginger root, powdered root, fresh root, liquid extracts, syrup, tea, tinctures, tablets and capsules, some of which now have a standardized gingerol content.

Main therapeutic properties: Most traditional Chinese Medicine prescriptions are combinations of many herbs, and ginger is used in nearly half of them. Ginger has been used in Asian medicine to treat arthritis, osteoarthritis and joint and muscle pain, and for stomach aches, nausea and diarrhoea. In Western medicine, fresh ginger is used for vomiting, coughs, abdominal distension and fever, but in today's Asia it is more commonly used to treat rheumatoid arthritis, migraine and sore throats, and to improve circulation and reduce fat deposits in the arteries.

In Ayurvedic medicine, ginger is used as a digestive and respiratory herb. Ayurvedic practitioners used it as a cure for cholera, anorexia and 'inflamed liver', and many of these traditional properties are supported by recent research.

In the West, ginger is generally considered good for colds and an appetite stimulant, anti-inflammatory, antiseptic, anti-emetic and carminative, circulatory and antitussive. In the US, ginger is frequently used as a herbal alternative to antihistamines. It is now used chiefly to alleviate post-surgery nausea, travel sickness, chemotherapy nausea and morning sickness. It is also used as an anti-inflammatory and to prevent blood clots and lower cholesterol and triglyceride levels.

Ginger has good antioxidant properties that are likely to contribute to slowing down ageing, as well as a strong potential to fight some cancers and aid resistance to diabetes. Research also indicates that ginger's shogaol component may benefit the neurological system of the unborn and the aged.

Cautions: Few side-effects are linked to ginger when it is taken in small doses, but gas, bloating, heartburn and nausea are sometimes associated with powdered ginger. An allergy to ginger usually takes the form of a rash. Those with gall-bladder disease should avoid taking ginger. Use caution when combining ginger herbal medicince with other anticoagulant herbs, medications and prescription drugs.

Coconut

Botanical name *Cocos nucifera*

Family Arecaceae

Description: The origin of the coconut is unknown and disputed, but it is believed to have spread from the Indian Ocean to Malaysia and Polynesia. The palm tree grows to around 25 m (80 ft) and, when fully grown at about 30 years, yields some 80 nuts a year, though different species produce more. The flowers have both male and female flowers in the same inflorescence, and the fruit is a large fibrous drupe, growing in bunches of 10–20.

The seed's outer shell (endocarp) and inner white flesh are the commercial product sold as coconut; 'coconut milk' is made from the dried meat (or copra) and water and then packaged for culinary use; the copra is desiccated and is also used to make coconut oil, which is employed in medicines and cosmetics.

Edible parts: Flesh of fruit.

History: Because of its economic importance, the coconut is cultivated in many tropical zones, including Africa and South-East Asia, both for decoration and for its many culinary and non-culinary uses. The outer fibres of the coconut are impervious to salt water so that, in former times, when fruits from plants growing at the water's edge dropped into the sea, they were taken by currents and tides to land and grow elsewhere. The coconut remains of great commercial significance, and is particularly important to the island communities of the Pacific.

It gets its name from *cocos*, Portuguese for 'monkey', and *nucifera*, meaning 'bearing nuts', because the coconut itself is thought to look like a monkey's face. In Thailand, monkeys are often bought as coconut-pickers because they can do the work ten times faster than humans. There are even training schools for the monkey nut-pickers!

Main therapeutic properties: Coconut is a highly antioxidant, nutritious food – if fattening. The 'meat' contains less fat than other dry nuts, such as peanuts and almonds, but has approximately

The fruit is another of the earth's gifts that comes with inbuilt protection, for the 'water' in coconuts is totally sterile until the fruit is opened. In the tropics, where coconut is sold on street stalls, the immature nut jelly is relished as a folk health remedy. It is also used as a face mask, and it may be *the* most rejuvenative and nourishing skin moisturizer obtainable straight from nature.

Coconut water, a highly nutritious food source containing sugar, fibre proteins and antioxidant vitamins and minerals, provides (via its isotonic solution) an electrolyte balance – consuming coconut water puts the cells of the body into a state of equilibrium with their surroundings, which makes for optimal health.

90 per cent saturated fat, which exceeds that of butter and lard. However, coconut meat contains less sugar and more protein than popular fruits such as bananas, apples and oranges. It is a good source of Vitamins C, B_5, B_1, B_3, B_6, B_2 and folate (B_9), and is high in iron, phosphorus and zinc, with magnesium, potassium and calcium.

Cautions: Coconut oil can cause an allergic reaction in some individuals, especially the solvent-extracted oil.

Hazelnut

Botanical name *Corylus avellana*

Family Betulaceae

Description: Hazel is a large deciduous shrub that is native to the northern hemisphere, from Europe to western Asia. It grows to about 3–5 m (10–15 ft) tall, with single-sex catkins barely showing long, bright-red styles. Each hazel 'nut' is within a shell and surrounded by a husk that partly encloses it. The nut is also known as the cob nut or filbert.

Description: Seeds.

History: The common name comes from the Anglo-Saxon word for bonnet, *haesel*;

and the genus name from the Greek *korys*, meaning 'helmet' or 'hood'. The hazelnut is surrounded in mystery and the occult. Forked branches were used as 'divining rods' for locating buried treasure, valuable ores and water, and continue to be used by traditional water-diviners. In Irish legend, the hazelnut was the fruit of wisdom and was used in meditation. In England, hazelnuts were hung in the house to bring good luck and were a symbol of fertility.

In Mediterranean countries, hazelnuts have been consumed in moderate quantities since ancient times (hazelnut oil is thought to have been extracted first during the Bronze Age). Frangelico, a traditional hazelnut liqueur drunk over ice or in coffee, was developed by 17th-century Christian monks living in Piedmont, northern Italy.

Main therapeutic properties: The hazelnut is rich in antioxidants and a super-source of the lead neutraceutical Vitamin E. It also contains Vitamin C, with lesser amounts of B_1, B_2 and B_6, which are essential to blood formation and mental health, especially for developing children, and of Vitamin K, A and folate. Hazelnut also contains manganese, copper, magnesium, phosphorus, iron, potassium, zinc, calcium and selenium, and the phytonutrient carotenoids lutein and zeaxanthin, plus phytosterols. It does not contain sodium or cholesterol.

High blood cholesterol is one of the main factors contributing to the increase in cardiovascular diseases, so such a special combination of oil, phytonutrients and nutrients puts the hazelnut is in a unique position to protect against heart disease. Its oleic acid prevents the rise of cholesterol in the blood, while beta-sitosterol, which is also abundant, is an important means of decreasing cholesterol and helps to prevent (breast and prostate) cancers.

Hazelnut's Vitamin E complement means that consuming just 25–30 g (about 1 oz) of them a day meets the recommended daily allowance for this vitamin. Nuts are a vital part of the Mediterranean diet (see page 118), and science has shown there to be a lower risk of cardiovascular disease in populations with frequent nut consumption, independent from other dietary components; this is also an excellent method to protect against heart-vein diseases and cancer.

Cautions: Do not eat hazelnuts if you are allergic to nuts in any form or if you have diarrhoea. Do not use hazelnut oil without the guidance of a qualified physician if you are pregnant, nursing or epileptic, or have liver or kidney damage or cancer.

Pumpkin seeds

Botanical name *Curcubita pepo*

Family Cucurbitaceae

Description: Pumpkin is an annual trailing vine with twining stems, which is thought to have originated in North America. It has lobed leaves, vibrant yellow flowers and large, grooved orange fruits, which generally weigh 4–8 kg (9–18 lb). The beautiful flowers, with petals like sunrays radiating out from the centre, are short-lived and may open for as little as one day. The seeds, also known as *pepitas*, are flat and dark green; some are encased in a creamy-white husk.

Edible parts: Seeds; flesh of fruits and flowers when cooked.

History: In North America, pumpkins were a precious food of the Native Americans, valued for both their dietary and medicinal properties. The cultivation of pumpkins was carried to many cultures of the Old World by the European explorers who visited the New World. The oldest evidence of the use of pumpkin seeds, dated to between 7000 and 5500 BCE, was found in Mexico.

Main therapeutic properties: The colour of pumpkin comes from its abundant antioxidant orange pigments, mainly lutein, which is protective of cataracts and age-related macular degeneration. Raw pumpkin seeds are nutritional powerhouses that contain a large amount of Vitamins A and K, folate and a lower amount of B_3; they are also a very good source of minerals: phosphorus, potassium, magnesium and, to a lesser extent, calcium, sodium, iron, zinc and selenium, with equal amounts of linoleic acid and omega-6, some omega-3 fatty acids and a full compliment of essential amino acids.

Science now corroborates some of the health benefits associated with pumpkin seeds in folk remedies. For example, their zinc content aids bone-mineral density against osteoporosis and reduces inflammation, which may assist arthritis. The seeds promote overall prostate health and may help to alleviate the difficult urination associated with an enlarged prostate and to lower the risk of certain types of kidney stones. In Central American herbal medicine the seeds are used as a treatment for nephritis and other problems of the urinary system, and in some studies (in animals) pumpkin seed was shown to improve bladder function. The ground seeds mixed with honey are an anthelmintic against tapeworm, and the oil remedies parasitic infestations of the intestinal tract.

Pumpkin seeds contain phytosterols, compounds shown to reduce levels of LDL or 'bad' cholesterol; they also protect against many cancers and help to prevent arteriosclerosis. Amino acid L-tryptophan, a natural anti-depressant compound, is also present in pumpkin seeds.

Pumpkin seed oil is a thick green oil produced from roasted pumpkin seeds (white seeds with shells produce a cheaper white oil). It is emollient, calming, and laxative and is used in cases of demineralization. It is reputed to be good for the lungs and the mucous membranes, and is commonly used to treat IBS. The oil is used in cooking in Eastern and Central Europe, generally mixed with other oils due to its robust flavour. However, cooking destroys its essential fatty acids.

Cautions: At the time of writing there are no known cautions for pumpkin seeds.

Sunflower seeds

Botanical name *Helianthus annuus*

Family Asteraceae

Description: The sunflower is a striking annual plant that is native to the Americas and is thought to have originated in Peru. Its stout, hairy stem can grow to 3 m (10 ft), bearing an amazingly large flowering head. The flowerheads can reach up to 30 cm (12 in) in diameter, producing the familiar huge, pale-grey seeds. In its bud stage the sunflower continuously faces and follows the sun, although the wild sunflower typically does not display this sun-worshipping behaviour.

Edible parts: Seeds; buds and sprouts when raw or cooked.

History: *Helianthus* means 'flower' (*anthos*) 'of the sun' (*helios*). In Peru, sunflower headdresses were worn by Inca priestesses, and flowers wrought in gold adorned the Inca temples of the

sun. Current evidence states that the sunflower was first domesticated in Mexico by at least 2600 BCE, while north of Mexico fully domesticated sunflowers were found in Tennessee dating back to *c*. 2300 BCE. After its introduction to North America, the sunflower found its way to the Mediterranean, Eastern Europe and Russia.

Traditionally herbalists used sunflower seeds for their expectorant and diuretic properties and for colds, coughs and bronchitis. It was also used as a substitute for quinine for malarial fever. In Russian medicine, decoctions of the seeds were given for jaundice, malaria, heart conditions, diarrhoea and other ailments. The seeds were also used for bronchial infections, and the whole plant for tuberculosis and malaria; chopped sunflower stems and heads, which have weak insecticidal properties, were macerated in vodka and consumed in order to create a sweat. The vodka-macerated flower head has also been used as a liniment rub for rheumatic sufferers, and a poultice of fresh leaves is another Russian folk fever remedy.

The oil is expressed from the crushed seeds, to obtain several different grades of oil. Raw sunflower buds and seed sprouts are added to salads, or the buds can be steamed and served as a vegetable.

Main therapeutic properties: Sunflower seeds have a high nutritional value. They contain 47 per cent fat and 24 per cent protein and are rich in dietary fibre and polyunsaturated fatty acids and low in saturated acids. They are an excellent source of Vitamins B_1, B_3, B_5 and B_6, as well as Vitamin E, magnesium, iron, phosphorus, selenium, calcium and zinc. They also contain a volatile oil, carbonate of potash and tannin.

The pale-yellow, delicately flavoured sunflower-seed oil is very high in polyunsaturated fat and low in saturated fat. The seeds are also processed into margarines, and the oil is used for cooking and salad dressings. Today, culinary use of phytosterol-rich sunflower oil helps to lower blood cholesterol levels and soothes irritated tissues. The mineral selenium aids DNA repair and is anti-cancerous. Research has also shown that sunflower oil in the diet may be helpful in the treatment of multiple sclerosis. The naturally occurring fatty acid CLA, which has been identified as a potentially key factor in weight management, can be derived from sunflowers.

Cautions: There are no known drug interactions or contraindications at the time of writing.

Walnuts

Botanical name *Juglans regia*

Family Juglandaceae

Description: The walnut is a deciduous tree that can grow to 300 years old and is native to the Americas, Eurasia and South-East Asia. It usually reaches a height of 10–40 m (30–130 ft), with robust, spreading limbs and a massive trunk clothed in a greyish-brown bark. The leaves have a strong, characteristic smell, while the fruits are green globe-like fleshy drupes.

Edible parts: Fruits (nuts).

History: The best-known member of the walnut family is the royal or Persian walnut (*J. regia*). Its name indicates Persian origins and, according to the UN's Food and Agriculture Organization, the Shahmirzad walnut orchard in Iran is the largest in the world.

The green husks of the immature fruit, which stain dark brown, were traditionally used for a yellow dye, and later as a do-it-yourself artificial skin-tan, initially by thespians on stage. Delicious 'pickled walnuts' made from green fruit are also anti-scorbutic.

Main therapeutic properties: Walnuts are a 'superfood' that are vitamin- and mineral-rich, containing B_6, B_5, B_3, B_1 and B_2, and especially selenium and manganese. They are also an excellent source of omega-3 fatty acids, which have many potential health benefits, ranging from cardiovascular protection to the promotion of better cognitive function; and anti-inflammatory benefits that are helpful in asthma, rheumatoid arthritis and inflammatory skin diseases. In addition, walnuts contain the super-antioxidant phenolic compound, which is known for its healing benefits, plus gallic and ellagic acids – the latter stimulates enzymes that detoxify carcinogens.

In traditional Chinese medicine, walnuts are primarily considered to be a kidney tonic and beneficial to the brain, back and skin; and to relieve constipation caused by dehydration. In the West, walnuts are traditionally used to treat dysentery and skin diseases. They have always been used to promote physical and mental strength (notice the inside of the nut even looks like a human brain), but are thought by many people to be fattening. However, research has proven this concept to be false and, in fact, people who eat nuts at least twice a week are far less likely to gain weight than those who almost never eat nuts. Walnuts also increase HDL or 'good' cholesterol in patients with type-2 diabetes.

Of late, the walnut has been referred to by the scientific fraternity as the 'heart nut' because of its fantastic antioxidant, nutrient and phytonutrient value. Eating walnuts after a meal that is high in unhealthy fats can reduce the damaging effects of such fats on the blood vessels.

Walnuts are also helping to remedy the serious brain disease of Alzheimer's, which causes confusion, memory loss, dementia and general demise. Walnut extract and its gallic and ellagic acids have been able to inhibit platelet aggregation and break down amyloid plaques in the brains of Alzheimer's-disease patients. They may also reduce the risk or delay the onset of Alzheimer's.

Cautions: Walnuts are generally recognized as safe when used as food, but very high dosages should be avoided, due to their unproven safety and efficacy. Walnut should not be used by nut-sensitive individuals.

Pine nuts

Botanical name *Pinus pinea*

Family Pinaceae

Description: Exuding a powerful resinous pine scent in the sun, the Mediterranean 'umbrella' or stone pine tree is symbolic of the Italian landscape, growing on average to around 12–20 m (40–65 ft). Some researchers believe it originated in the Near East and was spread by humans to Mediterranean locales, although it may only have existed in Spain and Portugal. The tree has a characteristic 'umbrella' shape, with a short trunk and very broad crown. Its mid-green 'needles' (leaves) are exceptionally long, in bundles of two. The seeds (pine nuts) are pale brown, with a powdery black coating that rubs off easily.

Edible parts: Seeds.

History: The pine tree has been naturalized and cultivated extensively for its edible seeds for at least 6,000 years throughout the Mediterranean region, which has made it a 'native'. Since about 1700 the tree had been introduced to other areas with similar climates, and is now naturalized in South Africa and planted in California, Australia and western Europe, extending northwards as far as southern Scotland, and other parts of the world.

The 'nuts' – often referred to as kernels – are reported to have been traded since prehistory. There are many species of pine tree grown commercially for their nuts, including the Korean pine (*P. koraiensis*) in north-east Asia, which is the most important species in international trade. Other species, including Siberian pine (*P. sibirica*), Siberian dwarf pine (*P. pumila*) and Chinese white pine (*P. armandii*), are also used to a lesser extent.

Harvesting pine kernels is manual, labour-intensive work. The pine kernel is expensive because it grows on soil that is difficult to fertilize, and the tree may be 15–25 years old before producing kernels, becoming really productive at 75 years. However, once established, the tree can be productive for 100 years. In North America and Mexico, the pine kernels were traditionally the main food of several Native American tribes, who, in many areas, have exclusive rights to the harvest.

In south-western parts of the US, it is thought that North American *pinon* tree kernels were eaten as a staple diet some 10,000 years ago. In Korea, China, Turkey, Pakistan and Afghanistan, the pine nut has been a traditional food of nomadic tribes. The pine is also mentioned in the Bible.

Mediterranean pine nuts have been used as a food ingredient by Italians, in particular, for more than 2,000 years.

Evidence found in the ruins of Pompeii, after the eruption of Vesuvius in 79 CE, shows that they were in wide use at that time, the ancient Romans using pine kernels in wine and sausages, and preserving them in honey. Several large forests of *Pinus pinea* were planted in Italy in response to papal decrees. One forest, established in 1666 near Fregeni at the initiative of Pope Clement IX, still exists today.

Pine nuts are still popular in Mediterranean and Arab cooking. They are frequently added to meat, fish and vegetable dishes, and go well with cheese and fruit. They are essential to Italian pesto sauce, and feature in the *salade landaise* of south-western France. Pine-nut dark roast coffee is peculiar to New Mexico.

Pine nut oil (also called pine seed oil or cedar nut oil) is extracted from the pressed seeds of several species of pine. It is valued for its mild nutty flavour and, with a relatively low smoke point, is more of a 'finishing' oil for flavouring than for overall cooking. However, it is reportedly an excellent bread preservative when added in small amounts to dough. Before the 1917 Russian Revolution, pine seed oil was used for cooking during Lent, in order to avoid eating animal fat. At that time, 10 per cent of hard currency in Russia was based on trade in pine seed oil, mostly with France.

Main therapeutic properties: Pine kernels are a highly nutritious, antioxidant food, high in fibre, Vitamins A and E, with B_2, B_3 and B_6. The nuts contain about 80 per cent of poly- or monounsaturated fats, and are a good source of magnesium, iron, copper, potassium, phosphorus, zinc and folic acid. Pine nuts are very high in protein, making them especially useful for vegetarians, and can be eaten raw and in salads for maximum nutritional benefit.

Pine-nut oil is important for conditions such as being overweight and obesity, helping to curb the appetite by stimulating the release of a hormone that functions as an appetite-suppressant – by up to 60 per cent for four hours. This property is readily understood in Siberia, where a handful of pine nuts (or a tablespoon of pine-nut oil) has traditionally been taken with (or instead of) a meal when food is scarce, to give a feeling of satiation.

Pine-nut oil also has antioxidants in high concentration, which can help to reduce the risk of peptic ulcers or gastritis, according to clinical studies in Russia and China, as a result of which

pine-nut oil is now considered a remedy for these conditions in both countries.

Furthermore, the pycnogenol found in pine-bark tea is water-soluble and moves freely through the body's bloodstream. It is one of the best antioxidants, and can block benzoprene (an inactive carcinogen in smoke) from being converted into a most deadly carcinogen. Pycnogenol is also one of the most effective substances for maintaining the integrity of collagen. It is 20 times more powerful

Pine nuts are popular in Mediterranean and Arab cooking, are highly nutritious and especially good for vegetarians due to their high protein content.

than Vitamin C, and 50 times more powerful than Vitamin E, and helps to neutralize free radicals that contribute to premature ageing.

Cautions: Pine kernels can become rancid quite quickly and require refrigeration or freezing for storage.

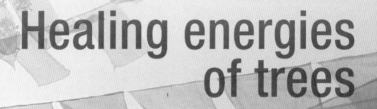

Healing energies
of trees

The tree: symbol and magic

Trees have long held a place of central importance in the human psyche. The mystic concept of the World Tree or Tree of Life is universal, found at the centre of archaic cosmological iconography in cultures worldwide.

The common theme holds that the tree's branches reach up to the divine sphere of the gods and uphold the heavens, stars and planets, with its roots stretching down into the dark, earthy Underworld, forming a portal to access the dead. The Tree of Life lives in and unites three worlds, and is both a feminine symbol, providing nourishment, and a masculine phallic symbol of fertility.

Worldwide interpretations of the Tree of Life

In the Hindu tradition, the World Tree is depicted upside-down. It is conceived as being rooted in the heavens and bearing its fruit on earth. All divine celestial beings inhabit its branches, the elements and cosmic principles, but each is rooted in Brahman, who represents the stem of the sacred tree.

Images of the World Tree represent the *axis mundi* (world axis), depicting the central pole around which all life rotates and spins its webs of destiny. They are found in the art and mythological traditions of cultures such as the Maya, Aztec, Izapan, Mixtec, Olmec and others, illustrating the interconnectedness between nature, humans and the gods.

In stylized images of the Tree of Life, the central stem may also represent the human spinal cord. The Tree of Paradise evolved from this ancient symbol and is the prototype from which the Egyptian, Islamic and Kabbalist Tree of Life concepts grew.

The Kabbalists' Tree of Life (*Etz haChayim*) in the system of Judaism, which claims insight into divine nature, is a mystical symbol within the esoteric

Worldwide, rags tied to trees express some form of votive offering to appease or supplicate.

Kabbalah, used to describe 'the path to God' and the way He created the world out of *nothing*, using the tree's 'map' of creation. It is believed by some Kabbalists to correspond to the Tree of Life mentioned in Genesis 2:9. However, in Judaeo-Christian mythology, the Tree of Heaven is the source of the primordial rivers that water the earth; whereas milk, honey and wine flow from the roots of the Tooba Tree of the Koran.

The Tree of Life was also central to Celtic spirituality. From the woods of sacred trees with magical properties to the practical provision of food and weapons, trees were the source of basic sustenance, both physical and spiritual.

The importance of trees is reflected in the Ogham alphabet, in which each symbol represented both a letter and a tree (these symbols are shown on the following pages wherever the tree in question was part of the Celtic world). Trees extended their *being* to the shamanic beliefs of the Druids, and in Celtic creation myths trees *were* the ancestors of human beings, the elders of wisdom. The oak *daur* was their chosen *axis mundi* and doorway to the Otherworld.

In virtually all cultures around the world it seems that trees have been viewed as the means of communication between worlds, and in some societies they were even made into magical totems.

Rituals of the sacred groves

The worship of trees as a spiritual healing force was fundamental to Druidism, the ancient Western pagan culture that worshipped especially in sacred groves. The Druids used evergreens during mysterious winter-solstice rituals, and holly and mistletoe as symbols of eternal life. Other cultures, such as the ancient Egyptians, treasured and worshipped evergreens too. When the winter solstice arrived, they brought green date-palm leaves into their homes to celebrate life's triumph over death. In the late Middle

Woodcut, c. 19th-century, of the Druids' ceremonial gathering of sacred mistletoe from holy oaks in the forest at the winter solstice.

Central Eastern Rainforest Reserves in Queensland, Australia, sacred to the Aborigines, the Lebanese Horsh Arz el-Rab (Forest of the Cedars of God), and a number of others that are a spiritual focus of their inhabitants.

In the frenzied modern world, ritual and secrecy persist in the sacred grove. In mid-July each year, Bohemian Grove in California – with a main camp area of 65 hectares (160 acres) of old-growth redwood trees in excess of 1,000 years old, some exceeding 91 m (300 ft) in height – hosts a three-week encampment of some of the most powerful men in politics and business.

A large wood carving of St John in clerical robes, with his index finger over his lips, stands at the shore of the lake in the grove, symbolizing the secrecy kept by its attendees throughout its history.

Therapeutic magic

In many parts of the world, the practical 'magic' of trees manifests in their being used as actual healers. In Lithuania

Ages, the Germans and Scandinavians placed evergreen trees inside their homes or outside their doors to demonstrate hope for the forthcoming spring – a forerunner of the Christian Christmas celebration of the fir tree.

The tradition of the sacred grove is commonly associated with secrecy and initiation rites, and such locations were considered 'untouchable'. Some significant groves have retained their importance. The World Heritage List of UNESCO includes several groves and forests known to be sites that are held to be sacred or holy, among them the huge oaks, lindens, mountain ashes and specific pine trees were worshipped for their healing powers. Historical sources reveal that sick people were passed through a hole in a tree formed by two branches, or supplicant sick children were taken to a tree whose branches had grown into a circle.

During the 16th and 17th centuries suffering people came from afar to an ancient oak tree in west Prussia, to heal the physically handicapped, the paralysed and those with lesser afflictions. They climbed onto ladders to push parts of the body into tree openings to be healed. Offerings of personal attire by women, and of money by men, were made to the tree, like the offerings of jewellery and gold left to statues representing the Virgin Mary or saints in churches by contemporary petitioners.

This part of the book explores the traditional spiritual and healing qualities associated with a range of different trees from around the world, together with the correspondences or attributes (such as the planet, deity, element, colour, stone, animal and virtue) that are associated with each tree.

Trees hung with red lanterns at the Chinese New Year's Lantern Festival of Quanzhou are called 'lantern trees' or 'spark trees'.

253

Fir

Botanical name *Abies* spp.

Family Pinaceae

Description: Native to the mountains of Europe, the silver fir (*Abies alba*) is known as the ideal Yule tree, with its conical narrow crown, balanced level branches with upturned tips, with red-brown ovate buds. In spring, resin is tapped from silver fir trees aged 60–80 years old and used in oil distillation.

History, mystery and spiritual healing: Silver fir is the species first chosen as the tree for merry-making at Christmas, the Christianized version of the pagan winter-solstice celebration. The Bremen Guild Chronicle of 1570 reports how a small fir erected in the guild house was decorated with apples, nuts, dates, pretzels and paper flowers for the benefit of the guild members' children, who collected the dainties on Christmas Day. By the early 19th century, the custom of decorating a tree became popular among the nobility and spread to royal courts as far as Russia.

Correspondences

The tree is sacred to the Druids and stands for 'hope assured'. It takes the Ogham letter A.

Ogham letter A

- **A (Ailm)** Clarity, achievement, energy
- **Planet** Jupiter, Moon
- **Deity** Dionysus, Bacchus, Artemis (Ishtar, Tamar, Astarte, Sumerian Inanna), Cybele, Druantia
- **Element** Air
- **Colour** Pale blue
- **Stone** Iolite, amber
- **Polarity** Feminine and masculine energy
- **Animal** Red cow
- **Virtue** Insight, objectivity, endurance
- **Association** Self-esteem, potential wisdom, strength, birth and rebirth, change; learning, choice and progress

Healing: In folk medicine the needles and/or resin are used to treat bronchitis, cystitis, leucorrhoea, ulcers and flatulent colic.

The bark is antiseptic and astringent. The buds are antibiotic, antiseptic and balsamic. The resin is antiseptic, balsamic, diuretic, eupeptic, expectorant, a vasoconstrictor and vulnerary. Either used as an inhalant or taken internally, both needles and resin are common ingredients in remedies for coughs and colds. The resin is also used externally in bath extracts, rubbing oils and so on, to treat rheumatic pains and neuralgia. The externally applied rubefacient oil of turpentine is occasionally used instead of leaves or resin for neuralgia, and is employed in medicine and veterinary work for sprains and bruises.

Silver Fir's essential oil is a thin, clear liquid tinged with yellow, which has a fresh, sweet, fruity-earthy, woody scent, with a delightfully balanced green incense-resinous bouquet, striking a harmonious, grounding chord upon which the delicate fir tree topnote rests. It is used in perfumery, and its buds' and scent in Baleneotherapy and in aromatherapy for arthritis, bronchitis, colds, coughs, flu, muscle aches, rheumatism and sinusitis.

Cautions: In high concentration, fir may cause skin irritation.

Baobab

Botanical name *Andasonia* spp.

Family Malvaceae/Bombacoideae

Description: The baobab, which may live to 1,000-plus years, is native to Madagascar. It behaves like a succulent and store masses of water inside its swollen, thick corky trunk to overcome drought conditions, and throws up branches that look like a root system, hence its other name of 'upside-down tree'. The enormous white flowers have only a single day of life. The large, hairy fruits resemble rats hanging by their tails, hence the nickname 'dead rat tree'.

History, mystery and spiritual healing:
Baobab fruit from West Africa was identified in the *Book of Roads and Kingdoms* by al-Bakri (1068), and the tree from the writings of early 14th- and 15th-century travellers such as Ibn Battuta, Leo Africanus and Portuguese navigators. The baobab is capable of providing shelter, food and water for animals and humans, and relief from sickness. Cut down an entire tree and it will simply re-sprout from the root. When a baobab tree dies, it collapses into a heap of soggy, fibrous pulp;

stories abound of how quickly decomposing trees burn up through 'spontaneous combustion'.

African myths and legends tell of how God planted baobabs upside-down; of how a disgruntled hyena was given the

Correspondences

Baobab means 'Father, sources'.

- **Planet** Earth, Sun
- **Deity** God the Creator, Thora (Kaang)
- **Element** Water
- **Colour** White
- **Stone** Tree agate (the stone of plenitude), sunstone (sun and protection)
- **Polarity** Male
- **Animal** Hyena (wisdom and cleverness)
- **Virtue** Courage, righteousness
- **Association** Omnipotence, safe haven

tree and planted it upside-down; of how the Bushmen's creator god took a dislike to it and threw it over the wall of paradise, but it continued to grow. Many Africans believe that spirits that dwell in the tree have to be placated. The *griots* or poets of West Africa are denied burial in the earth and are suspended in hollow baobabs, while in southern Africa the spirits of tribal chiefs live in the tree. African superstitions say that anyone who dares to pick a baobab flower will be eaten by a lion, but if they drink water in which the seeds have been soaked, they will be safe from crocodile attack.

Healing: Baobab leaves are used to fight inflammation; the dried leaf powder is used for anaemia, inflammation of the spine, dysentery, asthma and rheumatism. The fruit's pulp can also quell dysentery and guard against smallpox and measles. The bark combats fever and inflammation of the digestive tract. The tree's most healing gift of all is the provision of water in a drought.

It is noteworthy that, as a famine food, science has found the leaves of the boabab to be more nutritious than the fruit. There is also early scientific evidence for *A. digitata*'s beneficial effects on bronchial asthma and allergic skin disorders.

Cautions: At the time of writing there are no known contraindications for the use of this plant.

Neem tree

Botanical name *Azadirachta indica*

Family Meliaceae

Description: The neem tree, which belongs to the mahogany family, is a fast-growing evergreen that is native to Bangladesh, India, Myanmar and Pakistan. It has hard, fissured or scaly bark, feather-like leaves tinted with red and purple when young, and small white, fragrant star-shaped flowers. It normally contains one (rarely two or three) seeds with a brown seedcoat. Neem is one of very few shade-giving trees that thrive in drought-prone areas and is also valued for its anti-desertification properties.

History, mystery and spiritual healing: Neem's name derives from the Sanskrit *nimba* and it was known as the 'panacea for all diseases'. In India it is deeply imbued with spiritual meaning and is known as the 'divine tree'. The ancient Hindus believed that planting neem trees ensured a passage to heaven. Its curative properties were attributed to a few drops of heavenly nectar descending upon it.

Neem was, and still is, closely connected with Indians' everyday life, its pure, hygienic, decontaminating and

protective properties playing an important role in cradle-to-death care. Babies were bathed with neem water, given small doses of neem oil and the leaves were hung over their cradles. Smallpox and chickenpox were thought to be cured or held off by its use, for spiritually it was believed that Sithala, the goddess of smallpox, lived in the neem tree, as did the powerful mother goddess Kali.

Healing: In Ayurvedic, Unani and folklore traditional medicine, neem oil is used in India and Bangladesh as a treatment for leprosy and other skin diseases. It has also been used for malaria, ophthalmia and tuberculosis; in the treatment of tetanus, urticaria, eczema, scrofula and erysipelas; in hygiene products; and for inflammations and fevers. Neem twigs are used daily as bactericidal 'chew sticks' to clean the teeth.

Neem's three chief compounds range in use from cosmetics and toiletries to pharmaceuticals and agriculture. Its products have proven medicinal properties, being anthelmintic, antibacterial, antidiabetic, antifungal, antiviral, contra-infertility and sedative. It is particularly prescribed for skin diseases. Neem is also anti-inflammatory, anti-arthritic, antimalarial, antipyretic, antitumour, hypoglycaemic, diuretic,

pesticidal and spermicidal. Recently it has been investigated for its antioxidant and anticarcinogenic activities, for male contraception, and dermatological uses.

Cautions: There are some reports of allergic reactions to neem products. It is vital that the neem tree is not confused with the Chinaberry (*Melia azedarach*), which is very similar in appearance and all parts of which are toxic.

Correspondences

In East Africa neem is called the 'Tree of the 40', referring to its ability to treat 40 different diseases. In India it is known as 'heal-all', 'nature's drugstore', 'village pharmacy' and as the 'panacea for all diseases'.

- **Planet** Mars, Jupiter
- **Deity** Goddess Durga or Maa Kali, Yellamma, Sithala
- **Element** Fire/water
- **Colour** Indigo/violet
- **Stone** Amethyst
- **Polarity** Feminine
- **Animal** Snake
- **Virtue** Spirituality, healing
- **Association** Intuition and understanding; protection from spirits and diseases

Silver birch

Botanical name *Betula pendula*

Family Betulaeceae

Description: Silver birch is a prolific deciduous tree that is native to Britain, Ireland and most of Europe and parts of Asia. It has a slender crown of arched branches with drooping branchlets and wind-pollinated catkins, disintegrating at maturity to release the small fruits. The tree's tactile bark is a shining white. It was the first tree to colonize the earth's northern domain at the end of the last Ice Age about 12,000 years ago.

History, mystery and spiritual healing: Silver birch's fertility associations gave it strong connections to Druidic Beltane celebrations, and to Walpurgis Night in Germanic countries, with purification fires being kindled with birch. The Druidic Yule

Correspondences

The silver birch was known to the ancient Celts as the 'lady of the woods'. The proto-Germanic rune known as *berkanan* is named after the birch, which takes the Ogham letter B.

Ogham letter B

- **B (Beth)** Feminine enchantment, replacing lost innocence
- **Planet** Venus
- **Deity** Venus, Frigga, Freya, Eostre and Xawsós (goddess of the dawn)
- **Element** Air, water
- **Colour** White
- **Stone** Quartz crystal for communication and healing
- **Polarity** Feminine
- **Animal** White stag, white cow, pheasant
- **Virtue** Healing, luck
- **Association** Purification, new beginnings, inception

log burned at the winter solstice was traditionally birch, which would burn even when wet. A birch broom was also used to drive out the spirits of the old year and to 'beat the bounds' of property for protection. Cradles made of birch protected an infant from harm.

The birch is a national tree of Russia, where it was worshipped as a goddess during Semik (green week) in early June, now better known as Trinity week or Whitsuntide. At this time, handsome men wore birch charms, crosses or amulets to protect against the mythical Rusalka, mermaid-like fish-women, abducting them.

Healing: Silver birch is a healer of body, mind and spirit. Birch leaves, bark and oil have been used as an astringent, diuretic, anti-inflammatory, diaphoretic, bitter and tonic, and have mild laxative properties. Birch stimulates bile production and is slightly antiseptic, with a mild sedative effect. Birch tea is an effective remedy to combat cystitis, gout, rheumatism and arthritis, urinary problems and oedema. Birch charcoal absorbs poison, and is used commercially in water-jug purifiers and for stomach bloating. A decoction of leaves added to a bath is used as a 30-week treatment to revitalize the body 'inside and out', by osmosis and psychologically.

Xylitol, extracted from birch and used as a sugar replacement for dental chewing gum, is about as sweet as sucrose, but with only two-thirds the food energy. Chaga or clinker mushroom, which grows on silver birch, is a Russian folk medicine under research for its effective anticarcinogenic properties (see pages 62–63).

Cautions: No birch species should be used by those who are allergic to aspirin. Birch tar is currently believed to be potentially carcinogenic.

Cedar of Lebanon

Botanical name *Cedrus libani*

Family Coniferae

Description: Cedar of Lebanon is a large, stately evergreen tree that is one of two true cedars native to the Mediterranean region. It has a massive trunk when mature and wide-sweeping branches spreading out on all sides, with scented flowers and short, dark-green needles. It is incredibly long-lived, and species have been found that are more than 2,500 years old.

Correspondences

Cedar of Lebanon is also called *arbor vitae*, the Tree of Life. In Druidic terms it is sacred to the feast of Imbolc, halfway between the winter solstice and the spring equinox. Cedar means pride, greatness and power.

- **Planet** Sun, Mercury
- **Deity** God the Father, Amun Ra, Baalat, Cernunnos, Indra, Isis, Jupiter, Odin, Osiris, Pan, Poseidon, Wotan, Sezh, Wurusemu
- **Element** Fire, air
- **Colour** Red, gold
- **Stone** Chrysoprase, aventurine, moss agate, sunstone
- **Polarity** Male
- **Animal** Ewe, horse
- **Virtue** Surpassing excellence
- **Association** healing, longevity, purification, protection, preservation

History, mystery and spiritual healing: Cedars of Lebanon have been nominated as one of the new Seven Wonders of Nature. They are the most frequently mentioned tree in the Bible, and were commonly used for construction by the ancient Egyptians, Phoenicians, Greeks and Romans. The success of the Phoenician Empire had them firmly at its heart, for the trees provided strong wood for fishing boats and houses in the city of Byblos (founded *c*. 6000 BCE). Thereafter a strong, ongoing trade in cedar between the Egyptians and the Phoenicians continued.

The tree's history is also directly linked to one of the greatest mystics of all time, King Solomon, who was known for his wisdom, wealth and writings. His crowning achievement was the building

of the Holy Temple in Jerusalem with Lebanon cedars. Cedarwood was also used for 'smudging' to purify and protect living and working areas, and for sacred tools, especially among Native Americans. The Romans believed in the preservative content of its resin and used it to protect papyri from attacks of worms. The Egyptians used the oil of cedar of Lebanon for embalming.

Healing: Most modern use is of cedar's essential oil, steam-distilled from wood chips, generally from the *true* cedar species *Cedrus atlantica*. This is a wonderful healing oil and a preservative, and can be used for acne, arthritis and as a useful decongestant for the respiratory system. It also helps cystitis, dandruff and dermatitis, is an insect repellent and fungicide. Psychologically, it clears the mind and brain, aids nervous tension, stress and emotional release; a melatonin stimulant, it also enhances sleep. It is very good at dispelling negativity and helping to instil positivity.

Recent research provides evidence that inhaling cedar's cedrol affects the lungs and lower airway, which has a response effect on the cardiovascular system, suggesting a new target for drug therapy in hypertension.

Cautions: Do not use cedarwood oil (*C. atlantica, C. virginiana* or *Juniperus virginiana*) in pregnancy. In high concentrations, cedarwood oil may irritate the skin.

Hazel

Botanical name *Corylus avellana*
Family Coryloideae/Betulaceae

Description: Hazel, a member of the birch family, is a deciduous shrub that is native to Europe and western Asia. Typically a number of shoots or trunks branch out at (or just above) ground level, giving it a dense, spreading structure that has led to hazel's extensive use for coppicing. Its bark is a smooth, shiny, greyish-brown, and it has single-sex, wind-pollinated catkins. Fertilized female flowers grow into nuts (fruits), produced in clusters.

History, mystery and spiritual healing:
The Botanical name *Corylus* comes from *korus*, meaning 'helmet', regarding the shape and hardness of the nutshells. There is a legend that Joseph of Arimathea built the original English abbey of Glastonbury in Somerset from hurdles of hazel branches.

Hazel is said to be the quintessential Celtic tree because of its legendary position at the heart of the Otherworld, where nine magic hazel trees hang over the well of wisdom and drop their purple nuts into the water. Hazel is also the preferred wood for water divining and dowsing. In Celtic mythology, hazelnuts

Correspondences

Hazel takes the Ogham letter C.

Ogham letter C

- **C (Coll)** Creativity, purity, honesty
- **Planet** Mercury
- **Deity** Hermes/Mercury, Thor, Frey
- **Element** Air (fire and water)
- **Colour** Yellow
- **Stone** Apatite, ocean jasper
- **Polarity** Masculine (feminine energy)
- **Animal** Salmon
- **Virtue** Wisdom, honesty, understanding
- **Association** Luck, inspiration, poetry, science, intellect, creativity, mental alertness, intellectual growth, divination, clairvoyance, fertility, love, protection

into a paste, and extensively used in confectionery and more recently 'hazelnut butter'. Americans and Eastern Europeans are also partial to hazelnut vodka-based liqueurs, and aromatic hazelnut-flavoured coffee is popular in the West.

Healing: Hazel leaves have been used as a remedy to relieve haemorrhoidal symptoms and varicose veins. The antioxidant, cardio-protective nuts are a wonderful food containing two to three times more Vitamin E than olive oil, plus Vitamins C, B_3, B_2, B_1 and K, and fatty and amino acids. Its minerals include calcium, copper, iron, magnesium, manganese, phosphorus, selenium and zinc. Aromatic, nourishing hazelnut oil is slightly astringent, but is easily absorbed into the skin and is used for facial and body massages and in moisturizing products.

In January 2008, Italian researchers confirmed the presence in hazelnut shells of anticarcinogenic compounds (though less than in the leaves), which are considered waste material by many food industries.

equate to concentrated wisdom and poetic inspiration.

Hazel was used magically to protect against disease. In Ireland, a hazelnut in the pocket warded off rheumatism or lumbago, which was thought to be caused by 'elfshot'; a double-nut prevented toothache.

The delicious edible hazel kernel (seed) is used raw or roasted, or ground

Cautions: Those with allergies to nuts should avoid using hazelnuts and their products.

Hawthorn

Botanical names *Crataegus monogyna* and *Crataegus laevigata*

Family Rosaceae

Description: Common hawthorn or maythorn (*C. monogyna*) is native to Europe, north-west Africa and western Asia, while its near-relative Midland hawthorn (*C. laevigata*) is native to western and central Europe. The former is typically a shrub or short-trunked tree with a dense crown and dark longitudinal fissures in the bark, giving a rugged effect on older trees; it has sharp-thorned stems and dark-green leaves tinged reddish when young. The Midland hawthorn is

Correspondences

In Irish mythology, the hawthorn is directly linked with the Otherworld, and in Gaelic folklore it marks the entrance to the Otherworld. It takes the Ogham letter H.

Ogham letter H

- **H (Huath)** Contradiction, consequence, relationships, union of opposites, guardian
- **Planet** Mars
- **Deity** Hymen, Vulcan, Fulgora, Cardea, Maia, Blodeuwedd, Aine, Olwyn, the Virgin Mary
- **Element** Fire/water
- **Colour** Red/indigo
- **Stone** Ruby, garnet/azurite
- **Polarity** Feminine/masculine energy
- **Animal** Black crow, goat, dragon
- **Virtue** Love, restraint
- **Association** Hope, fertility, marriage, sex and procreation, renewal, duality, abstinence and excess (opposite rules of sexuality), *yin* and *yang* (concept)

characterized by spreading, deeply-lobed leaves and flowers with one solo style.

Maythorn's creamy-white flowers, with their attractive red stamens, dust the hedgerows in a froth of blossom in spring; their scent has been described as a pungent and slightly musky perfume, smelling of honey with a hint of almond; its deeper tones are said to have the sweet odour of death. Hawthorn derives its name from Old English haw meaning 'hedge', simply means 'thorny hedge'.

History, mystery and spiritual healing:
Folklore belief stating that it is bad luck to bring hawthorn into the house may be the reason why hawthorn trees were often left as landmarks. Traditionally hawthorns were grown, cut back and layered to form dense, prickly hedgerows.

Witches allegedly grew hawthorn in their gardens for protection, and as an ingredient for flying ointment, which is believed to be a mix of herbs

engendering an out-of-body-experience. The tree is also part of the fairy triad of Britain, 'oak, ash and thorn', and where all three trees grow together, it is said that one may see fairies. Celtic tree-lore informs us that it can be mortally unlucky to cut down a sacred hawthorn or 'faerie tree' except at specific times, such as when it is in bloom and at Beltane. Conversely, according to Serbian folklore, a hewn stake of hawthorn must be driven through the heart in order to slay vampires.

In ages past, both ancient Greeks and Romans viewed the hawthorn as symbolic of hope and marriage. May was the month of courtship and love-making after the winter's cold. The ancient Greeks used hawthorn wood for the marriage torch, and girls wore hawthorn crowns at weddings. The Romans placed its leaves in a newborn baby's hands for good luck. Hawthorn, born of lightning, was often grown alongside a house to protect it against that phenomenon and against damage to the house from severe storms. No evil ghosts (spirits) may enter into a house where hawthorn is present.

The hawthorn is sacred to the Celts, pagans and Christians alike. In the wilds of wind-lashed Argyll, in Scotland, there resides one of the few known 'wishing

The copper-coin-encrusted trunk of a solitary, wind-blasted hawthorn, a magical 'wishing tree' in the wilds of Argyll in Scotland.

trees', studded with token coins pressed into its bark by anxious travellers to support the granting of their wishes; sacred hawthorns also guard wishing wells in Ireland.

The famous Holy Thorn is said to have to have been planted at Glastonbury, in Somerset, by Joseph of Arimathea, after he landed in England following Christ's crucifixion. It is a symbol for Christ's crown of thorns, and flowers twice a year: once in late spring and once after midwinter has passed. The original tree was cut down by Puritans, but a cultivar was secretly propagated in the Glastonbury abbey grounds.

Healing: Hawthorn has always been a 'heart herb'. The flowers and fresh or dry fruits are a cardiac sedative, blood-vessel dilator and are blood-pressure-lowering. The leaves, flowers and berries have all been used as a cardiac tonic – the berries the most effective – working synergistically to normalize the heart, either stimulating or depressing. The blossom is drunk as a 'tonic tea' for the heart and circulation. Hawthorn is used in Russian herbal medicine as an antispasmodic, cardiac, sedative and vasodilatory. The Druids used the hawthorn's properties to strengthen the body in the frailty of old age.

In herbal use, the active ingredients in the flowers are tannins, flavonoids, essential oil, acids and purine derivatives; in the fruits they are tannins, flavonoids, pigments and vitamins.

In traditional Chinese Medicine, hawthorn or *shan zha* is sweet, sour, warm and applied to the liver, spleen and stomach meridian. The fruit is used to reduce food stagnation, to transform blood stasis, to dissipate clots (Buerger's disease) and for hypertension. In China, dried hawthorn fruits (either whole or as flakes) are eaten as sweets, and the jelly or flakes are used to aid the digestion of meats.

In magic healing, hawthorn is added to water to clean the home, to protect and purify and to still negative vibrations. Wiping the face with a facecloth on May Day morning that had been left overnight on Hawthorn flowers to absorb the dew was still a practice in Britain into the late 1930s and beyond. These days, hawthorn leaves and flowers are used to make liquid extracts, usually with water and alcohol. The tree's edible young leaves are good in salads, and the 'haws' are used to make wine, jelly and to flavour brandy.

Cautions: Hawthorn may interact with existing prescription drugs, and medicinal use of it should be professionally supervised. It is considered safe for most adults for short periods of time and side-effects are usually mild (upset stomach, headache and dizziness), but the evidence is limited.

Eucalyptus blue gum

Botanical name *Eucalyptus globulus*

Family Myrtaceae

Description: Eucalyptus blue gum belongs to the myrtle family and is native to Tasmania and Australia. It is a tall, straight, evergreen tree that is mainly cultivated in unhealthy low-lying or swampy districts. Its rough, deeply furrowed bark can be grey-blue or reddish and peels off in large strips, hence the name 'stringy bark tree'. The juvenile leaves are broad and a waxy whitish-green, but are succeeded by a mature, dark blueish-green, sickle-shaped form. Its almost stalkless flowers bloom singly or in clusters and produce copious nectar. The fruit is a woody capsule with valves that open on the top, shedding numerous small seeds.

History, mystery and spiritual healing:
Eucalyptus blue gum was first collected on the south-east coast of Tasmania in 1792–3 by Jacques Labillardière and described by him in 1799. It is said that he named it *E. globulus* because its spherical, waxy fruit bore a strong resemblance to a kind of round button then worn in France. Much later, on 27 November 1962, the tree was

proclaimed the official floral emblem of Tasmania, but is seldom used.

In the Dreamtime, the Koori people have a myth about Australia's Murray River and how it was created, which involves the eucalyptus gum tree. Totyerguil was a mighty hunter and one day, having thrown all his spears and lost the huge fish he had hunted, he landed upon a river bank, where he set his

Correspondences

- **Planet** Moon
- **Deity** Ogun
- **Element** Water
- **Colour** Green (white)
- **Stone** Opal (pearl)
- **Polarity** Masculine
- **Animal** Snake
- **Virtue** Healing
- **Association** Australian Aboriginal Magic (divination, dream magic), healing, protection

canoe on end and stuck his paddle upright in the ground. The canoe became a huge gum tree and the paddle a Murray pine. It is these species of trees that the descendants of Totyerguil still use in making their canoes and paddles.

Believed to be the world's oldest wind instrument, the didgeridoo, or *yidaki*, is traditionally made from eucalpytus and is used by Aborigines for healing, ceremonies, initiation rites and social gatherings.

Before the biological process of the malarial mosquito's ability to spread the disease was understood, the eucalyptus blue gum was an axis of superstition. It was an Aboriginal belief that the tree released a magical essence that purified the air of fever germs – a very reasonable assumption, given the disinfectant nature of the leaves' oils emanating into the atmosphere. However, the benefit is actually derived from the capacity of the eucalyptus to absorb water from the swampy ground, culminating in the loss of suitable mosquito-breeding habitats.

Healing: One aspect of the eucalyptus's healing power is the didgeridoo as a form of vibrational medicine. It gives both psychological and physical benefits from the sound: it influences the brainwaves directly and, as a result, can put the player or listener into an altered state of consciousness. Science proves that regular didgeridoo playing is an effective and well-accepted treatment for obstructive sleep apnoea. Reportedly, medical research has shown that healing with the didgeridoo aids aggressiveness, behavioural disorders, energetic blockages, hysteria, phobias, speech impediments, severe inhibitions and traumatic burdens; it also helps bone, muscle and hormone function and lowers the heart rate and blood pressure.

An aboriginal man playing the didgeridoo in the Australian outback, creating its distinctive penetrating healing sounds.

Although eucalyptus's properties have been renowned for more than 150 years in the Western world, the Aborigines used eucalyptus medicinally long before any colonists. Northern Aborigines crushed eucalyptus leaves as a 'sniffing' medicine, and the *kino* or tannin-rich 'gum' was also used by Aborigines to make an antiseptic wash for burns and skin infections. Boiled in an iron pot, *kino* yielded a black die used for ink and staining leather.

It was common Aboriginal knowledge that bathing in lakeside places where eucalyptus trees cast their leaves into the water offered skin-healing properties. And to treat diarrhoea, water from eucalyptus's 'manna' – made from the leaves and young bark of various eucalyptus species – was greatly valued by Bushmen and early colonists alike.

Antibacterial, anti-Candidiasis, antifungal, antimicrobial, antiseptic and antiviral, *E. globulus* essential oil is used for countless complaints, from halitosis and rheumatics to tuberculosis and viral infections. The lead compound, eucalyptol, is noted for its anaesthetic, analgesic, antibronchitic, anticatarrhal, antilaryngitic, stimulatory and expectorant properties, among much else. Used in aromatherapy, vaporized eucalyptus has an excellent record as an inhalant for the sinus and bronchial congestions of bronchitis, whooping cough, colds, asthma, influenza and other respiratory illnesses. The German Commission E approves the internal use of eucalyptus oil for treating catarrh (mucous) of the respiratory tract, and externally for use against bone and joint pain.

Eucalyptus oil was listed in the 1885 edition of the British Pharmacopoeia, in the British Pharmaceutical Codex of 1973 and in the British Herbal Pharmacopoeia of 1996. The oil's therapeutic uses have been integrated into traditional medicine systems, including traditional Chinese medicine, Indian Ayurvedic and Western medicine. Eucalyptus is included in the Indian Pharmacopoeia as a counter-irritant and mild expectorant; in the Chinese Pharmacopoeia as a skin irritant used in nerve pain; and in the present Ayurvedic Pharmacopoeia for its topical application for headaches due to colds.

Cautions: Eucalyptus oil is contraindicated for internal use during pregnancy. Avoid it if you have high blood pressure or epilepsy. It may interact with existing prescription drugs. The oil should be diluted before internal or external use. Eucalyptus preparations should not be applied to the face, especially the nose, of infants and children.

Common beech

Botanical name *Fagus sylvatica*

Family Fagaceae

Description: The beech is a magnificent large, deciduous tree, which is broadly native to most of temperate Europe as far as north-west Turkey. It matures at 120 years, with an average lifespan of 150–200 years, and has a long, smooth-barked trunk, with erect branches up to a slender crown. The golden-green leaves darken to stunning yellows, reds and oranges in autumn. The seeds form small triangular 'beech mast', with two nuts to each 'cupule' (hardened bract).

Correspondences

Sacred to Obraash the Sun lord, the beech is a chieftan tree and takes Ogham letter AE (sometimes X or Xi).

Ogham letter AE

- **AE (Amhancholl or Eamhancholl)** Contra all forms of negativity
- **Planet** Mercury, Saturn
- **Deity** Obraash, Thoth, Apollo, Mercury, Odin, Athena, Zeus, Diana, Fagus, Ogma
- **Element** Air, fire, earth
- **Colour** Sky-blue, green
- **Stone** Turquoise, blue topaz, lapis lazuli
- **Polarity** Masculine
- **Animal** Eagle, fox
- **Virtue** Tolerance, insight, solidity
- **Association** Arcane knowledge, learning, understanding, divination, sustenance, preservation, renewal

History, mystery and spiritual healing: The word 'beech' is Anglo-Saxon. In several north-western European cultures the word for 'book' and 'beech' was identical. Recent evidence indicates that the beech arrived in England *c.* 4,000 BCE, following the Ice Ages. Mythologically and historically, beech is connected with learning and intellect. It is said that its wood provided the first 'paper' – slivers or tablets of beech used to inscribe runes

and literature – and it is likely that it helped to form the first-ever book.

The beech has been valued for its mast, used to feed pigs (and an important food source for birds and small mammals). The pale-brown, hardwood is not generally suitable for outdoor use, but is used for furniture, plywood and veneers, toys, craftsmen's tools, chopping blocks, clothes pegs, parquet-flooring and was used in France for wooden clogs or *sabots*.

Healing: In traditional medicine, a strong infusion of cooling, astringent beech leaves was used to bathe sores and wounds; a leaf poultice helped to reduce hot swellings and heal scabs. Stuffing a sickbed mattress with beech leaves was thought to aid the healing process, while natural water collected from the hollows of ancient beeches was believed to heal skin complaints. The bark was also used to help reduce fever, and a tea made from the powdered bark and leaves was used as a tonic to aid stomach troubles, ulcers, diabetes and to improve the appetite and to benefit the liver, kidneys, and bladder. Beech ground charcoal was also used in vermifuge remedies for tapeworms and roundworms.

Initially used by herbalists, the fresh wood is used by the pharmaceutical industry for distillation to produce an antiseptic, stimulating tar, known medicinally as 'creosote', an ingredient of medicinal soaps, salves and balms for skin conditions such as eczema and psoriasis.

Beech is one of the 39 Bach Flower Remedies. It is recommended to enhance sympathy, and physical, mental and emotional tolerance for conditions, people, places and things (see pages 356–357).

Cautions: At the time of writing there are no known contraindications for the correct use of this plant.

Ash

Botanical name *Fraxinus excelsior*

Family Oleaceae

Description: The European or common ash is a large, handsome deciduous tree, found in Europe, North Africa and Asia, with a lofty, domed crown. The sturdy shoots are light greenish-grey, with jet-black buds, and the pale grey bark of young trees becomes fissured into deep grooves in older specimens. The dark-purple, wind-pollinated female flowers, rather longer than the male flowers, open before the leaves. The fruit or 'ash key' often hangs in bunches throughout the winter.

History, mystery and spiritual healing: Ash wood is the sorcerer's favourite for a magic wand, and is thought to have been used by the Druids and others to direct positive healing energies and aid communication and wisdom. Traditionally it is the wood of the writer, poet and scholar.

To the Vikings' ancestors, the ash was Yggdrasil, the Tree of Life, its branches spreading over the entire world; atop it sat an eagle, and coiled among its roots in the Underworld was a dragon or serpent. Anciently, it was believed that the first

Correspondences

The ash tree takes the Ogham letter N.

Ogham letter N

- **N (Nuinn)** Connection and wisdom
- **Planet** Neptune
- **Deity** Odin, Nemesis, Poseidon
- **Element** Air, water
- **Colour** White
- **Stone** Turquoise (stone of contentment, one of the oldest protection amulets)
- **Polarity** Feminine (female and effeminate male energy are present, 18 February to 17 March)
- **Animal** Snake
- **Virtue** Stability
- **Association** Balance, inner peace

human was created from the ash tree. In Norse mythology the ash was the tree of the god Odin, who in order to receive the important divination tool of the Futhark runes of prophecy put himself into a trance by hanging himself on Yggdrasil, during which act he lost an eye to ravens.

Healing: In sympathetic magic, a cure for children's rickets was to pass the body of the sick child three times at sunrise through an ash sapling that had been split lengthways; the sapling would then be tightly bound and, if it healed, the child would be cured.

Both the ash bark and leaves have medicinal uses. The decocted leaves were traditionally used internally for constipation, dropsy, cystitis, feverish conditions, arthritis and rheumatic pain; externally they were applied in compresses for suppurating cuts and sores. The bark is collected from both the trunk and root – but preferably the root, which scientific investigation now shows to contain the glucoside fraxin, a colourless crystalline substance, as well as fraxin-related chemicals that are antioxidant. Polish research shows that ash used in medicine for degenerative rheumatics is successful in reducing the intake of non-steroidal anti-inflammatory drugs, and the effect of the herb's performance in Moroccan animal studies bodes well for its future use in treating diabetes.

Cautions: At the time of writing there are no known contraindications for the correct use of this plant.

European holly

Botanical name *Ilex aquifolium*

Family Aquifoliaceae

Description: Holly is an evergreen shrub or tree that is native to western and central Europe, north-west Africa and south-west Asia. It grows at a slow rate, and has smooth grey bark and greenish twigs, leaves with three to five sharp spines on each side, sweetly scented, minute white flowers and shiny red drupes (fruit).

Correspondences

The holly tree takes the Ogham letter T.

Ogham letter T

- **T (Tinne)** Goodwill, happiness
- **Planet** Mars, Saturn
- **Deity** Thor, Taranis, Lugh, Jesus Christ
- **Element** Fire
- **Colour** Red, green
- **Stone** Ruby, chalcedony (fire agate)
- **Polarity** Masculine
- **Animal** War horse, ram
- **Virtue** Justice
- **Association** Hope, the home, protection, energy, strength and power, balance

History, mystery and spiritual healing:

For Christians, prickly holly is symbolic of Jesus' crown of thorns, and holly berries with drops of the blood shed for mankind's salvation. Holly has long and varying associations with Christmas. The holly bush classically brightened the dark days of Yule, centuries before the introduction of the fir Christmas tree (see page 254). Indeed, the Romans considered the plant to belong to the god Saturn, who was celebrated at the 'Feast of Sol Invictus' on 25 December.

Cuileann (holly) was also the most sacred tree to the Celtic Druids and conjoined with the gigantic Holly King of Celtic mythology, who ruled from the summer solstice until the winter solstice, ending in a great celebration.

Healing: Holly leaf contains active components such as tannin, bitter principle, ursolic and ilexic acids, and has a mildly diuretic effect; it alleviates fever and stimulates sweating. Holly leaves are dried and used as teas for fevers, bladder problems and bronchitis. Leaf infusions are used against the common cold, flu, rheumatism and arthritis, and the juice of the fresh leaf is helpful in jaundice treatment.

Recently Chinese research has revealed that the root of *I. pubescens* had a successful result (on animals) for the anti-inflammatory and analgesic effects of its component 'purified saponin faction'. In coronary cases, trials have shown that at least 90 per cent of sufferers were relieved of agonizing chest pain or it was much reduced.

South American holly (*I. paraguariensis*) is made into *yerba maté* tea, which is the reinvigorating national drink in Argentina, Paraguay and Uruguay. It contains stimulants including caffeine, and is made by steeping dried holly leaves in boiling water. A transient energy-booster, *maté* quickens the nervous system, temporarily raising mental potency, and is slightly analgesic. It assists fatigue, headaches, migraine, neuralgic and rheumatic pain, and is used to alleviate ancillary melancholy.

Cautions: No contraindications with drugs have yet been identified, but the use of holly during pregnancy and when lactating should be avoided. Ingestion of the berries can cause vomiting, diarrhoea, stupor, dehydration and electrolyte imbalance. Side-effects may occur from drinking *yerba maté* and it should not be taken during pregnancy or when breastfeeding. Consult your healthcare provider if you have diabetes, high blood pressure, alcohol dependence or liver disease, or before giving it to young children.

Sausage tree

Botanical name *Kigelia africana*

Family Bignoniaceae

Description: The deciduous sausage tree is found throughout tropical Africa, and its Afrikaans name *worsboom* ('sausage tree') refers to its long, sausage-shaped fruit. This medium-sized tree has smooth grey bark, thick branches and velvety, bell-shaped flowers that stay open for one solitary night, coloured orange to blood-red, purplish-green or maroon, from which Sunbirds sip sweet nectar. The hard grey pendulous fruit is a thin-skinned woody berry, with fibrous, soft and spongy pulp containing numerous seeds.

History, mystery and spiritual healing:

The sausage tree is important to African tribes because it is used in medicine, food, beer, religious ritual and magic, and for shade. It provides dugout canoes, animal fodder and is ornamental. On the night in 1855 before he first saw Victoria Falls, David Livingstone, the African explorer, pitched camp beneath a sausage tree and carved his initials on its bark.

Sausage-tree fruits are hung in African homes to ward off whirlwinds and to encourage crops to grow well. If a member of the Ndebele tribe in Zimbabwe dies abroad, the grieving family digs a grave for the absent person and buries a sausage-tree fruit in their place. Zulu warriors use the tree's leaves to polish the handles of their spears, and drink a sausage-tree fruit infusion to give themselves strength and courage in battle. The home-brewed beer confers power on the women, instead of the men who drink it; their daughters inherit secret recipes and brewing methods.

Healing: In traditional African magic-medicine, healers paint sausage-tree fruits and use them to diagnose the causes of disease; the fruits can also ward off evil spirits. The tree's fruit, bark, leaves and roots are believed to cure almost any ailment that afflicts human beings. Science shows that the plant's natural sterols help a range of skin conditions, particularly eczema. The flavonoids have hygroscopic and fungicidal properties. Internally, the fruit is used to treat a variety of conditions including dysentery, ringworm, tapeworm, post-partum haemorrhaging, malaria, diabetes, pneumonia and toothache, plus many types of inflammation, nutritional and skin disorders, pain, poisoning and disorders in pregnancy and birth.

Anecdotal evidence indicates that antioxidant and anti-inflammatory *Kigelia* is an effective treatment of solar keratosis, skin cancer and the HIV-related Kaposi's sarcoma. Today, a significant body of scientific literature confirms the validity of many traditional uses of sausage-tree fruit extract for treating skin cancer.

The Tonga women of the Zambezian Valley use cosmetic preparations of the fruit facially to ensure a blemish-free complexion. *Kigelia* has also found European and Far Eastern markets with its active ingredient in breast-firming and skin-tightening formulations, including facial creams to which some sausage-tree steroid chemicals are added, and other products such as shampoos.

Cautions: At the time of writing there are no known contraindications for the correct use of this plant.

Correspondences

The fruit *ipfungwani* can represent 'man'.

- **Planet** Sun, Pluto
- **Deity** Pluto, Mercury, Chonganda (African creator of flora), Nyamia Ama (Senegalese invisible sky god of storms, rain and lightning)
- **Element** Fire
- **Colour** Red
- **Stone** Garnet, fire agate
- **Polarity** Masculine
- **Animal** Eland bull
- **Virtue** Justice
- **Association** Hope and healing, guarding and protecting against evil, especially the evils of ignorance and prejudice, with strength and courage in battle

Myrtle tree

Botanical name *Myrtus communis*

Family Myrtaceae

Description: Myrtle (also called 'true myrtle') is an evergreen shrub or small tree that is native to the Mediterranean region and found in western Asia. It is covered in a deep-greyish, fissured bark, with smooth and shiny, deep-green leaves, which when crushed exude a strong scent and yield an essential oil. The myrtle has fragrant, starry, usually white flowers and edible, spherical, blue-black berries containing several seeds.

History, mystery and spiritual healing: A sacred flowering tree, myrtle was dedicated to Aphrodite, goddess of love in ancient Greece, and brides garlanded themselves with myrtle leaves. Myrtle was also linked to the Roman festival of Verenalia, when women requested divine intervention in their relations with men, ritually removed jewellery from the statue of the goddess Venus, cleansed her and adorned her with flowers.

Biblical references to myrtle, such as 'The man that stood among the myrtle trees' (Zechariah 1:10), are many. For the Jews, myrtle was a token of peace, which is why it became a bridal decoration. Used for its pleasant aroma, it is also one of the four sacred

Correspondences

Floriographic meanings of myrtle are joy, love, love in absence, heartfelt love, love and marriage; it is the Hebrew emblem of marriage. Its flower day is 4 May.

- **Planet** Venus
- **Deity** Aphrodite, Artemis, Ashtoreth, Astarte, Hathor, Marian, Venus
- **Element** Water
- **Colour** Green, red/pink and white
- **Stone** Watermelon tourmaline, Herkimer diamond
- **Polarity** Feminine
- **Animal** Swan
- **Virtue** Providence and caring, purity and sincerity
- **Association** Love, fertility, youth, peace, money

plants of Sukkot, the Feast of Tabernacles: the leaves are held by the worshippers in the synagogue during prayers. In the Muslim tradition, myrtle was among 'the pure things' carried by Adam out of the Garden of Eden. Myrtle has also been held as the emblem of honour and authority, and was worn by the Athenian judges when exercising their duties.

Healing: A medicinal plant of the ancients, myrtle played a prominent part in writings of Hippocrates, Pliny, Dioscorides, Galen and the Arbabian writers. Ancient Egyptians used crushed myrtle leaves added to wine to treat fever and infections. This was also used by Dioscorides for stomach, bladder and pulmonary infections.

In the 19th century myrtle was used for bronchial infections, genito-urinary problems and haemorrhoids. It was practically obsolete in modern therapeutics until it was revived in 1876 by medical doctor, researcher and author Dr Jean Delioux de Savignac, who recommended diluted tincture of myrtle leaves as an astringent lotion, and used the powder internally for chronic catarrh of the bladder and menorrhagia, and in infusion for chronic bronchitis.

Modern research finds the plant astringent, with antioxidant and antigenotoxic activities that may be chemo-preventive. Myrtle contains tannins, flavonoids and phenols, among other compounds; the essential oil contains mainly alpha-pinene, cineole and myrtenol, and is used for asthma, coughs and sore throats.

Cautions: At the time of writing there are no known cautions.

Scots pine

Botanical name *Pinus sylvestris*

Family Pinaceae

Description: The Scots pine is a large, evergreen, coniferous tree that is native to Europe and Asia. Mature trees have bare, cylindrical, straight trunks with a flattish top of massed foliage, composed of pairs of stiff, bluish-green needles. In winter the male flowers are yellowish buds that release their pollen in the spring; the female flowers (seed cones) contain blackish seeds that are released the following spring.

History, mystery and spiritual healing: Sir James Frazer's *The Golden Bough* (1890) recounts how the ancient Egyptians buried an image of the god Osiris in the hollowed-out centre of a pine tree, which symbolized the tree being inhabited by a spiritual 'life form'.

In the description of the ancient Greek 'pine goddess' Pitthea, the tree was a symbol of royalty. Greeks carried pine-cone-tipped wands, a symbol of fertility among worshippers of Bacchus. The tree itself was an object of worship by the ancient Romans during the spring equinox festival.

A folk-healing ritual of 'transfer magic' credited the pine tree with healing by absorbing the pain of whoever was afflicted. In Russia 'shaman forests' – Scots pine groves found across Siberia – were reverenced by the Mongolian Buryat people for the gods and spirits of the wood.

Healing: Pine needles are astringent, diuretic, irritant and rubefacient. Fresh pine needle shoot tea is a bladder and kidney remedy, and used for urinary tract infections. Decocted, bruised fresh pine shoots in the bath ease aches and pains, breathing disorders and skin complaints.

The essential oil distilled from the pine needles is antiseptic, antiviral, bactericidal, decongestant, deodorant, diuretic and expectorant. It is used for coughs and colds (especially inhalations) and other respiratory conditions, also a rubefacient for muscle stiffness. Pine oil's fragrance is in toiletries, detergents and disinfectants. Today, highly antioxidant pine oil is used for 'Sick Building Syndrome' – its fungicidal activity is used against airborne micro-organisms. *P. sylvestris* oil of turpentine is used externally in ointments and liniment plasters, as a stimulant for rheumatic swellings, sprains and bruises and to kill parasites.

Pine Bach Flower Remedy is taken for guilt (real or assumed) and self-reproach leading to dissatisfaction with the self, and is used contra-despondency and negativity (see page 356–357).

Cautions: There are no known safety issues or interactions associated with pine, with the exception of rare allergic reactions. However, do not use pine oil internally except under professional supervision. Its safety in young children, pregnant and nursing women and those with severe liver or kidney disease is not known, and it is contraindicated for certain respiratory conditions, some specific skin diseases and abnormally tense muscles.

Correspondences

Pine takes the Ogham letter A.

Ogham letter A

- **A (Ailm)** 'pine'
- **Planet** Mars (Sun)
- **Deity** Artemis, Astarte, Pitthea, Cybele, Attis, Bacchus, Dionysus
- **Element** Air (fire)
- **Colour** Red (green, gold)
- **Stone** Black agate, amber
- **Polarity** Feminine
- **Animal** Badger, horse
- **Virtue** Courage, resilience, endurance
- **Association** Healing, purification, protection, serenity, inner peace, foresight, objectivity, self-esteem, strength, dispelling of negative energy, prosperity

Aspen

Botanical name *Populus tremula*

Family Salicaceae

Description: The aspen is a medium-sized, hardy, deciduous tree that is native to cool temperate regions of Europe and Asia. It is crowned with shimmering green leaves in summer and soft golds and yellows in autumn, which tremble in the slightest breeze. The male and female catkins appear on different trees; the capsules contain numerous tiny seeds shrouded in fluff, which assists wind dispersal.

History, mystery and spiritual healing: The aspen – which is world-renowned for its quivering, 'whispering' leaves – is often confused with its poplar relatives. Hades, god of the Underworld, planted an aspen tree in the Elysian Fields to honour his mistress, the nymph Leuce. The colourful aspen is also sacred to Persephone in her role as goddess of regeneration.

The aspen tree has been called the 'Judas tree', because it was said to be the wood used for the cross at the crucifixion of Jesus Christ. It is noticeable that trees

Correspondences

The aspen aids speech and communication, and overcoming fear. It takes the Ogham letter E.

Ogham letter E

- **E (Eado, Eadha)** Transformation, vision, victory
- **Planet** Pluto, Mercury, Saturn
- **Deity** Persephone, Hades, Demeter, Epona, Heracles (divine hero)
- **Element** Air, water
- **Colour** Silver and white, red
- **Stone** Black agate (aids overcoming flaws, fears and loneliness)
- **Polarity** Feminine
- **Animal** White mare
- **Virtue** Courage, endurance
- **Association** Regeneration, reason, overcoming negative situations

important to pagan religions appear to have been deliberately demonized in later Christian teaching. The aspen is a holy tree and it has been suggested that its constant trembling may be construed as awe at the grave honour bestowed upon it for supporting the earthly body of Jesus in his crucifixion agonies.

Celts made fighting shields from aspen wood for protection from physical and psychic harm. Basque shepherds carved signs into aspen trees as a means of communication and to record events. Most carvings are lost as the average above-ground lifespan of aspen trees is less than 100 years.

The aspen is an esoteric tree. Its pith is star-shaped, providing a pentagram symbol for what is up in the heavens (the macrosphere) connected to the microsphere of human life on earth.

Healing: Formerly, aspen was used in magic to cure fevers. A sick person's nail clippings were placed in a hole in the tree's trunk, which was then covered and sealed – a cure that reportedly worked only if done at night. A member of the willow family, aspen's bark and fresh dried leaves have been used herbally as an anodyne, anti-inflammatory, diuretic, expectorant, febrifuge and stimulant. Today it is generally used as a Bach Flower Remedy to treat 'vague fears of unknown origin', anxiety and apprehension (see page 356–357). The scientifically derived ingredients tremulacin, salicyltremuloidin and salicin are used in a few proprietary medicines for chronic prostate and bladder disorders. In 2007, research showed that Aspen could be used as a reasonable substitute for drugs that alleviate the pain and swelling of arthritis inflammation.

Cautions: At the time of writing there are no known contraindications for the correct use of this plant.

Cherry

Botanical name *Prunus avium*

Family Rosaceae

Description: The wild cherry is a small, vigorous, deciduous tree that is native to Europe, north-west Africa and western Asia. It has a broadly rounded crown, smooth grey-brown bark and showy white flowers that blossom in early spring. The fruit is a sweet, red to dark-red drupe that matures early to mid-summer.

History, mystery and spiritual healing: The seeds of a number of cherry species have been found in Bronze Age and Roman archeological sites throughout Europe. Crossing the Atlantic Ocean, sweet cherry trees landed in North America with English colonists in 1629, and were later introduced to California by Spanish missionaries.

Cherries are beloved as fruit by adults and children alike, but poetry and paintings honour the beauty of cherry blossom, which has much symbolism. In China, cherry blossom signifies feminine beauty. In Japan, the blossom represents the fast-moving accumulation and dispersal of clouds, mirroring the ephemeral nature of life, and is associated with the Buddhist religion. The crowded cherry blossom festivals in Japan (*hanami matsuri*) attract the Japanese spiritual mind, which looks for harmony in all things animate and inanimate, as viewers contemplate the psyche-soothing blooms.

Healing: Bird cherry was used medicinally during the Middle Ages, when bark placed at the door was supposed to ward off the plague. Sweet cherries and bird cherries were both used to flavour alcoholic drinks, especially cherry brandy – kirsch takes its name from the word *karshu*, given to the first cultivated cherries in Mesopotamia in 8 BCE – and German 'cherry water' aged in ash barrels; both are good for heart-warming during a cold winter.

Highly toxic in excessive dosages, wild bird-cherry bark was used by Cherokee women for labour pains; other Native Americans used it for coughs and colds, haemorrhoids and diarrhoea. Early American colonists used it to treat bronchitis and made the stalks into various medicinal tonics. Formerly used by children as chewing gum, the tree resin dissolved in wine reportedly treated coughs, gall stones and kidney stones.

Currently the antioxidant value of bright-red and black cherry pigments (anthocyanins) is key to its ability to help relieve the inflammation of gout. Consuming cherries and cherry juice on a regular basis may help to lower the risk of heart attacks and strokes. Scientists are studying the benefits of cherry juice and potential direct applications in the treatment and prevention of cancer.

Correspondences

The cherry tree stands for 'good education', and cherry blossom for 'spiritual beauty' and 'truth'.

- **Planet** Venus
- **Deity** Aphrodite, Guanyin
- **Element** Water
- **Colour** Purple, violet
- **Stone** Amethyst (unifies all life; brings forth trust in inner truths)
- **Polarity** Feminine
- **Animal** Heron
- **Virtue** Understanding, love
- **Association** psychic energy, divination, spiritual awareness, meditation, balance

Cautions: At the time of writing there are no known contraindications for the correct use of sweet or sour cherries' flesh and juice. However, the seeds (pips) contain poisonous cyanides, mainly in the form of cyanogenic glycosides as a defence against herbivores – as few in a cherry pie cause no harm, but consumed in excess can be lethal. Mild poisoning symptoms include headache, dizziness, confusion, anxiety, and vomiting.

Blackthorn

Botanical name *Prunus spinosa*

Family Rosaceae

Description: Blackthorn, the herald of spring, is a many-branched deciduous shrub or small tree that is native to Europe and western Asia. The twigs have short lateral, spiny shoots and blackish bark, and often form dense, thorny thickets. The five-petalled flowers dust the hedgerows with a creamy-white confetti. The spherical autumn sloes (fruits) are black-skinned, thin-fleshed drupes with a purple-blue bloom.

Correspondences

Blackthorn is a Chieftain tree, being a tutor about life's lessons. It takes the Ogham letter Str.

Ogham letter Str

- **Str (Straiff)** Discipline, control, perspective
- **Planet** Mars, Saturn
- **Deity** The White Goddess, Morrigan, Bel, Dagda
- **Element** Fire
- **Colour** Bright purple
- **Stone** Red jasper (brings consolation), ametrine (disperses negativity)
- **Polarity** Feminine-masculine
- **Animal** Wolf, toad, black cat
- **Virtue** Unity, strength in adversity, protection
- **Association** Challenges, strife, unexpected changes, confusion, developing courage and overcoming negativities

History, mystery and spiritual healing:

Blackthorn is equally the black and the white of life, and is considered both sacred and unlucky. A fairy tree, its blossom is the 'white light' of hope and the promise of renewal; its darkness celebrates Samhain, the eve of winter, and opens the pathway to the Underworld and its deities.

The plant's naked black bark is stark in barren winter, the standing-still period of the earth, yet tough and determined – like Mars

with its fighting spirit, it strives against all negativities before announcing the rebirth of spring. Known as the thorny 'flesh-tearer', in Ireland it is cut-up to make multi-knotted walking canes and cudgels like the Shillelagh, a one-time vicious stick now mainly used in the Irish martial art of stick-fighting.

Healing: Blackthorn contains several flavonoids and is being scientifically investigated for its antioxidant properties. Medicinally, it is chiefly an astringent, aperient, diaphoretic, diuretic and stomachic in action.

In folk medicine, sloe is a curative cornucopia, being used for diarrhoea, blood purification, convalescence, exhaustion and fatigue, rashes and skin disorders. Currently, a flower extract is also used in a body moisturizer. The juice, which contains a high quantity of tannins, acids and Vitamin C, is used externally to stimulate the skin's self-strengthening and metabolic functions. Blackthorn fruit and bark teas with wild-plum bark extract have also been used for cramps, bloating and indigestion, as a poultice and for wounds.

Blackthorn berries are listed in the German Commission E monographs for treating mild inflammation of the oral or pharyngeal mucosa; as well as preparations containing the flowers for treating common colds, diseases of the respiratory tract, as a laxative, for diarrhoea, gastric spasms, bloating, intestinal diseases and dyspepsia.

Homoeopathic remedy *P. spinosa* is used for nerve pain, urinary problems, weak heart and nervous headaches, and for fatigue from interrupted sleep.

Cautions: At the time of writing there are no known contraindications for the correct use of this plant. However, as with all the Prunus plant family, its seeds contain poisonous cyanides that can be lethal consumed in excess.

Oak

Botanical name *Quercus robur*

Family Fagaceae

Description: Native to most of Europe, Asia Minor, the Caucasus and parts of North Africa, the English oak is a massive, long-lived, deciduous tree with a wide-spreading head of rugged branches. Its green leaves turn gold to brown in autumn. The male flowers are pendulous catkins, while the female flowers are arranged in a spike. The fruits are acorns (nuts), green when young, turning a shiny golden-brown when mature.

History, mystery and spiritual healing: Held in high esteem throughout the major cultures of Europe, the oak was the most venerated tree to the Greeks, Romans, Celts, Slavs and Teutonic tribes. It is associated with their respective gods that had dominion over rain, thunder and lightning. In bygone times rulers wore oak-leaf crowns, symbolic of the god they represented on earth; Roman commanders were also presented with them as a sign of victory. Triumphal oak leaves continue to be insignias of military prowess.

From the time of the Tudors, oak wood lay at the heart of Britain's building construction and

Correspondences

Oak takes the Ogham letter D.

Ogham letter D

- **D (Duir)** 'Men of oak'
- **Planet** Jupiter, Sun
- **Deity** Zeus, Thor, Perun, Jupiter, the Dagda, Taranis, Esus
- **Element** Fire
- **Colour** Green (white)
- **Stone** Diamond
- **Polarity** Masculine
- **Animal** Lion, white horse
- **Virtue** Courage, honesty, nobility, endurance
- **Association** Fertility, generosity, hospitality, potency, prosperity, protection, strength and triumph

externally as a decoction and applied as a wash, lotion or ointment to bathe weeping eczema and for skin eruptions, dermatitis, sweaty feet, ringworm, ulcers, varicose veins and haemorrhoids. It is also used as a compress for inflamed eyes, as a gargle or mouthwash for throat and mouth infections, and as a vaginal douche. Internally the drug is used in some proprietary medicines for diarrhoea, flatulence and dyspepsia, and for a prolapsed uterus or anus. Recently, American research into methanol extracts of *Q. robur* found that they demonstrated high activity against both thrombin (a blood-clot promoter) and cancer.

In homoeopathy, oak-bark essence is used for disorders of the spleen and gall bladder; it is also reputed to cause alcoholics an aversion to intoxicating drinks. In 2001, research on 41 cases of Cushing's disease in animals concluded that *Q. robur* used homoeopathically may lend itself to the treatment of this disease.

Oak Bach Flower Remedy is used to promote common sense and inner strength, and to improve the ability to cope with worry and stress.

industry and the fabrication of Queen Elizabeth I's conquering ships. Following the Battle of Worcester in 1651, when King Charles II famously hid from the Roundheads in a large oak at Boscobel, Royal Oak Day celebrated the restoration of the monarchy. More recently, in 2001, the oak was adopted as the national tree of the US.

Healing: Oak bark, galls and acorns contain bitters, abundant tannins and are strongly astringent, antiseptic and anti-inflammatory; they are used to control bleeding. English oak bark is used

Cautions: Common oak bark should not be taken internally without professional advice and supervision.

White Willow

Botanical name *Salix alba*

Family Salicaceae

Description: White willow is a deciduous tree that is native to much of Europe. It has ascending branches, deeply fissured grey bark and olive-green leaves covered with silvery-grey hairs. The male and female catkins appear with the leaves on separate trees, the female catkins becoming downy airborne seeds dispersed by wind and water. The fruit is a capsule.

History, mystery and spiritual healing: The willow's ability to grow from coppiced or pollarded trees earned it the title 'tree of immortality'. For its spiritual, visionary and consciousness-altering affects, it was called the 'tree of enchantment and mysteries' by the ancient Celts.

The willow tree's leaves and bark were mentioned in ancient texts from Assyria, Sumer and Egypt for aches and fever. The use of its salicylic acid to reduce pain dates back at least to Hippocrates (440–377 BCE). It was also used by Dioscorides in the 1st century CE for lower back-pain. It was forgotten during the Middle Ages, but was used again as an internal styptic by the 17th-century English herbalist Nicholas Culpeper for its pain-relieving effects.

Healing: The dried bark from three- to six-year-old willow contains many compounds, including the healing glycoside salicin, tannin and resin. It is analgesic, anti-inflammatory, anti-neuralgic, anti-rheumatic, astringent, a febrifuge and styptic. It is used for arthritis, the common cold and other feverish conditions, cystitis, headache, neuralgia and rheumatism. A decoction is used externally for slow-healing abrasions, ulcers and burns.

Homeopathically, an essence of willow bark is used for the same complaints. Willow eases sorrow and the loss of love, and its Bach Flower Remedy restores the balance of optimism and a sense of humour to the disappointed.

Willow's yield of salicylic acid was reported by the Reverend Edward Stone to the Royal Society in England and published in 1763. In 1897 Felix Hoffmann created a synthetic version of salicin. The drug was named 'aspirin' by the company Bayer AG and initiated the class of drugs known as NSAIDs.

Recent research confirms that *S. alba* is not only useful for lower back pain, but – alone or combined with feverfew (see pages 94–95) – reduces the frequency of migraine attacks and their intensity and duration. Natural willow spring water has also been shown to aid skin and other conditions. Native Americans also relied upon various species of willow as the basis of their medicine.

Cautions: White-willow bark should not be taken with aspirin or NSAIDs, or if you have an ulcer, other gastrointestinal disorder or tinnitus. Consult your healthcare professional if you are pregnant or breastfeeding. As with aspirin, never give white willow bark to a child under the age of 16 who has cold, flu or chickenpox symptoms.

Correspondences

Willow takes the Ogham letter S.

Ogham letter S

- **S (Saille)** Willow tree
- **Planet** Moon
- **Deity** Artemis, Brigantia, Diana, Hecate, Helice, Luna, Orpheus, Selene
- **Element** Water
- **Colour** Silver, white
- **Stone** Moonstone, quartz crystal
- **Polarity** Feminine
- **Animal** Hare
- **Virtue** Healing, wisdom
- **Association** Divination, dowsing, flexibility, growth, healing, imagination, immortality, intuition, renewal, visions and vitality

Rowan

Botanical name *Sorbus aucuparia*

Family Rosaceae

Description: Rowan, or mountain ash, is a deciduous tree that is native to most of Europe's northern hemisphere except the far south, and to northern Asia. It has a slender crown, graceful upward-swept branches with a smooth greyish bark, white flowers, and foliage that displays crimson colours in autumn. The globular fruit is bright red and dispersed mainly by birds.

History, mystery and spiritual healing: Mountain ash appears in Greek mythology as created from the feathers and blood shed by an eagle, sent by the gods to assist in the recovery of Hebe's magical chalice that dispensed the elixir of youth to them. In Irish and Norse mythology, mountain ash was the tree from which the first woman was made, and also saved the life of the god Thor.

Known as a 'faerie tree' for its white flowers, the rowan is sacred to the English goddess Brigantia and to the Celtic Brigid or Brighid, as the goddess of spring. It also has a long reputation as an antidote to witchcraft: its berries, bearing a tiny five-pointed star (pentagram), and their vibrant red colour

Correspondences

Rowan was the chosen wood on which runes were inscribed. It takes the Ogham letter L.

Ogham letter L

- **L (Luis)** Rowan
- **Planet** Sun (Uranus, Venus)
- **Deity** Aphrodite, Brigantia, Brigid, Hebe, Thor
- **Element** Fire
- **Colour** Red, green
- **Stone** Peridot, Rubellite (red tourmaline)
- **Polarity** Feminine (masculine energy)
- **Animal** Crane, quail (dragon)
- **Virtue** Spiritual strength
- **Association** High protection, divine and creative inspiration, providence

In folkloric remedies the dried flowers are used for herbal teas, being mildly diuretic, purgative and stimulatory to menstrual discharge; an infusion of them and/or the dried fruits, or a compote prepared from them, is given against constipation, menstrual and rheumatic pains and as an aid in the treatment of kidney disorders.

Rowan berries also contain a flavonoid called quercitin or meletin, which is used to treat abnormal capillary fragility. It is antioxidant, antiviral and is reported to help allergies, prostate inflammation, cystitis, atherosclerosis and cataracts.

are ancient symbols of protection. Pieces of the tree were carried in pockets, and equal-armed rowan crosses were sewn into clothing or hung in cattle barns as protective charms.

Scandinavians regard rowans – for not growing 'in' the ground, but 'out' of elevated places such as rock clefts – as having magical powers and call them 'flying rowans'.

Healing: Rowan berries are a renowned source of Vitamin C and a cure for scurvy. Infusions and decoctions of them can be used as a gargle for sore throats and inflamed tonsils. The fumes of the burned leaves, if inhaled, aid asthma.

Cautions: Rowan's bitter seeds should be removed as they are considered poisonous. The berries should be treated before the fruit is used for medicine or food. They contain parasorbic acid in their raw form, which is toxic, but on cooking the acid is converted into harmless, digestible sorbic acid. Rowan should not be used by those taking anticoagulant or anti-platelet medication.

Yew

Botanical name *Taxus baccata*

Family Taxaceae

Description: Often a churchyard sentinel of the dead, the yew is renowned for its longevity and may live for over 2,000 years. Native to western, central and southern Europe and to Asia Minor, it is a slow-growing evergreen, with flattened, needle-type, dark-green leaves. The female trees produce fruits that are modified seed cones. Most parts of the tree, including the leaves and bitter seeds, are poisonous.

History, mystery and spiritual healing:

The yew tree has many forms of spiritual meaning. In Georgia it is called the 'tree of life' and, when wounded, continually bleeds red sap. In Japan the yew species is connected with the creator gods who live on mountaintops. The Celts believed that yews contained the spirits of our ancestors, with their pagan myth crossing over into Norse mythology as the tree from which Odin hung himself until he saw the runes in its branches that gave him wisdom and purpose. This mirrors the Gnostic Bible's meaning of Jesus, the Great Mystic, bestowing the powers of yew, overseer of light and clairvoyance, to Mary and the disciples.

The yew's poison works fast and is very effective; in his *Gallic Wars* Julius Caesar narrates that Catuvolcus, chief of the Eburones, poisoned himself with yew rather than submit to Rome. In England, Edward III (1312–77) made it compulsory for every able-bodied man to practise archery. The resultant use of yew for weaponry decimated the country's forests.

Healing: Anciently, yew was used for snake bites and rabies, obstructions of the liver and bilious complaints. Although extremely poisonous, the powdered leaves were used by herbalists for epilepsy. Clandestinely, despairing women used yew as an abortifacient to stimulate spasms in the womb.

As early as 1021 the Persian physician Avicenna introduced the phytotherapeutic use of yew in *The Canon of Medicine*. He called the herbal drug that he used as a cardiac remedy *zarnab*; it was the first known use of a calcium-channel blocker to decrease blood pressure, and did not reappear in widespread use in the Western world until the 1960s.

Shamans use yew to enhance magical and psychic abilities, and to induce visions. In conventional medicine, the precursors of commercial chemotherapy drugs can now be derived from the leaves of the European yew species, *T. brevifolia*.

Cautions: Yew leaves and seeds are highly poisonous.

Correspondences

In Druid tradition, yew is the tree of the seer and opens doorways into the Otherworld. It takes the Ogham letter I.

Ogham letter I

- **I (Idad)** Transference, passage, illusion
- **Planet** Mercury, Saturn
- **Deity** Odin, Wotan, Mercury (elvish Islaar), Hecate
- **Element** Earth, water
- **Colour** Black, dark green
- **Stone** Black onyx, obsidian (Apache tears)
- **Polarity** Feminine (masculine energy)
- **Animal** Spider
- **Virtue** Renewal, knowledge, articulacy
- **Association** Immortality, eternity, resurrection (death and rebirth), change and regeneration, helpful spirits, guides and ancestors.

Lime or linden

Botanical name *Tilia cordata*

Family Malvaceae/Tilioideae

Description: *Tilias* are generally called 'lime' in Britain and 'linden' in North America and parts of Europe. *T. cordata*, the small-leaved lime, is native to much of Europe and western Asia. A lofty, elegant tree, it was used to line broad avenues and boulevards in many cities in Europe. It has mostly hairless leaves, small and heavily scented, yellow-green flowers and its fruit is a dry downy drupe that becomes smooth at maturity.

History, mystery and spiritual healing: Both the ancient Greeks and the Slavs considered the lime to be the abode of their goddess of love and beauty, Aphrodite and Lada respectively. Homer, Horace, Virgil and Pliny mentioned the linden and its virtues. In Roman mythology the lime tree was a symbol of conjugal love and fidelity.

The linden tree was (and is) regarded as the tree of all peoples with Slavic ancestry. Its golden branches grace the flag of the Czech Republic's presidential flag and became fixed as a national symbol after the break-up of

Correspondences

Linden takes the Ogham letter U.

Ogham letter U

- **U (Ura)** Generosity and persistence
- **Planet** Venus (Mercury)
- **Deity** Shava (queen of stars and love), Lada, Venus and Aphrodite, Ishtar and Isis, Rhiannon and Arianrhod
- **Element** Air (Earth)
- **Colour** Pearl-white
- **Stone** Alabaster, tree agate
- **Polarity** Feminine
- **Animal** Turtle dove, hind (bee)
- **Virtue** Godliness, cleanliness, seeker of truth
- **Association** Purity, beauty, peace, light and love, luck

the Austro-Hungarian Empire. In Germany, the linden was used by communities as a meeting place for dance, celebration and dispensing judgement, and so became associated with peace and harmony.

Bast obtained from inner bark of lime trees has been used by the Japanese Ainu, a people of prehistoric origin, to weave their traditional clothing, the *attus*. Its fibres can also be used to make ropes, nets and bags.

Healing: In folkloric medicine, because of its heart-shaped leaves, the lime tree was dedicated to Venus and was said to cure all diseases classified under the goddess and the planet named after her. In ancient Indian Ayurveda, Venus's diseases were bronchial problems, whooping cough, asthma, dyspepsia and so on. Linden's use also corresponds to mercurial complaints, such as nervous diseases, restlessness and irritation.

Lime flowers have been used in bath infusions for hysteria, and the sweet sap made into wine. Herbal tea made from the dried flowers is considered good for nerve-related conditions, such as headaches, restlessness, insomnia and anxiety. The German Commission E has approved linden flowers for colds and cold-related coughs. The British Herbal Compendium indicates its use for upper respiratory catarrh, common colds, irritable coughs, hypertension and restlessness.

In 2008 two sets of Mexican scientists demonstrated the fresh or stored flowers of the Mexican linden (*T. Americana* var. *Mexicana*) to be non-toxic and supported their use as a tranquillizer in traditional medicine, as well as confirming the anxiety-reducing effect of a rich flavonoid component, without affecting motor activity.

Cautions: No safety information is available for linden-blossom absolute.

Elm

Botanical name *Ulmus glabra*

Family Ulmaceae

Description: The deciduous elm, wych elm or Scots elm, which is native to Europe, Asia Minor and the Caucasus, grows along roadsides, in hedges, at the margins of woods and in the Scottish Highlands. It has a broad crown supported by a short bole, with robust, supple young shoots and rough-surfaced leaves. Produced in clusters of 10–20, its flowers appear before the leaves in early spring.

History, mystery and spiritual healing: In Greek mythology, the elm's link to Orpheus and his lute are well known. In Norse myth, the first man and woman were made from the ash and the elm tree, while Teutonic myth states that the elm was given a soul by the god Odin, senses by Hoenir, and blood and warmth by Lodur, becoming the first woman. In Finno-Ugric mythology, elms were believed to be the mothers of the fire goddess, Ut. The Celts believed

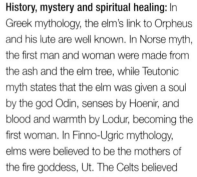

that the falling of elm leaves out of season predicted murrain (cattle disease), which they cured by means of the elm 'need fire', through whose fumigatory smoke the cattle were driven.

In Britain, the wych elm is associated with the Mother aspect of the Goddess, with elves who were said to guard Celtic burial mounds, their dead and their passage to the Otherworld.

Dutch Elm Disease has proved a scourge to elm trees

worldwide, decimating populations in northern Europe, the US and Canada.

Healing: The dried, young inner bark of English elm (*U. procera*) is an astringent, anti-inflammatory and mild diuretic. Homoeopathically, fresh bark essence was given for eczema. An infusion of shredded bark is used for diarrhoea, arthritis and rheumatic pain (slightly stronger to bathe inflamed wounds, haemorrhoids and mouth inflammations). Traditionally, Wych elm leaves were used as a poultice for swellings, and its inner bark for skin and venereal infections.

The North American Slippery elm (*U. fulva*), well-known medically and to herbalists, was used by the Cherokee for coughs, skin conditions and as an eye-wash. The multi-healing secretion from the tree's bark was used in poultices for infected wounds, in salves for wounds, boils, ulcers, burns and even nappy rash. Slippery elm is recognized by the FDA as a safe and effective medicinal option for sore throats and respiratory symptoms, such as coughs. Science has found that Canadian slippery elm possesses potent antioxidant and DNA-protective activity, properties common to natural anti-cancer agents.

Cautions: At the time of writing there are no known contraindications for this plant. However, slippery elm should not be used in cases of impacted bowel or bowel blockage of any origin. Prescription medications should be taken at an alternate time to consuming slippery elm bark.

Correspondences

The elm takes the Ogham letter AHL-m.

Ogham letter AHL-m

- **AHL-m (Ailm)** Connection, wisdom
- **Planet** Saturn
- **Deity** Mother goddess, Mother Earth, Briah, Cerridwen (Am-Mesh)
- **Element** Water, (slippery elm) air
- **Colour** Silver
- **Stone** Black onyx, black jade
- **Polarity** Feminine
- **Animal** Raven, goat
- **Virtue** (Masculine) solidity, stability, nobility; (feminine) rebirth, metamorphosis, endurance
- **Association** Grounding energy and focus; childbirth (Embla), the universe

Plants for
spiritual healing

The soul healers

Plants interact with and aid our psycho-emotional balance and harmony, transforming the often-polluted physical, mental and spiritual environments of the modern world in which we live, and – both directly and indirectly – touching and healing our very souls.

The colours, scents and alchemical, curative physical and incorporeal components of plants nurture and foster our spiritual well-being in many different ways. Although many seers, diviners and mystics do not require a psychoactive 'key' in order to gain entrance to the supernatural, throughout the history of humankind psychotropic (or mood-altering) substances have been ingested or inhaled during spiritual rites and rituals for this purpose. In the past, such plants were not used irreverently as they are today, when they are frequently used for dangerous *unguided* frolic, whereby narcotics absorbed into the subconscious may re-emerge capable of causing grave mental and sometimes bodily harm.

Young woman attuning her soul with Nature by meditating outdoors in the warm sunshine sitting in a half-Lotus position.

Opening the 'doors of perception'

Ancient Egyptian priests and priestesses, and ancient Greek and Roman oracles, ingested and inhaled psychoactive plants and their substances, going beyond the medicinal painkilling use of opiates or of the myrrh offered to Christ on the cross as an intoxicant to make crucifixion more bearable. A sacred plant's contents were taken ritually to open the 'doors of perception'; to enter and interface with a spiritual world, in order to experience and witness *what is* on all different levels and dimensions, both within human beings and within every living entity that surrounds us – *all* energies (crude or subtle), *everything* seen and normally unseen in our environment.

The symmetry and profundity of the virginal pure white water-lily is used here as a focus for meditation.

The traditional purpose of hallucinogenic participation was to go beyond the self and to communicate with otherworlds and those beings within them, guided – according to culture – by a spiritual leader. Hallucinogenics were taken to enlighten the spirit while travelling along earth's road towards attaining spiritual perfection.

This chapter explores a range of plants from different cultures and traditions that have been considered of specific benefit for spiritual development.

Fly agaric

Botanical name *Amanita muscaria*

Family Amanitaceae

Description: Fly agaric is a large 'fairytale' mushroom, which is native to birch, pine, spruce, fir and cedar woodlands throughout the northern hemisphere, and was introduced to Australia, South Africa and New Zealand via pine trees imported from Europe. It has an umbrella-like, bright-red cap covered in white scales (remnants of its membranous universal veil).

On emerging from the soil, fly agaric's fruiting bodies look like warty white eggs. As the fungus grows, the conspicuous red colour breaks though the veil. The cap changes to become hemispherical, then a flat plate 8–20 cm (3–8 in) in diameter in mature specimens. Its oval spores are white.

History and symbolism: Fly agaric may be among the earliest psychoactive substances used for spiritual purposes.

Archeologically, the oldest evidence found (3500 BCE) regarding humans' use of mushrooms is seen in a cave painting in Tassili in Algeria, which depicts them in association with electrified auras outlining dancing shamans.

Believed by some to be the original Indian *soma* plant used to create hallucinations in religious ceremonies, fly agaric is a sacred offering to Agni, the Indian god of fire. The Maya people call it *kukulja*, meaning 'thunder', and, in the Lacandón jungle, *eh kib lu'um*, meaning 'light of the earth'.

Slovenian folklore tells of the Germanic god Wotan (Odin in Norse mythology) riding his stallion Sleipnir, pursued by devils, and of how red and white flecks of blood and foam sprayed like spores from the horse's mouth and fell onto the ground, whereupon fly-agaric toadstools magically arose.

In Germany, to celebrate New Year, the *Glückspilz* (lucky mushroom) – one of five quintessential symbols of good fortune – is incorporated into chocolate and marzipan decorations.

Healing properties/other: Fly agaric is used by shamans to enter a clairvoyant trance state and mobilize their shamanic powers of healing, but in order to minimize its toxic effects, it is dried, smoked or made into a drink or ointment. Celtic Druids traditionally fasted, drinking only water, before using fly agaric. Siberian shamans also fasted, then ate the mushroom, and celebrants would then drink the shamans' urine, from which most of the toxins had been naturally filtered out.

Similarly, in Lapland, reindeer were fed the mushroom and their urine was then collected for consumption. In Siberia, the Koryak people obtained the same effects from eating 'high' reindeer meat.

Modern research shows that fly agaric's two active chemical compounds can inhibit fear and the 'fight or flight' reflex within the brain. This might explain the use of fly agaric by Viking berserker warriors before going into battle, as well as their legendary fearlessness.

Cautions: The fungus is listed as a poison by the US Food and Drug Administration (FDA). It contains two toxins that are responsible for its hallucinogenic effects. It can cause violent intoxication and delirium, and can fatally compromise any heart condition, known or otherwise. Do not ingest this plant or introduce it into the body in any form.

Ayahuasca

Botanical name *Banisteriopsis caapi*

Family Malpighiaceae

Description: Ayahuasca is pronounced 'aja'waska', 'Aya' means 'vine' while *huasca* or 'waska' means 'spirit' in Quechua, is the Incan name for this spiritual vine plant, also called 'vine of the soul', and 'vine with a soul'. Originally taken from the wild, it is cultivated throughout the moist tropical Amazon basin of Peru, Ecuador, Colombia and Brazil. It may refer to the plant itself or to a hallucinogenic brew called *ayahuasca*, which is made from the bark and stems of any of the 40 identified varieties of ayahuasca vine of the genus *Banisteriopsis*, especially *B. caapi*; these are mixed with other psychotropic plants and used in shamanistic rituals by certain Amazonian Indian peoples.

Ayahuasca's woody stems are very long and branch repeatedly. The vine has huge green, round-ovate leaves, which are pointed at the end. Flowering only rarely and exclusively in moist tropical climates, its inflorescences consist of small, five-sepalled white or pink individual flowers.

History and symbolism: Ayahuasca and its medicinal draught belong to the mysterious shamanic zone of parapsychological healing. Some early missionaries to South America mentioned it in their writings, but it only became known in the West much later on. Indeed, ayahuasca was not described academically until the early 1950s, by Richard Evans Schultes – often called the Father of Modern Ethnobotany – who found it being used for both divinatory and healing purposes by the Amerindians.

Favoured by many traditional peoples of South America, ayahuasca has become the focus of a major new religious movement in Brazil, and its use spread among neo-shamanistic groups in North America and Europe during the 1990s.

Shamanic healing is seen as a natural resource and is a tool unfamiliar to the West. According to native *ayahuasqueros* (frequent drinkers of the herb), *B. caapi* is considered to be the most important 'plant teacher'.

Healing properties/other: Proper ritual use of sacred *ayahuasca*, which creates altered states of consciousness, is said to be non-addictive. In 1992, attempting to fight the modern world's demon of drug addiction by offering one of the ancient world's oldest traditions, maverick doctor Jacques Mabit founded Takiwasi (meaning 'The Chanting House') on the outskirts of Tarapoto in Peru. Its shamanic treatment involves both physical and psychic detoxification, or 'emotional cleansing', after which mystical ayahuasca treatment sessions take place at night, in the middle of the jungle, to the sound of shamanistic chanting to traditional songs known as *ikaros*. These treatments reportedly have a 70 per cent success rate.

Cautions: Do not use psychoactive 'gateway' unsupervised. The plant itself is not illegal, but some constituents of it and the brew are; individuals must determine the legal status of ayahuasca in their respective countries.

Frankincense

Botanical name *Boswellia carterii*

Family Burseraceae

Description: Frankincense, or olibanum, is the purified aromatic resin obtained from small trees and thorny bushes belonging to the Burseraceae family, which usually grow in mountainous climates on rocks, often with only morning dew for moisture. *B. carterii* is found in parts of North Africa, especially Somalia, and in some areas of Saudi Arabia.

It is a leafy, deciduous, but hardy forest tree, about 7–8 m (23–26 ft) tall, branching at the base, with white or pale-rose flowers. Its resin is harvested two to three times a year by tapping the trees. An incision is made that bleeds out the gum for about two weeks; this gum turns golden as it hardens into a resin known as 'tears', which are then scraped from the wound. The 'tears' are purified and used for healing or perfumery.

Frankincense oil, which is used in both aromatherapy and perfumery, is extracted by steam distillation from the gum-resin. An absolute is also produced, but is mainly used as a fixative.

History and symbolism: Frankincense is one of the oldest aromatic materials to have been used by humankind. Having been traded on the Arabian peninsula and in North Africa for more than 5,000 years, it was subsequently used as incense in Mesopotamia, Egypt, Greece and Rome – a use that was later adopted by the Catholic Church and continues in church services today.

At Queen Hatshepsut's Luxor temple, reliefs dating from 1512–1482 BCE portray frankincense being grown in pots for use in cosmetic face masks.

Both a form of currency and a source of wealth during the Roman Empire, 'tears' of frankincense were as valuable as gems or precious metals, and were chosen as a gift of the Magi to honour the birth of Jesus.

Healing properties/other: Frankincense has been used in both ancient and modern times as incense and as a herbal remedy for many health problems. It is significant in the Ayurvedic system of healing.

Being antimicrobial, anti-inflammatory and spiritually uplifting, frankincense is an aid to all kinds of respiratory problems, and is also a super-relaxant for the purposes of meditation.

New research by Johns Hopkins University and the Hebrew University of Jerusalem has found that frankincense smoke, which contains the chemical compound known as incensole acetate, is a psychoactive drug that may in future be used to relieve depression and anxiety.

Cautions: Do not use frankincense during pregnancy, and avoid all contact with the eyes and mucous membranes. The safety of frankincense in young children, nursing women and those with severe liver or kidney disease it not known. Rare side-effects are occasional allergic reactions of mild gastrointestinal distress.

Copal

Botanical name *Bursera microphylla*

Family Burseraceae

Description: The extraordinary copal, or 'elephant tree', is native to northern Mexico and the south-western United States, but grows throughout tropical America, north-east Africa and Madagascar, the Galapagos islands and Malaysia.

It is an intricately branched, small shrubby tree with a short, thick trunk, and reaches up to 4.8 m (16 ft) in height. Its bark is light grey to white, and when cut it exudes a resin, which is left to harden before collection. Younger branches have a reddish hue. The aromatic foliage has long, straight, flat, long, straight, flat, camphor-scented leaves composed of paired leaflets. The flowers open from yellow buds to starry white or cream blooms with five petals each and yellow stamens. The fruit is a hanging drupe measuring 6 mm (¼ in) long, which splits into three to reveal a single yellow stone.

History and symbolism: Copal's precious golden, black or whitish resins have been used by ancient civilizations – from the Egyptians to the native tribes of pre-Columbian Mesoamerica, including the Maya and the Aztecs – as a ceremonial sacred incense.

Native Mesoamericans, both today and in the past, have seen a powerful symbolic connection between maize and copal, connected with copal's use as 'food for the gods'. Seed corn was traditionally passed through copal smoke dressed with sacrificial blood before burning, to increase its productivity.

Copal smoke was also used by shamans to induce trances and for divination. And Guatemalan Christians recite the 23rd Psalm while burning copal, in gratitude for blessings received.

In the sacred book known as the Popol Vuh, written *c.* 1550 in the classical Quiché language of highland Guatemala, copal is described as a 'seeing instrument'. It was believed that its sacred smoke could lift the veil between people and the spirit world and carry messages to the world beyond.

Copal is often added to love and purification incenses. Pieces of copal sometimes represent the heart in poppets (dolls representing human beings) used for magic spells.

Copal is still used today in sweat lodges, a type of ceremonial sauna, in both Mexico and Central America.

Healing properties/other: Copal resins have numerous uses besides incense, ranging from glue to medicine. Tinctures, which may be made from twigs and leaves as well as from gum, are used for periodontitis, herpes, cystitis and other conditions. According to the Cahuilla, a tribe of Native Americans who have inhabited California for more than 2,000 years, the red sap of the 'elephant tree' was used as a panacea.

In the late 1960s American scientists working in Arizona isolated a compound called deoxypodophyllotoxin from *B. microphylla* that is one of several anti-tumour agents to be found in the plant.

Cautions: At the time of writing there are no known cautions for this plant.

Cannabis

Botanical name *Cannabis sativa*

Family Cannabaceae

Description: An annual plant, Cannabis's origin has been genetically traced to the 'Heavenly Mountains', Tien Shan, Kazakhstan, where the indigenous people have used it for 2,500 years.

It has slightly branched, erect stems with greyish-green hairs. The palmate, sharply serrated leaves with five to seven leaflets are dark green and smooth-surfaced, with downy, lighter green undersides. The small flowers are unisexual, those of the female plant producing hundreds of seeds; male plants shed their pollen and die. The fruit is small, smooth, light brownish-grey and entirely filled by the seed.

During their vegetative growth phase, cannabis plants require more than 12 hours of light daily. The flowering plant requires at least 12 hours daily.

History and symbolism: Historically, it has been used variously, as food and fibre (hemp), for its oil, as a drug, medicine, and for spiritual and recreational purposes. Evidence of cannabis smoking has been found in Romania dating from the third millennium BCE.

Earlier, cannabis was associated with the sacred, intoxicating hallucinogen known as *soma* in the ancient Sanskrit texts, the Vedas. The Rastafari movement (which was founded in 1930) has used cannabis smoking as a form of sacrament.

Healing properties/other: Cannabis is the most popular recreational hallucinogenic drug worldwide. Therapeutically, it is chiefly used to ease pain and induce sleep, and for soothing nervous disorders, neuralgia, gout, rheumatism, delirium tremens and so on.

New research states that cannabis primarily developed its THC psychoactive agent, a natural defence mechanism against predation, from ultraviolet light at altitude.

Cautions: Overuse may cause paranoia. Its use by children of 15 years or under causes a 6 per cent risk of schizophrenia, compared with 1 per cent risk for those in their twenties.

Myrrh

Botanical name *Commiphora myrrha*

Family Burseraceae

Description: *C. myrrha* is indigenous to eastern Mediterranean countries and north-eastern Africa: Somalia, Ethiopia, Eritrea, Yemen and southern Arabia. Its aromatic reddish-brown, walnut-sized globules of gum-resin are obtained naturally, from the dried yellow-brown sap that has seeped out of pale-grey bark ducts; collectors may also make incisions to increase the tree's yield.

Myrrh averages about 2.7 m (9 ft) in height, but may reach as much as 10 m (32 ft). It has knotted branches, and branchlets that stand out at right-angles, ending in sharp thorns. The scanty leaves, which are small and single, are alternate. Its tiny inconspicuous flowers produce smooth brown, ovate fruits, somewhat larger than a pea.

History and symbolism: Ancient Egyptians imported myrrh during the Fifth Dynasty (*c.* 2470–2350 BCE), and this trade continued sporadically for more than a thousand years. In around 1200 BCE the domestication of camels stimulated growth of the incense trade with Egypt, and eventually with Greece and Rome.

Myrrh's golden resin – known as the 'tears of Horus', after the god that symbolizes power and renewal – provided the ancient Egyptians with oil for embalming and for use as an antiseptic; and its sacred incense was burned for religious sacrifice, and to honour the sun god Ra daily at noon.

Myrrh's perfume, embodying all the finest qualities of femininity, was dedicated to Hathor and purified the temples of Isis (the embodiment of female sexuality and beauty). Charged with eroticism, its ministrations prepared wives-to-be of the Persian king Darius the Great (*c.* 549–486 BCE) for the initial six months of their year in purdah.

A symbol of wealth, more precious than gold, myrrh appears no fewer than 22 times in the Bible, from Moses to the Magi's gift to the baby Jesus and Christ's crucifixion.

Healing properties/other: Ancient Greek and Roman physicians used myrrh for wounds, infections, digestive and menstruation problems. It remained an embalming ointment until about the 15th century.

Myrrh is used in traditional Chinese medicine, Ayurveda, Unani and Western herbalism, aromatherapy and in perfumes worldwide; also in some liniments, healing salves, modern lotions, remedial dental toiletries and treatments. Non-toxic and listed by the FDA as a safe herb, myrrh is also approved by the German Commission E for mild oral and pharyngeal inflammations.

In today's stressful world, myrrh's incense purifies the environment and lifts the spiritual ambience. When inhaled, it aids contemplation and meditation, and creates inner peace.

Cautions: Myrrh's essential oil must not be used internally and the mucous membranes (such as the eyes, nose or mouth) must not be exposed to it. Avoid myrrh in pregnancy and when lactating, or if you have kidney problems or stomach pain. Diabetics and others using medicinal therapy for glucose tolerance and to lower cholesterol, or taking acne or liver drugs, should consult their healthcare professional before use.

Angel's trumpet

Botanical name *Datura inoxia*

Family Solanaceae

Description: Members of the *Datura* genus belong to the nightshade family, and researchers believe they originated in Mexico and the American south-west. Angel's trumpet is an annual shrubby plant. Its stems and leaves are covered with soft silvery hairs, which give it a greyish appearance. The long, pleasantly fragranced, night-blooming flowers first grow erect, then incline downwards. The fruit is a spiny, burr-like capsule, splitting open when ripe to disperse its seeds. All parts of the plant emit a foul odour when bruised or crushed.

Daturas are normally short-lived, but are quickly replaced by self-seeding. The seeds can virtually hibernate in the soil, and some that were stored for 39 years were still 90 per cent fertile. Heavily scented at dusk, their floral fragrance has developed a rather musky tone, mirroring the moths' sex pheromone, with a sweet note that promises nectar, in order to attract pollinating nocturnal moths.

History and symbolism: In the 11th century, the Persian polymath Avicenna gave the earliest account on record of a *Datura* plant, which was later translated by Dioscorides.

The 16th-century English herbalist John Gerard believed that *Datura* was used to induce the prophetic state of Apollo's priests in ancient Greece. His view was reflected in the plant's spiritual and mysterious uses in the New World. In Mexico, for example, various tribes used angel's trumpet, or *toloache* in religious rituals; some smoked the dried weed, leaving them on a 'high' and causing total relaxation of the body, as well as hallucinations.

Healing properties/other: In Avicenna's day, angel's trumpet was used as an efficacious painkiller. In China, *Datura* was used to treat colds and nervous conditions, and in Europe's days of witchcraft it was used in salves or ointments.

Datura was known to the ancient Hindu physicians, who regarded it as intoxicant, emetic, digestive and heating. The whole plant is considered to be narcotic, anodyne and antispasmodic.

In his East Indies work in 1578, the Portuguese Cristóbal de Acosta recorded *Datura* being used as an aphrodisiac: the seeds, when ground to a powder and added to wine, were said to be precious treasures of *enamorades*, or 'infatuated' Hindus. He also reported that the plant was given to young girls when brought into prostitution, as well as to their clients.

Cautions: Homoeopathically, *Datura* is used mainly for neurological and neurotic afflictions, from confusion to trauma. All parts of *Datura* plants contain dangerous levels of poison and may be fatal if ingested by humans or animals. The entire plant and its seeds are hallucinogenic, with a high probability of overdose.

Sacred fig

Botanical name *Ficus religiosa*

Family Moraceae

Description: The sacred fig is a large, dry-season deciduous or semi-evergreen tree that is native to India, Nepal, Sri Lanka, Myanmar, south-west China and Indochina east to Vietnam. It grows up to 30 m (100 ft) tall, with graceful, heart-shaped leaves and small green fruits ('figs') that turn purple as they ripen. The seeds are dispersed by fruit-eating birds and become embedded in the crevices of a host tree, where they germinate as air plants (epiphytes).

The plant is a species of banyan fig, all of which have the habit of putting out aerial shoots that grow down into the soil. Banyans, like other fig species, have a unique fruit structure and

lifecycle that depend upon fig wasps for reproduction. Older banyans form aerial prop-roots that grow into thick, woody trunks able to cover a wide area; indeed, they may envelop the host tree and become indistinguishable from the main trunk – hence the tree's nickname of strangler fig. 'Banyan' is also the English name for *banians* or Hindu merchants who set up markets in the shade of these enormous multi-trunked trees.

History and symbolism: Early peoples living close to nature were animists – some of them worshipped trees, and all had an inborn reverence for plants. The Indian sacred fig continues to be holy to followers of Hinduism, Jainism and Buddhism, its locale often being the site of religious and animist shrines.

The sacred fig is not the oldest tree on earth, though one particular sacred fig is the oldest known living tree in the world to have been planted by humans. In the 3rd century BCE, a sapling from the original bodhi tree at Bodhgaya in India under which Buddha attained *nirvana* (enlightenment) and developed his philosophy, was transported to Sri Lanka by Thera, daughter of the Indian emperor Asoka. According to the Mahavamsa ('Great Chronicle'), it was planted in 288 BCE in the Mahameghavana Park in Anuradhapura by King Devanampiya Tissa.

The site at Bodhgaya is traditionally known as Bodhimanda ('ground around the bodhi tree'). It is the most important of the four main Buddhist pilgrimage sites, and its revered Mahabodhi Temple became a UNESCO World Heritage site in 2002.

Healing properties/other: The sacred fig or bo tree also appears in Hindu symbolism. It is shown encircling the kalpa tree (palmyra palm), which means 'desire' and represents the Tree of Life of the Hindu paradise. This image of 'the bo-tree united in marriage with the palm' represents generative activity, combining male and female elements.

Mainly regarded as a place of pilgrimage for meditation and enlightenment, the Buddhist bo tree is where worshippers leave their flowers and votive offerings. Hindu *sadhus* still meditate below this tree of eternal life, and its 'fire sticks' are used in their sacrificial fires. Indian research shows anticonvulsant fig extract to be a potential treatment for epilepsy.

Cautions: At the time of writing there are no known cautions for this plant.

Hibiscus

Botanical name *Hibiscus spps.*

Family Malvoideae/Malvaceae

Description: Hibiscus (*H. sabdariffa* var. *sabdariffa*) is native to, and commonly cultivated in, areas ranging from India to Malaysia (where it is the national flower). It is an annual or perennial, erect, bushy, herbaceous subshrub up to 2.4 m (8 ft) tall, with mainly smooth, red stems. The long leaves are green with reddish veins. The showy flowers are yellow or buff with a rose or maroon eye, turning pink as they wither at the day's end, at which point the red calyx around the flower base begins to swell, enclosing a velvety capsule.

The Chinese hibiscus (*H. rosa-sinensis*) is native to East Asia. Widely grown as an ornamental plant, it is now pantropic in cultivation. It is an evergreen flowering shrub with large, showy flowers that are generally red and lack any scent. It rarely produces fruit.

History and symbolism: The seeds of *H. sabdariffa* are said to have been transported to the New World by African slaves. In the 17th century the plant grew in Brazil, and it was recorded growing in Jamaica in 1707. It was being cultivated as a foodstuff in Guatemala before 1840, and by 1899 large baskets of dried hibiscus calyces were seen in the markets of Guadalajara, Mexico.

The Chinese hibiscus, with its many attractive hybrids, is the most popular flower. In Hindu worship it is a holy offering to the mother-goddess Kali and to Lord Ganesha; devotion to whom extends to Jains, Buddhists and beyond. It is also used for Devi worship (the female principle, or *shakti*).

According to legend, the hibiscus is sacred to the island of Kayangel in the Pacific, which was created when a woman, after an ordeal at sea, was told by the gods to stick a hibiscus branch into the bottom of the sea and cover it with a coconut shell. From this the atoll emerged, and the sacred flower still grows there. In Hawaii, the beautiful hibiscus known as *ma'o hau hele* is the state flower. Women wear it singly, tucked behind the ear, denoting their availability for marriage.

Healing properties/other: *H. sabdariffa* is widely used for herbal teas. As a vegetable it is a delicacy in Mexico, and in the Caribbean it is used for jam. The flowers are popular in cocktails. In Egypt and the Sudan, hibiscus-petal tea is (like the plant) called *karkadé*. Research into the properties of the plant's calyces shows them to be antioxidant, lipid-lowering drugs, which are good for the heart.

The Chinese hibiscus is used as an antifungal and emmenagogue, with emollient and refrigerant effects. In southern India and the Pacific Islands the red flower and leaf extracts are used for hair care. In Ayurvedic medicine white hibiscus buds aid digestion; the flowers dried in the shade of a neem tree and powdered are used against cancers; the roots make decoctions for a variety of ailments and when boiled are also used for cancerous wounds.

Cautions: There are no known toxicities, aside from hibiscus's action as a contraceptive for both sexes. However, avoid hibiscus during pregnancy.

Morning glory

Botanical name *Ipomoea violacea*

Family Convolvulaceae

Description: *I. violacea* is a perennial species of morning glory, which is cultivated as a garden annual. It occurs throughout the tropics, particularly in coastal regions. It is a common ornamental twining vine with a tuberous root and heart-shaped green leaves. It grows up to about 3–6 m (10–20 ft) long, with bright white, pink, blue or purple funnel-shaped flowers – pollinated by hummingbirds and other birds, butterflies, bees and other insects – that produce small, black seeds. Entwining itself around any available object, it forms a riot of flowers, especially when it canopy-covers an old or dead tree. Although it is considered an invasive bindweed by many, its beautiful flowers have encouraged horticulturalists to produce varieties that show stunning flower patterns of vivid colours, one of which is 'Heavenly Blue'.

History and symbolism: Historically, morning glory has a rich foundation in psychedelic and visionary practices, having been used for thousands of years by Central American Indians in shamanic and traditional ceremonies. In the mid-16th century Spanish chroniclers reported the divinatory use of morning glory seeds. Known as *badoh negro* in South America, the seeds were used by the Chontal Indians of Oaxaca in Mexico, and by the Aztecs in the pre-Hispanic era, who called them *tlitliltzin* (Nahuatl for 'black') and used them to connect with the sun gods.

The Mazatec people of Mexico continue to use *I. violacea* as a means of communicating with their gods. They utilize several 'teacher plants' (including morning glory) in their religion and rituals, believing – as do Native North Americans – that spirits live in all matter, especially plants and animals, connecting them to Mother Earth both physically and spiritually.

Healing properties/other: The appropriate use by shamans of morning glory as a ritual for healing is vastly different to the misuse of it, which can distort the perception of time and space and create illusions or hallucinations that could be dangerous or undesirable.

Morning glory's wonderfully diverse range of blue and violet hues can psychologically uplift the mind and the spirits – enjoy it by growing it safely in your garden and revelling in its beauty.

Cautions: Commercial gardening seeds are usually coated with emetic poisons to discourage their purchase for intoxication. The seeds may have dangerous side-effects for many conditions and in association with other products, and should not be ingested.

Jasmine

Botanical name *Jasminum grandiflorum*

Family Oleaceae

Description: Common white jasmine is a hardy woody climber that is native to northern India and Persia and has been introduced to other parts of the world. It is acclimatized in central and southern Europe, and has been extensively cultivated for the perfume industry.

It grows to around 3.6–6 m (12–20 ft), with feathery, dark green leaves, and with leaflets in three pairs plus a larger terminal one. The fragrant white flowers open at dawn and close at dusk.

History and symbolism: Jasmine bears a Persian girl's name – Yasmin meaning 'a gift from God' – and is ranked as the 'queen of flowers'. The plant is believed to have been in Egypt before 1000 BCE, and is said to have reached China during the Northern Sung Dynasty.

Over time, the perfumery varieties of jasmine spread along the sea-trading routes, beginning with the regions along the Arabian Sea, crossing the Red Sea into Egypt and, after that, reaching the area around the Aegean, into Turkey and Greece. Jasmine then spread into and around the Mediterranean basin, through Egypt, Algeria and Morocco, subsequently reaching western Europe via Spain and the Moors.

In Egypt, jasmine was symbolic of Isis, the moon goddess, possessor of secrets, magic and healing. Its nocturnal habit also links it with Nyx, goddess of the night; and its commanding aphrodisiacal aroma links it to Aphrodite Philopannyx, 'who loves the whole night'. Morning-blooming *J. grandiflorum* belongs to Aurora, goddess of the dawn.

Healing properties/other: The multi-use of Jasmine's plants extends worldwide. The main western use of *J. grandiflorum* is aromatherapeutic. The aroma works on the psyche, soul and emotions, and it relieves stress and lifts the spirits – a solace, to make the heart sing again.

Cautions: While generally safe, the jasmine species may cause allergic sensitivity in some individuals.

Bay laurel

Botanical name *Laurus nobilis*

Family Lauraceae

Description: Wreathed in myth and history, bay laurel is a large aromatic evergreen shrub or small tree, which is native to the Mediterranean region and is also cultivated in areas with similar or oceanic climates. It is lovingly nurtured as an ornamental plant and herb in gardens and pots, on patios and doorsteps, or as an indoor plant in many cooler areas of the world.

It reaches about 10–18 m (30–60 ft) and has flavoursome, glossy green leaves, which are well known to cuisines worldwide. It has pale yellowy-green male and female flowers, which are borne in pairs beside a leaf on separate plants. It is pollinated by bees, and the resultant fruit is a small black berry containing a single seed.

History and symbolism: In Greek mythology the bay laurel tree was sacred to Apollo, the Olympian Greek god of prophecy, poetry and healing, and it became his symbol when the nymph Daphne changed into one to escape his lustful pursuit. The roof of Apollo's temple at Delphi was covered in bay leaves for protection against physical disease, spiritual witchcraft and lightning. According to legend, prior to expounding, the Delphic Oracle chewed bay leaves (which are slightly narcotic in high dosages) or inhaled the burning leaves' fumes, to promote her visionary trances.

In ancient Greece, the leaves of bay trees planted in sacred groves near the healing temples were woven into laurel wreaths – symbolic of wisdom and glory – which were first presented at the Pythian Games as a mark of excellence to honour artists, scientists, musicians and poets; later they were given to victorious athletes. The plant thus contributed phrases such as 'poet laureate' (meaning 'crowned with laurels') and 'rest on one's laurels'.

In ancient Rome, the laurel wreath symbolized the crowning glory awarded to emperors and heroes who were triumphant in martial conquests, elevating the victor and boosting the public's morale.

Healing properties/other: Bay laurel is a classical Greco-Romano medicinal herb and a modern antimicrobial food preservative. Bay-leaf tea can soothe minor stomach upsets, relieve flatulence and, anecdotally, may aid arthritis.

The herbaceous, fruity, fresh, camphor-scented leaf oil reputedly relieves rheumatic aches and pains, sprains, bruises and skin rashes.

Cautions: Bay-leaf oil can be narcotic and cause dermatitis. It should not be used in pregnancy.

Peyote

Botanical name *Lophophora williamsii*

Family Cactaceae

Description: Peyote (its name deriving from the Aztec word *peyotl*) is native to southern North America. It is a small, spineless cactus that inhabits primarily desert scrub, particularly thorn scrub, and is most commonly found on or near limestone hills, but rarely above 1,500 m (4,920 ft).

Peyote is extremely slow-growing and flowers sporadically, producing small, edible pink fruit with black seeds. The top of the cactus growing above ground is called the 'crown'. Poor harvesting of the disc-shaped 'buttons' of peyote, which are cut from the roots and dried, will cause the plant to die. This has caused a scarcity where peyote grows naturally in south Texas, so that the plant is now listed as an endangered species.

History and symbolism: Archaeological digs reveal that peyote has been used since the mid-Archaic period (8000–1000 BCE) in the Americas by the Oshara Tradition people. It was used at least 5,500 years ago in Texas, and between 810 and 1070 CE in Mexico.

Initially the Mescalero and Kiowa (Athabaskans) started the practice of peyote religion north of Mexico, later introducing it to Northern Plains' migrants, the Comanche and the Kiowa. The practice was taken up by many tribal groups that were native to, or had relocated to, the Southern Plains states of Oklahoma and Texas.

When the Spanish conquistadors arrived in northern Mexico, the Huichol (who were traditional users of the peyote cactus) together with the Tarahumara retreated to the Sierra Madre Occidental mountains, taking the peyote religion with them. The Spanish found peyote use to be more widespread than its limited areas of growth suggested, and on 29 June 1620 published a prohibition order. It failed, and today the ritual use of peyote is protected by the Native American (Peyote) Church.

Healing properties/other: Peyote's psychoactive substance, mescaline, is mild in fresh peyote 'buttons', but strong when dried. A tool for

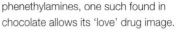

transcendence, it has been used in meditation, psychonautics (exploring altered states of consciousness), art projects and psychedelic psychotherapy. It also contains phenethylamines, one such found in chocolate allows its 'love' drug image.

The Huichols' annual peyote collection is a sacred pilgrimage, led by a spiritual leader who is in contact with, and accompanied by, the god Peyote, or Tatewari, the sacred fire. He takes the people on a journey to the San Luis Potosi desert, where peyote grows. After partaking of the peyote, while their spiritual leader heals the sick or divines the future, followers are metaphysically transported to a state of 'adventurous synaesthetic' linkings, with vibrant coloured images and auric visions surrounding all living things, to trigger and facilitate deep states of introspection and insight.

Cautions: Do not use peyote without a professional guide. Do not take it if contemplating pregnancy, or when pregnant or lactating.

Mandrake

Botanical name *Mandragora officinalis*

Family Solanaceae

Description: Mandrake belongs to the nightshade family, and inhabits open woodlands, deserted fields, stony places and dappled shade. It is a native of southern Europe and the Levant, and its natural range includes India (the

Himalayas) and China. Nowadays it is grown universally in frost-free gardens.

Mandrake is a self-fertile hardy perennial, growing 10–30 cm (3–12 in) tall, with large, dark-green, fetid-smelling leaves growing from its rosette crown. The flowers stem from its centre, each stalk producing a purple, bluish or greenish-white hermaphrodite flower, which is pollinated by insects. The orange-to-red smooth, globular, pulpy fruits, about the size of a plum, contain seeds and have a strong apple-like scent when ripe. The mandrake famously has large brown roots, like a parsnip, reaching deep into the ground, which are either single or divided into two to three branches.

History and symbolism: The plant's root crudely resembles the human form and is imbued with ancient mysticism, magic and superstition. Ancient Egyptian priests combined it with other psychoactive drugs for astral travel. Biblical Hebrews used it for infertility (Genesis 30:14) and the aphrodisiac fruits' scent was mentioned in Solomon's Song of Songs (Canticles 7:13); and as the Arabic *luffâh* or *beid el-jinn* ('genie's eggs'), it ensured conception. Both medieval witchcraft and modern neo-pagan magic (such as that of Wicca and Odinism) have used mandrake root.

In 200 BCE the Carthaginians used mandrake in an ancient form of bio-warfare. They left wine laced with *Mandragora*, which was drunk by the invading Romans, rendering them insensible; the Carthaginians then slaughtered them.

Healing properties/other: The potency of *M. officinalis* was known to Dioscorides, Pliny, Josephus, Galen and Isidorus, and it has a long history of medicinal use as emetic, hallucinogenic and narcotic. The plant on its own, or infused in alcohol, was employed as an anaesthetic in early surgery. But its root contains poisonous alkaloids, including atropine and hyoscine, which prevent much usage in modern herbalism.

Today, mandrake is used homeopathically for to ease coughs and asthma; its hyoscine content forms part of standard pre-operative medication that is given to soothe and reduce bronchial secretions. It was once viewed as exciting delirium and madness, but it now aids restless excitability and can also help sufferers of epilepsy.

Cautions: All parts of the mandrake plant are poisonous. It may have legal restrictions in some countries.

Indian lotus

Botanical name *Nelumbo nucifera*

Family Nelumbonaceae

Description: The Indian lotus is an aquatic perennial. Native from modern Vietnam to Afghanistan, *N. nucifera* spread extensively as an ornamental food plant. Now rare or extinct in the wild in Africa, it is naturalized in southern Asia and Australia, where it is commonly cultivated in water gardens.

Its cultivars' flower colours vary from snow-white through yellow to light pink. The plant grows on average up to about 1.5 m (5 ft) tall, and occasionally taller, with large leaves and flowers. Remarkably, the oldest seed to be germinated came from a 1,300-year-old lotus fruit, recovered from a dry lake-bed at Xipaozi in north-eastern China in 1995.

History and symbolism: Unknown to ancient Egypt, the Indian lotus was introduced by Persian invaders in around 525 BCE). Like other species of lotus, it came to represent Upper Egypt as symbolized in the hieroglyph Sema, which bound a lotus and papyrus and stood for the unification of Egypt that took place in 3100 BCE.

The lotus flower closes at night, submerges and then re-emerges blooming in the morning, making it a natural symbol of the sun, creation and rebirth. It is the national flower of India and Vietnam, and is associated with the Hindu deities: Krishna, the 'Lotus-Eyed One'; Brahma and Lakshmi, deities of potency and wealth; Vishnu, the supreme god; and Sarasvati, goddess of knowledge and the fine arts.

In Buddhism, the lotus signifies the progress of the soul from the primeval mud of materialism, through the waters of experience, into the bright sunshine of enlightenment.

In the West, poetic knowledge of the Greek nymph Lotis – who transformed herself into a 'lotus tree' to escape being raped by Priapus, the embodiment of male sexual domination – long preceded English naturalist Sir Joseph Banks's horticultural introduction of the living plant into Western Europe in 1787.

Healing properties/other: In the West, the intensely floral, deeply relaxing white and pink lotus oil is used in aromatherapy for

its ability to calm and soothe. It may have the effect of opening up a person's nature to being more forgiving and kind. In Asia, the roots and seeds of the lotus are an important, healthy food and the seeds are used extensively (for 'clearing heat') in traditional Chinese Medicine, but the major healing value of the lotus is as a teacher of the mind.

Cautions: Do not use lotus oil or absolute if pregnant. Medicinal use of the seed is contraindicated in abdominal bloating with constipation.

Sacred blue lily

Botanical name *Nymphaea nouchali* var. *caerulea*

Family Nymphaeceae

Description: The sacred blue lily is a beautiful aquatic plant, a water-lily with sky-blue flowers that flourishes in sunny positions on the shores of lakes and rivers. It grows along the River Nile, in Thailand, and is indigenous to Tanzania and Kenya.

It is a clump-forming perennial with thick, black, spongy, tuberous rhizomes anchored by spreading roots in the mud. Its large, flat, round or oval-shaped leaves with notched edges are cleft almost to the centre, where the leaf stalks, which arise from the rhizome,

are attached. Initially a soft, shiny green, the ageing leaves develop light-brown or purple splodges as they deteriorate, turning yellow and then brown, before they eventually submerge and die back.

History and symbolism: The sacrerd blue lily – one of the world's most sacred plants – was revered by the ancient Egyptians, Nubians, Abyssinians and African civilizations. Its mysterious blue flower (which was believed to be a gift from the sun god Ra to the moon goddess Isis), and its reputation for psychoactive effects, made it a contender for the 'lotus-eaters' (the Lotophagi) in Homer's *Odyssey*.

The sacred blue lily's flowers, buds and leaves, which are depicted on many ancient monuments, murals, pottery and furniture, aroused further interest after the flowers were found scattered over Tutankhamen's body in 1922. Moreover, analysis of the ritual and sacred iconography of dynastic Egypt, on stelae, vessels and magical papyri, showed that ancient Egyptians possessed a profound knowledge of plant lore and altered states of consciousness.

In 2000 an investigation was carried out on Azru, an Egyptian mummy dating to 2700 BCE and a noblewoman of Thebes. A ministrant to the god Khonsu at Karnak, her role involved using the sacred flower's tincture or extract. Forensic analysts found no drugs in the mummy, but did discover phosphodiesterase (which is the active ingredient of Viagra), from the sacred blue lily.

Healing properties/other: In the ancient Egyptian and the Mayan cultures, the sacred blue lily was used to induce an ecstatic state, and as an aphrodisiac for both sexes. It was also a cure-all, being traditionally and effectively used to relieve pain, increase memory and circulation, and as a key to good health, sex and rebirth.

Recent American research shows the blue lily to be antioxidant. The sacred blue lily has a marked synergy with alcohol, enhancing its effects. In modern culture, the flowers are steeped in wine and Martini, made into a cordial or liqueur, or used to make blue-lily tea. Blue lotus absolute in grape alcohol is reportedly non-toxic, non-irritant and non-sensitizing. The dried leaves can be smoked and are sometimes blended with other herbs to add flavour and a euphoric effect.

Cautions: At the time of writing there are no known cautions for this plant, however those contemplating pregnancy, or who are pregnant or lactating, should avoid using it.

Peach

Botanical name *Prunus persica*

Family Rosaceae

Description: The term 'peach' may refer to the tree or the fruit. It belongs to the *Prunus* genus, which includes plums, cherries and apricots, and is a member of the rose family. Chinese in origin, the peach became native to the Mediterranean basin, the Middle East and Asian countries, and is now cropped commercially in North America, Canada and Australia, and is espaliered in gardens worldwide.

The peach is a small deciduous tree, 5–10 m (16–33 ft) tall, with spreading branches and sharp-pointed, veined green leaves. The succulent fruit is a drupe, covered in a velvety skin and slightly grooved on one side, containing delicately perfumed yellow or whitish flesh, and a single large seed.

History and symbolism: Documented in China from the 10th century BCE, peaches journeyed through different cultures and countries to Persia and the Mediterranean regions along the Silk Road. Evidence suggests that its espaliered form may date back to ancient Egypt.

Peaches are a popular fruit, which are rich in folktales and tradition in China, Japan, Korea, Laos and Vietnam. In Taoism, the peach is the Tao and the symbol of longevity. Its stone is an ancient symbol of female genitalia.

The mother of the Jade Emperor, the Queen Mother of the West, as the goddess Seiobo cultivated a garden of peach trees that blossom only every 1,000 years, ensured the gods' everlasting existence by feeding them the peaches of immortality.

To ancient Romans, peaches were the fruit of Venus, who was also associated with immortality, truth and sincerity.

Healing properties/other: Although the leaves, bark, flowers and kernels of the peach all have medicinal values and are used in herbalism, but even just the sight of a peach tree blossoming in spring can gladden the heart and heal the spirit.

A syrup and infusion of peach flowers was formerly recognized as a mild purgative for children or those in weak health. Peach Flower Essence aids those who are egocentric to 'open up' and become less selfish (see pages 354–355). Research carried out in 1993 suggests that peach skin may be protective of the kidney and liver, and that the flesh extract may ameliorate some drug toxicity in cancer patients.

Cautions: Eat the fruit only. Use any other parts of the peach only if they are prescribed by a medical professional.

Magic mushroom

Botanical name *Psilocybe zapotecorum*

Family Strophariaceae

Description: 'Magic mushrooms' are fungi that mainly belong to the *Psilocybe* genus, which are best known for the species that contain the psychedelic substances psilocybin and psilocin, however, most species do not contain these hallucinogenic compounds. *P. zapotecorum* is native to Mexico and is known to occur in Argentina, Brazil, Chile, Colombia, Mexico and Peru. It is named for the Zapotec Indians, the 'Cloud People', an indigenous pre-Columbian civilization that flourished in Mexico's Valley of Oaxaca.

Psilocybe means 'bare-headed', referring to the mushroom's plain cap. The nondescript fruiting bodies are typically small and brown to yellow-brown, with a spore-print colour ranging from lilac-brown to dark purple-brown, though rusty-brown varieties also occur. The bruised bodies of hallucinogenic species show a blue stain.

History and symbolism: The magic mushroom is a symbol of cosmic vision. Its magical powers are prehistoric, and it is possible that it formed part of early hominids' diet. Mushroom-shaped statuettes found at archeological sites also tell us that the ritual use of hallucinogenic mushrooms is quite ancient. The first-known experimentations date back 7,000–9,000 years in the Sahara Desert.

Known to the aboriginal Mexicans as *teónanácatl* (literally 'god flesh'), *P. zapotecorum* was reportedly served at the Aztec coronation of Montezuma II in 1502. The Mazatec people of Oaxaca state call the mushrooms *nti-si-tho*, meaning 'worshipful object that springs forth', relating to their apparently miraculous appearance where there were none before.

Healing properties/other: From pre-Columbian times until the present day, hallucinogenic species of *Psilocybe* have been used by the native peoples of Mesoamerica for religious communion, divination and healing. Mexican-American women and indigenous Mesoamerican natives continue to use *cuaraderos* (native healers), who employ magic mushrooms for diagnosis and as part of psychological counselling.

Although *Psilocybin* has no recognized medicinal uses, since 1961 investigations have continued into its therapeutic application as experimental treatment for several disorders, including obsessive-compulsive disorder (OCD).

Currently *Psilocybin* is being researched for supportive care to ease the psychological suffering associated with cancer, for depressive symptoms and anxiety, and as a palliative treatment for terminal diagnoses.

Cautions: Like all hallucinogens, magic mushrooms should not be taken unguided and alone. Avoid driving, operating machinery or using the plant in conjunction with other prescribed drugs. Use of magic mushrooms may aggravate or trigger emotional or psychological problems.

Diviner's sage

Botanical name *Salvia divinorum*

Family Lamiaceae

Description: A member of the mint family, *S. divinorum* is a perennial psychoactive herb. It is endemic to the sierras inhabited by the Mazatec people of Oaxaca, and its distribution is anthropogenic. This plant grows in isolated, shaded, moist conditions, often trailing along rocky stream-banks, sometimes in running water.

It has vigorous shoots arising from the rooted nodes of runners, broken stems, degenerating or almost dead woody pieces, in a layering habit. It has large green leaves, hollow square stems and occasional racemes of white and purple flowers.

It is a mysterious plant, producing few seeds (nutlets) – and those that do appear seldom germinate. It is thought to be a cultigen: a result of artificial selection, not occurring in a wild state. Although isolated stands of *S. divinorum* do exist, it is unknown whether these were secretly created and nurtured by people.

History and symbolism: *Salvia divinorum* translates as 'diviner's sage' or 'sage of the seers', its genus *Salvia* coming from the Latin *salvare*, meaning 'to heal' or 'to save'. *S. divinorum* has been used for centuries by the Mazatec Indian shamans of Oaxaca, in rituals and for healing during spirit journeys. It is also the first of the three divinatory plants employed in their shamanic training, the other two being morning-glory seeds and magic mushrooms. The Mazatec religion is a synthesis of traditional beliefs (including the cultivation of psychoactive substances for spiritual purposes) and Christian beliefs (brought by the Spanish conquistadors). The Mazatec people call diviner's sage *ska María Pastora* and always show it reverence, believing it to be an incarnation of the Virgin Mary.

Healing properties/other: In remedial low dosages, the herb is prescribed for anaemia, as a diuretic for diarrhoea, for headaches, rheumatism and a semi-magical disease called *panzón de borrego* (swollen or 'lamb' belly).

The plant has become both increasingly well known and available in modern cultures. Its active chemical, Salvinorin A, is unique in that it is an agonist (a substance that initiates a physiological response) of neuroreceptors that are largely ignored by other known drugs.

Cautions: Generally, diviner's sage appears not to be toxic or addictive, but research is limited.

Iboga

Botanical name *Tabernanthe iboga*

Family Apocynaceae

Description: Iboga is a perennial, evergreen rainforest shrub that is native to Gabon, Cameroon, Zaire, the Congo and Angola, and is cultivated throughout west central Africa. It normally grows to 2 m (6½ ft), but, if given favourable conditions, can become a grow up to 10 m (33 ft) tall. It has small green leaves, with pink and white flowers, producing orange, oval-shaped fruits, whose seed may have a brainlike seed-coat.

The strong, yellow-coloured, heavily branching roots contain indole alkaloids, notably ibogaine, the psychoactive material that is harvested from living plants. Only part of the root is taken, so the plant remains alive and can regenerate more roots.

History and symbolism: Iboga is 'a bridge to the ancestors', which is used in ritual ceremonies by several indigenous peoples living in west central Africa, including the Babonga, Mistsogo and Fangs. For some 150 years, it has been used by the Bwiti cult, whose religion is virtually based on this powerful plant.

Some believe that iboga is the tree of knowledge from the Garden of Eden, given to them to recognize God and to access the secrets of Paradise.

The modern Bwiti religion is syncretistic – incorporating animism, ancestor worship and Christianity into its belief system – and the herb has a central role in the rite of passage into this religion. Iboga is taken in enormous doses by initiates to induce a visionary 'living dream' state, and is used in smaller doses in connection with other ceremonies and tribal dances. The initiate reportedly travels into the land of the dead, a journey that embraces regression, prescient experience (insight into the future) and the ability to see their true higher self.

Healing properties/other: Since unrecorded history, iboga has been used for divination, to diagnose illnesses and as a stimulant. Its bitter taste causes an anaesthetic sensation in the mouth and systemic numbness to the skin, while also stimulating the central nervous system.

In Bwiti culture, iboga is administered by male or female spiritual leaders known as *N'ganga*, who are pillars of the community, with extensive knowledge of traditional healing practices, as well as hexes and spells.

Cautions: Iboga can cause paralysis and eventually death. Do not experiment with this plant. At the time of writing it is outlawed or restricted in Australia, Belgium, Denmark, France, Sweden, Switzerland and the US.

Cacao

Botanical name *Theobroma cacao*
Family Sterculioideae/Malvaceae

Description: *Theobroma cacao* is native to the deep tropical region of the Americas. Recent genetic studies show that it originated in the Amazon and was distributed by humans throughout Central America and Mesoamerica.

This small evergreen tree grows to about 4–8 m (15–26 ft), with a brown-barked trunk and bright-green lance-shaped leaves. Its small reddish, almost odourless flowers are pollinated by tiny flies. Its smooth yellowy-red fruits are borne with the tree's leaves and flower all year round. They contain capsules of about 25 seeds, which rattle when ripe. After fermentation and separation, the seeds (the cocoa beans) are sun-dried.

History and symbolism: The genus name *Theobroma* means 'food of the gods'. Mexicans called the pounded seeds 'chocolate' – a word derived from the Nahuatl *xocolatl*, from the words for bitter and water. During the Aztec period, cacao beans were used as currency for small transactions. In places such as the Yucatán, this continued into the 1840s.

The mythological Plumed Serpent (symbolic of the Aztec god Quetzalcoatl) is reputed to have given cacao to the Maya people. To celebrate, every April ceremonial blood sacrifices and offerings of cacao, feathers and incense were made to the cacao god, Ek Chuah. With the addition of some aphrodisiacal chilli, many cups of 'hot chocolate' daily helped the Aztec emperor Montezuma II (*c.* 1480–1520) to keep his numerous concubines happy.

Healing properties/other: Cocaine is extracted by stimulating cacao leaves. The leaves are widely chewed to overcome altitude sickness, and this is also a homeopathic remedy. Dark chocolate may boost women's libido, and has circulatory benefits. Cocoa-based prescription drugs could potentially help treat diabetes, dementia and other diseases.

Cautions: Too much chocolate is an obesity risk, and may cause acne and toxicity in animals that are unable to metabolize theobromine.

European mistletoe

Botanical name *Viscum album*

Family Santalaceae

Description: Mistletoe is native to Europe and northern Asia, and has ranges from Scandinavia to North Africa, Turkey, India and Pakistan, central Asia, China and Japan. It inhabits orchards, light woodlands and gardens, and grows in dappled shade on the branches of many trees, especially old apple trees, and sometimes on the hallowed oak, but not on conifers. Thriving on soft-barked deciduous trees, it forms pendant bushes 2–5 m (6–16 ft) in diameter.

It is a yellowish-green, evergreen, hemi-parasitic shrub, with smooth, freely forked, jointed stems and dull leathery, textured, strap-shaped leaves in opposite pairs. The inconspicuous flowers produce globular, smooth, translucent white or ivory berries (fruits) containing several seeds embedded in a sticky, glutinous fruit pulp. Most seeds are spread by birds, such as the mistle thrush in Europe.

History and symbolism: Mistletoe is the Roman Virgil's 'golden bough', the Welsh 'tree of gold' and it is dedicated to the pagan goddess Freya. The pagan custom of hanging mistletoe in the house is a symbol of peace, friendship and goodwill, while kissing beneath it at Christmas is supposed to bring good fortune.

The Druids' worshipful use of mistletoe made it holy. Chief of their seven sacred herbs, protecting its possessor from all evil, mistletoe was held in awe for its capacity to renew itself when cut. It was reverentially harvested with golden sickles on the sixth day of the moon, to be used in Druidic ceremonies.

Growing high up in sacred trees, as if suspended in space, mistletoe's ability to alter levels of consciousness represents a portal of connection to the Otherworld, revealing beautiful dreams amid the sombre forces of dark midwinter, which holds back the life-force of sunlight.

Healing properties/other: The ancient Celts, and other peoples, knew of mistletoe's homeopathic value for neurological, heart and other conditions. Today, *V. album* is still employed homeopathically, for complaints relating to the left side of the body and asthma.

Often referred to as *All heal* in old texts and folklore, research has barely scratched the surface of Mistletoe's promise and potential for healing and medical applications. The German Commission E Monographs recommend mistletoe as a treatment for degenerative inflammation of the joints, and as a palliative therapy for malignant tumours. In 1999, American research showed that a Mistletoe extract may also be used to aid immuno-suppressed patients with HIV and AIDS.

Mistletoe's spiritual energy can open the soul to the deepest lessons, so that it becomes a teacher and guide.

Cautions: All parts of raw, unprocessed mistletoe are poisonous, though the toxicity level is slight. Avoid during pregnancy or when lactating. Do not use with other drugs without professional supervision. In North and Latin America, *Phoradendron* rather than *Viscum* is the genus used.

Flower essences

The power of flowers

The knowledge that the flowers of plants hold potent energetic healing qualities is not new but rather something that ancient peoples were acutely aware of, and used to the full, in their systems of medicine.

What are flower essences?

For those not familiar with the concept of flower essences, in contrast to essential oils, they are the infusion of the energetic imprint of the flowering part of the plant. A flower essence is a plant's unique signature – its quality of vibrational healing potential – suspended in a solution of water and alcohol.

The practice of encapsulating the potent healing qualities of flowers in water is an ancient art discovered by indigenous peoples throughout the world when they noticed that the morning dew

on flower petals, which had been potentized by the first rays of the sun, not only lifted their spirits but also had a profound healing effect on all levels. This insight led them to continue to explore these effects in greater depth.

Flower therapy of the ancients

Flower remedies as a healing therapy is not new, for both medically and historically many ancient cultures possessed the knowledge of the therapeutic qualities of flowers. Documented evidence of their effective use has been discovered dating back to the time of the Egyptian civilization, some 7,520 years ago. It was said that the high priests honoured flowers and their essences for their sacredness and used them extensively in their healing ceremonies and rituals, because they believed that the flowers' positive, life-enhancing energy corrected any imbalance in the body at whatever levels

Flower essences can be combined with essentail oils to create a refreshing, uplifting therapeutic mist to enhance mood.

were needed – physical, emotional or spiritual. They documented the specific therapeutic values of each plant species.

Flower essences were recognized and used to treat emotional states by civilizations in South America, the Far East and Africa. In Crete, at spiritual ceremonies, the Minoans floated specially chosen flowers in water during their ceremonial rites, sipping the flower water to cleanse themselves of negative thoughts and feelings, so that they were left feeling refreshed, renewed and transformed.

The waterlily was discovered in Asia, and is found gently floating in water. Revered for its purity, it inspires intimacy and love.

The history of flower essences

The Swiss alchemist Paracelsus (1493–1541), who developed the Doctrine of Signatures (see page 12), rediscovered flower therapy in the 1500s and apparently collected dew on blossom to treat his patients' emotional imbalances. He believed that if there was harmony between the mental, emotional and spiritual aspects of an individual, then there would be no space for illness.

Bach Flower Remedies

Dr Edward Bach (1886–1936), a Harley Street physician in London, revived the art of flower therapy during the 1920s. Dissatisfied with the medicine of his time, which treated the symptoms and not the cause of an ailment, he rediscovered flower remedies by searching for a simple system of medicine that treated the underlying root of the illness, guided by the insights and observations gained through his clinical consultancy. He understood that stress and shock, at whatever level, were the causative factors of illness and he intuitively looked to nature for healing qualities and answers, particularly from flowers and trees.

It was said that Bach used himself as a form of experiential laboratory, creating intense negative mental and emotional states and then intuitively allowing himself to be drawn to a particular flower, which gave him the opposite, positive emotion. This is how he developed a repertoire of 38 remedies that now form a widely used, complete system, which has specifically evolved to address different personality types and their responses to stressful events.

A quiet revolution

Since Dr Bach's rediscovery of flower essences this field has developed profoundly. In the last 25 years in particular, the scope and availability of essences for a wide range of health issues have gone from strength to strength. A quiet revolution has occurred, with many people responding to the need for remedies in our increasingly stressful lives by investigating the healing qualities of other flowers, especially those that are indigenous to their own country. Two of some of the first pioneers of the 21st century are Richard Katz and Patricia Kaminski, of the Flower Essences Society in California. To date they have researched and documented more than 200 essences for their therapeutic use.

In Australia, the Aboriginal healing tradition has been continued by a fifth-generation herbalist called Ian White, who has developed the Australian Bush Flower Essences range. These remedies focus on the interconnection between the mind and emotions, and how problems in these areas can result in physical ill health. Both Australian Bush Flower proponents and the Flower Essences Society have conducted major research into the efficacy of flower essences.

Dr Edward Bach is considered to be the father of Flower Essence therapy and the Aborigines are believed to be the grandfathers.

How to use flower essences

We are facing increasing health problems in today's stressful world. Flower essences are useful tools for handling the demands of a faster pace of life.

First choose the essence, or combination remedy, that is the closest match to the condition or situation that you would like to treat. See pages 360–377 for more on using remedies for a variety of problems, including insomnia, stress and low energy. Flower essences can be administered in various ways.

Internal use

Most people will experience a sense of calm after taking a flower essence, and situations that would normally create tension can be handled without stress. However, when taking flower remedies it is important to realize that we are all unique and respond in a highly individualistic way.

The recommended method for taking flower essences is placing drops under the tongue.

The traditional way of taking flower essences is to drop them under the tongue – a method that seems to enhance their absorption. You should avoid letting the dropper touch your tongue, as this tends to create bacterial

growth in the essence. If preferred, drops can be added to drinks such as spring water, juices or herbal teas (but not to coffee or tea).

It is important to take a remedy regularly to reap the full benefits. Seven drops taken directly in the mouth, first thing in the morning before rising and last thing at night on retiring, are the rule of thumb. Keep your chosen remedy beside your bed, so that you are less likely to forget to take it. In more deep-seated cases, use the remedy more frequently by taking an extra seven drops at midday.

Normally a one- to two-month course is followed, and towards the end you may need to take the essence less frequently. If you forget to take it altogether, this usually signifies that you no longer need that particular essence or combination.

Remedies are self-adjusting; a slow, continuous course is more effective than a rapid one. More is not necessarily better, except in an emergency situation.

External use

Flower essences do not have to be administered internally. If alcohol sensitivity is a problem, or when treating babies or children, the remedies are equally effective when rubbed gently onto the skin, on the inner side of the wrists or the soles of the feet.

An alternative method is to add a few drops of flower essence to a bath of warm water. Relax and soak for half an hour, while the energy of the essences is absorbed though the skin.

Quick fixes

If you are feeing tired or stressed, try the following essences for a quick boost:

- **Emergency Combination Essences or Rescue Remedy** (see pages 360–361) is a refreshing and revitalizing pick-me-up after a long, fraught day at work.

- **White Chestnut** (see page 365) or **Elm** (see page 374) is a useful essence to clear the mind and promote relaxation.

- **Dynamis** (see pages 376–377) is a morning pick-me-up that helps to counter lethargy and get you going.

Abbreviations used

Bach = Bach Flower Remedies
Aus Bush = Australian Bush Flower Essences
FES = Flower Essences Services

First-aid remedies

Flower essence remedies that act quickly to provide first aid in acute situations are invaluable and can be carried in a handbag or first-aid travel kit. They activate self-healing to kick in immediately, when the shock caused by a traumatic incident can inhibit the body's natural self-healing mechanism from functioning.

Most people are introduced to flower remedies through first-aid combinations for emergency situations. The most well known and loved is Bach's Rescue Remedy, but the Australian Bush equivalent, Emergency Combination Essences, is becoming ever more popular. Both assist recovery from surgery, as well as acute situations of fear and panic.

Rescue Remedy and Five-Flower Remedy (Bach)

This gentle but potent combination of flower essences contains star of Bethlehem (*Ornithogalum umbellatum*) for shock, cherry plum (*Malus sylvestris*) for loss of control, clematis (*Clematis vitalba*) for unconsciousness, rock rose (*Helianthemum nummularium)* for panic and terror and impatiens *(Impatiens glandulifera)* for stress. It is a tried-and-

tested shock remedy that is effective for children as well as animals and the elderly.

Administer seven drops of Rescue Remedy every hour, or every 10–15 minutes if necessary. In severe panic attacks, take every five minutes.

Emergency Combination Essences (Aus Bush)

This swift-acting remedy contains crowea (*Crowea saligna*), dog rose of the wild forces (*Bauera sessiliflora*), fringed violet (*Thysanotus tuberosus*), grey spider flower (*Grevillea buxifolia*), sundew (*Drosera spathulata*), waratah (*Telopea speciosissima*) and angelword (*Lobelia gibbosa*). It can be used in acute and extreme situations and is considered by some to be like 'Bach Remedies on steroids', due to the intensity of the environment where the flowers are grown and harvested – the

Waratah means 'most beautiful' and is unique to Australia. The Aborigines consider it to be their most sacred flower.

harsh climate of the Australian Bush.

This emergency essence is excellent for any emotional or physical upset, calming the mind, body and emotions during a crisis. It eases distress, fear, severe mental or physical stress, nervous tension and pain, helping your coping ability. This combination is also invaluable if someone needs specialized medical help, as it can provide comfort until treatment is available. Emergency Combination Essences has also proved effective during acute asthmatic attacks.

Administer seven drops of Emergency Combination Essences every hour, or every 10–15 minutes if necessary. Take every five minutes in severe panic attacks.

Caution

Flower essences should not be used as a substitute for emergency medical care. Consult a medically qualified practitioner as a first course of action in emergency situations.

Depression

Depression can manifest in various forms, from mild to severe. It may be due to exhaustion, trauma, loneliness and isolation or be a result of frustration and anger.

Depression can vary in degree from mild, which is not so easy to detect, to major, which in extreme cases can lead to suicidal tendencies. It is important to address depression before this extreme situation develops.

Tall Yellow Top (*Senecio magnificus*) (Aus Bush)

Use this flower essence for depression due to a sense of abandonment, isolation and loneliness and when there is no connection felt to family, country or oneself. A feeling of displacement can bring its own degree of depression and melancholy, but this remedy creates a sense of belonging and of knowing that you are 'home', an acceptance of oneself and others and an ability to reach out.

Mustard (*Sinapis arvensis*) (Bach)

This is an important remedy for overwhelming feelings of gloom and despair, where they are not connected to any obvious situation or circumstances and seem to come from unknown origins. It works well both for chronic, low-grade sadness and to clear the all-consuming black cloud of depression linked to a deep melancholy, which can lift as unexpectedly as it descends. It is useful in complex states of depression, especially bi-polar mood swings.

Mustard brings equilibrium and clears the sense of hopelessness, strengthening the ability to survive whatever life throws at you. It brings the realization that every day is an opportunity to get more deeply in touch with yourself, to grieve for what is amiss so that healing can occur, in preparation for new growth.

Waratah (*Telopea speciosissima*) (Aus Bush)

This essence is considered a powerful survival remedy by the Aborigines, who still honour the waratah as their most

Caution

Depression can be a very serious illness and should be treated by a medically qualified doctor.

sacred flower. It is a quick-acting remedy for those going through despair, deep depression and an inability to cope in a crisis. It brings courage, tenacity, endurance, survival skills and a feeling of hope. Its powerful qualities are perfect for those in total despair, who feel that there is nowhere for them to go.

Waratah fosters adaptability and the capacity to cope with any emergency situation. It gives you the power to call on the inner strength that you already possess and encourages tenacity in dealing with your problems. It enables you to tap into previously learned survival skills, teaching you to discover the reservoir of inner faith and courage that is only to be found deep within.

Depression can effect us all at some point and taking the appropriate essences can lift us out of the gloom.

363

Insomnia

One of nature's great healers is sleep. It is the body's inbuilt mechanism to conserve energy and to repair, rebuild and rebalance the body's energy systems. Having a good sleeping rhythm should be as natural as breathing, but it is not something that everyone is able to achieve, especially in times of stress.

Natural sleep patterns are set in the early years and the way a baby sleeps often dictates that person's sleep patterns as an adult. It seems that those babies who are forced to sleep – who are put down to sleep at a set time before they are ready and left to cry for long periods at bedtime – may develop a sleeping problem later on in life. Encouraging the development of healthy sleeping habits, by understanding a child's natural rhythm and working with it (within reason), can avoid problems later on.

Some people are naturally night owls, working best till the small hours of the morning when all is quiet; others are morning birds, who wake up early feeling bright-eyed and bushy-tailed. While some people need a regular nine hours' sleep, others can function perfectly well on just five hours – it's how you handle your energy that is the key. Stress and nervous tension, anxiety, over-tiredness and mental overload are some of the main reasons for insomnia. And when the brain is not able to properly rest, it can drain the body of its serotonin levels.

Regaining a natural sleep rhythm and waking up refreshed in the morning is achievable with the right flower remedy.

White Chestnut (*Aesculus hippocastanum*) (Bach)

This is an essence that encourages mental relaxation, clearing the mind of chatter – the persistent unwanted thoughts and obsessive thinking that is the result of external pressure. It is good for over-excitement as the tried-and-tested Calm and Clear Bush Combination Essence (see page 369).

Morning Glory (*Ipomoea purpurea*) (FES)

This is for night owls with erratic eating and sleeping rhythms, who have difficulty getting up in the morning and an inability to enter the body fully. Feeling hungover, dull and toxic may make night owls susceptible to nervous depletion and poor immunity. Morning glory essence also encourages attunement with your natural sleeping rhythms to restore normal energy levels. A sparkling life force develops, with a feeling of being refreshed, alive and in touch with life.

Caution

Consult a medically qualified practitioner if insomnia persists.

Grief and loss

No one is ever fully prepared for the impact of the death of a loved one – whether that death is expected or not. The shock and grief take their inevitable toll. This is part of life and something that we will need to cope with, if we haven't already done so.

However death is handled, the experience has a marked effect on us. There is no set formula for grieving, but the emotion of grief and a sense of loss are the overriding emotions. We have all heard of couples who have spent their lifetime together, and when one dies, the other quickly follows – the grief seems to weaken their immune system. This physical effect may be behind the saying 'To die of a broken heart'.

In acute situations, on receiving news of a death and just after the death, Grief Relief Combination Spray (FES) is invaluable, for not only does it clear the shock of the loss, but it helps the recipient with the grief. Two other remedies are given below.

Sturt Desert Pea (*Clianthus formosus*) (Aus Bush)

This essence deals with the immediate grief and the emotional anguish of separation. One of the effects of a recent death is that it reveals deep-seated sadness, old emotional wounds and memories of previous grief that were physically locked in the body. According to traditional Chinese Medicine, the lungs are most associated with and affected by grief, hence the tendency to catch viruses affecting the bronchial passages and lungs when loss has occurred.

This remedy is multifaceted. It helps to fight viruses and bacterial infections and is a good general support for the physical body during a time of grief and loss.

Transition Combination Essence (Aus Bush)

This remedy helps with difficulties in the transition phase of a loved one passing

Coming to terms with the death of a loved one and healing the grief is something we all need to be able to cope with.

over from the physical plane to the spiritual world. It is a combination of bauhinia (*Lysiphyllum cunninghamii*), bottlebrush (*Callistemon linearis*), bush iris (*Patersonia longifolia*), lichen (*Parmelia s. lat.*), mint bush (*Prostanthera striatiflora*), red grevillea (*Grevillea speciosa*) and silver princess (*Eucalyptus caesia*).

Transition Combination Essence is an interesting and helpful remedy for those caring for, and with, their loved ones when they are dying. Not only does it aid the transition, but it helps both patients

Caution

Consult a medically qualified practitioner if grief persists.

and carers to come to terms with the fear and apprehension of approaching death. It enables people to let go, for death is just as much about letting your loved one go as it is about a peaceful transition on their part.

Stress and feeling overwhelmed

In our increasingly stressful world there is hardly anyone who isn't touched by stress in one form or other, whether it manifests itself on the physical, mental, emotional or spiritual plane. Not all stress is counter-productive, for a certain amount of stress can – if used creatively – challenge us to make positive life changes. The art is to cope with and manage stress positively and creatively.

The most obvious sources of stress are the big, shocking changes like the death of a partner, divorce, the loss of a job and moving house. Equally, however, stress can be caused by less obvious, insidious states of mind, such as feeling lonely, overwhelmed and depressed or aimless. How we react depends on our stress backlog and our threshold levels – our response to stress is relative and highly individual.

Stress is now being recognized as a medical condition. Scientists at Harvard University, researching the effect of stress on the body, have discovered that the mind and body are linked by shared interactive chemicals, especially in relation to the nervous, immune and endocrine systems, as well as the skin. A precursor to (and often at the root of) many physical problems, stress must be handled efficiently.

Indian Pink (*Silene californica*) (FES)

This is a remedy for those who take on too many activities at once, becoming tense, emotionally volatile, depleted of energy and easily fragmented by too much going on in their lives. The remedy assists you in becoming centred and focused, even under stress or high levels of activity, helping you to manage and coordinate diverse activities.

Caution

Consult a medically
qualified practitioner if the
symptoms of stress persist.

Calm and Clear Combination (Aus Bush)

This is a combination of boronia
(*Boronia ledifolia*), bottlebrush
(*Callistemon linearis*), bush
fuchsia (*Epacris longiflora*),
crowea (*Crowea saligna*),
jacaranda (*Jacaranda
mimosaefolia*), little flannel flower
(*Actinotus minor*), paw paw
(*Carica papaya*) and a black-
eyed Susan (*Tetratheca
ericifolia*). Calm and Clear
Combination is a remedy for
being over-committed, rushing
around, always on the go and
suffering from mental tension and
tiredness. It enhances the ability to find
space and have time for oneself, to relax
and unwind without getting caught up in
external pressures and demands.

Black-eyed Susan in particular
balances the adrenal glands. It helps to

The stress and rushing around that comes with modern living is taking its toll on our physical, emotional and mental well-being.

deal with anxiety, impatience, irritability
and with feeling out of control, resulting in
a lack of focus. It encourages clarity and
calmness, clearing indecision, frustration,
stress-related stomach problems and
anxiety, plus obsessive thoughts that
result in the inability to unwind at night.

Shock and trauma

Flower essences excel in shock situations. The effect of sudden shock on the body may be imagined as a pebble thrown into a calm pond, sending ripples reverberating through the water. However, shock may also act in a more insidious way, having a long, slow and ongoing effect that is harder to recognize.

Either way, shock can have a devastating effect on the body's energy systems. Unless steps are taken to rebalance these, the disruptive impact can become deep-seated. The greater the build-up of unresolved shock, the deeper it resides. The different types of shock – traumatic or long and slow – are treated in different ways.

Traumatic shock

The world is full of distressing events, from natural disasters to car accidents and bomb blasts. We will all experience some form of sudden and unexpected traumatic shock that shakes us to our very core. If not addressed, the symptoms of shock can last a lifetime and even manifest in symptoms that seem to have no apparent cause. Recognizing its effect on physical and psychological well-being, the medical

profession uses the term 'post-traumatic stress disorder' for the aftermath of shock.

Fringed Violet (*Thysanotus tuberosus*) (Aus Bush)

This flower essence is for shock and trauma, damage to the aura and lack of psychic protection that allows vitality to be drained from us by other people and by environmental factors such as radiation. It removes the effect of recent and old trauma, reintegrates the subtle energy system after shock and provides psychic and energetic protection.

Long, slow shock

We are often unaware of the existence of long, slow shock, which is more insidious than traumatic shock, for it becomes an integral part of our lives. It can take its toll even before we are born, in our mother's

Clearing the system of shock and trauma by reducing the build-up is key to boosting the body's self-healing processes.

anxieties about the pregnancy and apprehensions about the birth. Any long, ongoing situation of tension or subtle abuse can also contribute to slow shock.

Star of Bethlehem (*Ornithogalum umbellatum*) (Bach)

Take this for all forms of shock, but particularly for long, slow shock that has built up over a period of time, delayed from the past or the shock of birth. It clears shock from the system, bringing a sense of being centred, soothed and comforted, and restores the body's self-healing mechanisms. It also aids recovery from deep-seated strain and ongoing traumatic situations.

Caution

Flower essences should not be used as a substitute for emergency medical care. Consult a medically qualified practitioner as a first course of action in emergency situations and if symptoms of shock persist.

371

Anxiety, fear and panic

We all have moments of anxiety, apprehension and niggling fears, usually brought on by mental overload, tiredness and the general stresses of life. More severe forms of fear can develop in those who are of a nervous constitution, so that stress develops into extreme anxiety and even panic attacks. Panic attacks can be alarming and may be confused with asthma attacks or even mild forms of heart attack.

Crowea (*Crowea saligna*) (Aus Bush)

This remedy is for individuals who continually worry, feeling anxious and out of balance. It helps to dissolve the build-up of stress and brings peace, calm, vitality and a sense of being centred and balanced.

Panic, fear and anxiety attacks are often the result of high stress levels and overload.

Dog Rose (*Bauera rubioides*) (Aus Bush)

A remedy for those who tend to dwell on their fears and insecurities, and who are affected by nervousness that has been picked up from other people or stimulated by the environment, or by events that trigger deep subconscious fears. It encourages a positive, fearless attitude and helps people to be unafraid of new challenges.

Grey Spider Orchid (*Grevillea buxifolia*) (Aus Bush)

This is excellent in acute panic when the adrenalin reaction creates an anxiety overload and has a direct physical effect on the body, such as being unable to move, paralysed by fear. This can spill over after the trauma to the type of fear and panic that lead to claustrophobia. This remedy helps to release paralysing fear and bring courage and calm, plus a feeling of being more in control.

Fearless Combination Spray (FES)

This remedy consists of red clover (*Trifolium pratense*), mountain pride (*Penstemon newberryi*), Californian valerian (*Valeriana capitata),* Oregon grape *(Berberis aquifolium),* mimulus *(Mimulus guttatus),* rock rose

Caution

Consult a medically qualified practitioner if you experience panic attacks and if anxiety symptoms persist.

(Helianthemum nummularium) and green rose *(Rosa chinensis viridiflora).*

Red clover helps acute states of panic and high anxiety triggered by social or environmental stimuli, calming and stabilizing the heart. Mountain pride builds strength and courage when confronted by adversarial conditions. Californian valerian provides a fortifying sheath for the nerves during times of agitation and chaos. Oregon grape counteracts paranoid states, promoting a calm centre of objective awareness. Mimulus helps when there is a tendency to withdraw due to fear and anxiety, giving the ability to take risks and learn from demanding situations. Rock rose helps terror or extreme fright, enabling positive grounding and internal anchoring in times of stress. Green rose nourishes a turbulence of the heart, helping to counteract fear with the positive forces of compassion and connection to the environment.

Low energy and exhaustion

We are all unique in terms of our energy levels and the way we use the energy we are born with. The Chinese call this ancestral energy *qi* and believe it is stored in the kidneys. Managing our energy levels is an art. Some have a natural abundance of *qi* energy and accomplish a lot, with very little need for recharging; others seem to have a finite source of *qi* and are not able to bounce back so readily.

When there has been a drain on the adrenal glands – from illness or a period of long, ongoing stress that creates adrenal exhaustion – replenishment is particularly important, otherwise this can be a precursor to physical illness. With lowered vitality, our resistance is also lowered and the immune system becomes more vulnerable to viruses and infections.

Below are some remedies for when you are feeling overwhelmed by day-to-day responsibilities or by not being able to measure up to your own view of a responsible person. Flower essences can make it possible to tap into an inner reservoir of energy in order to recoup.

Elm (*Ulmus procera*) (Bach)

Elm is for capable people who shoulder responsibility and occasionally take on tasks that prove to be unreasonably demanding, making them feel drained, exhausted, overwhelmed and temporarily inadequate. It enables people to let go and let others handle the excess responsibility, so that they are free to enjoy life as well – otherwise life would seem to be one long struggle.

Olive (*Olea europea*) (Bach)

This is used for total mental and physical exhaustion, especially after prolonged illness or during a period of convalescence. It is an aid to

Exhaustion and burn-out is all too common today. Essences are said to help recharge and rejuvenate our energy system.

combating the negative effects of overwork, stress and too much worry, and helps people get through crises such as divorce or conflict that may have weakened the system.

Macrocarpa (*Eucalyptus macrocarpa*) (Aus Bush)

This flower essence is for those who are physically, mentally or emotionally exhausted and, as a result, have poor immune resistance. It is a quick pick-me-up that regenerates the adrenal glands,

restoring energy, strength and vitality. It is useful for poor recuperation after a long illness, to recharge the adrenal glands and bounce back to full health and energy levels.

Caution

Consult a medically qualified practitioner if low energy levels persist.

375

Colds and flu

Preventive action is just as vital as remedial action when we catch a viral or bacterial infection. Factors that lay us open to infection increase when we are overstretched, tired and therefore less able to handle the stresses of life, our reserve tanks running on empty. We are then prey to the different strains of cold and flu that are especially prevalent during the winter months.

Antibiotics have important uses when administered appropriately, but the practice of doctors giving out antibiotics for viruses is a trend that has not helped build strong immune systems. And not everyone knows how to rebuild the healthy bacteria in their intestinal flora, to bring their system back into balance after a course of antibiotics. As it is in the nature of viruses to constantly adapt and mutate into completely new forms, it seems sensible to protect and boost the immune system in any way we can.

Ian White, the creator of Australian Bush Flower Essences, has discovered that flower essences from the bio-diverse Australian outback have a profound effect on managing immune health, particularly where stress has compromised its efficiency. He has formulated the Dynamis combination essence to address this problem.

Dynamis Combination Essences (Aus Bush)

Excellent when feeling drained and exhausted, this remedy combines banksia robur (*Banksia robur*), crowea

Maintaining a healthy balanced immune system is a sensible precaution against colds and flu, given the prevalance of these viruses today.

Caution

It is wise to consult a medically qualified practitioner if you experience symptoms that are worse than those of the common cold or flu.

(*Crowea saligna*), illawarra flame tree (*Brachychiton acerifolius*), macrocarpa (*Eucalyptus macrocarpa*), old man banksia (*Banksia serrata*) and yellow cowslip orchid (*Caladenia flava*).

Dynamis is very helpful for those times when it is hard to bounce back and recoup your energy levels, especially after setbacks and illness. It harmonizes and stimulates the major endocrine glands, in turn strengthening a weakened immune system. One of its main effects is to help you deal effectively with burn-out due to adrenal stress, as a result of the adrenal glands being overstimulated. It acts as a quick pick-me-up to harmonize vital forces, boost energy levels when down and boost the immune system when compromised.

Glossary

absolute: A concentrated, highly aromatic, oily mixture extracted from plants, using solvent techniques or, more traditionally, through enfleurage.

acetylcholine (ACh): A chemcial compound and neurotransmitter in both the perhipheral nervous system (PNS) and the central nervous system (CNS); it is severely diminished in the brains of people with Alzheimer's disease.

adaptogen: A plant which improves physical energy, and increases the body's immunity to minor infections, stress and anxiety.

agonist: A plant that interacts with a cell receptor to trigger a physiological or a pharmacological response by the receptor, for example, contraction.

alkaloid: Part of a large, varied group of complex nitrogen-containing compounds (usually alkaline) that react with acids to form soluble salts, many of which have physiological effects on humans; they include nicotine, cocaine, caffeine, etc.

allergen: An antigenic substance that causes an acute defensive reaction in a person's immune system (an allergy). Common allergens are pet dander, smoke and pollen.

allopathic: The conventional method of medicine that combats disease by using active techniques specifically against the disease, usually with drugs.

alterative: A substance that produces a gradual, beneficial change in the body.

anabolic: Strengthens and builds body tissue and encourages weight gain or anabolism.

analgesic: A medication that reduces or eliminates pain.

andandamide: A chemical with marijuana-like properties, isolated from brain tissue.

androgenetic alopecia: Hair loss resulting from a genetic predisposition, often linked to DHT. It is also termed female/male pattern baldness, hereditary alopecia and common baldness.

animism: From the Latin *anima*, meaning 'soul' or 'life'. Commonly refers to belief systems that attribute souls or spirits to animals, plants, rocks and natural phenomena.

anodyne: A medicine or agent that relieves or soothes pain.

anthelmintic: A substance that expels or destroys intestinal worms (also called a vermifuge).

anthocyanins: Natural pigments that occur in plants. They are water soluble and belong to a group of antioxidant plant compounds called flavonoids.

anthropogenic: Of, or related to, the influence of human beings or their ancestors on natural objects.

antiandrogen: A substance that blocks the action of androgens, the hormones responsible for male characteristics; it is used to treat prostate cancers that require male hormones for growth.

anti-angiogenic (anti-tumour): A substance that blocks, or helps to reduce, the formation of new blood vessels, used to treat cancer.

anti-arrhythmic: A drug used to treat abnormal or irregular heart rhythm (arrhythmia).

anti-atherosclerotic: A substance or drug used to treat atherosclerosis, the process of progressive thickening and hardening of the walls of the heart's arteries from fat deposits on their inner lining.

anticholesterolemic: Contra 'cholesterolemia', the presence of elevated levels of cholesterol in the blood.

anticonvulsant: A drug used to treat or prevent convulsions (as in epilepsy).

anti-ecchymotic: A substance to treat ecchymoses, commonly known as bruises, a discoloration and tenderness of the skin due to the leakage of blood from an injured blood vessel into the tissues.

anti-emetic: A drug that prevents or alleviates nausea and vomiting.

antigenotoxic: an agent that destroys genotoxins, toxic agents that damage DNA molecules in genes, causing mutations and tumors.

antihalitotic: A treatment for bad breath (halitosis).

antihidrotic: An agent that reduces or suppresses perspiration.

antilaryngitic: An agent which soothes and treats laryngitis, the inflammation of the larynx, resulting in hoarseness of the voice.

antimicrobial: A substance that kills or inhibits the growth of micro-organisms such as bacteria or fungi.

antiphlogistic: is a traditional term designating a plant or remedy that counteracts, reduces or prevents inflammation (anti-inflammatory).

antiprotozoal: A substance that kills or inhibits the growth of single-celled micro-organisms called protozoa, which cause diseases such as malaria.

antipyretic: A medicine that lowers body temperature to prevent or alleviate fever.

antiscorbutic: A substance that helps to prevent or cure imbalances of Vitamin C deficiency.

antiretroviral: The group of medications used to treat HIV/AIDS.

antiscrophulatic: An agent to treat scrofula, a form of tuberculosis affecting the lymph nodes of the neck and resulting in chronic inflammations of the skin.

antitussive: Inhibits the cough reflex.

antivenin: An antitoxin used in the treatment of venomous bites or stings.

antivertigo: Treatment of vertigo - a sensation of dizziness, moving or spinning. It is commonly caused by a problem with the balance mechanisms within the inner ear.

antivinous: An anti-intoxicant substance that treats addiction to alcohol.

apathae: Ulcers occurring in the mouth, on the tongue and inside the cheeks.

aperient: A laxative medicine or food.

aporphine: One of a class of quinoline alkaloids; one commonly used aporphine derivative is apomorphine, which is used to treat Parkinson's disease, erectile dysfunction and sexual-arousal disorder.

astral travel: The experience, whether spontaneous or induced, of travelling through the astral realm in the form of the astral body, for spiritual journeys — often during sleep, but sometimes as 'out-of-body-experiences' (OBEs).

asymmetrical: Not symmetrical, or lacking the symmetry that characterizes balance among the parts of something.

atropine: A poisonous crystalline alkaloid extracted from the nightshade family, used as an antispasmodic, eye-pupil dilator.

Australian Bush Flower Essences: A range of flower essences developed by fifth-generation herbalist Ian White, which focuses on the mind and emotional interconnection and how this can result in physical ill health.

axillary: Of, or relating to, the axil or upper angle between an axis and an offshoot such as a branch or leaf stalk.

ayurveda: The traditional Hindu science of health and medicine, which uses diet, herbal remedies and the power of body, mind, and spirit to prevent and treat disease.

Bach Flower Remedies: Dilutions of flower material developed by English physician and homeopath Dr Edward Bach (1886-1936) during the 1930s, used primarily for emotional and spiritual conditions, such as depression, anxiety, insomnia and stress.

bactericidal: Any substance capable of killing bacteria.

balsamic: A substance that contains resins and benzoic acid and is used to treat colds and abrasions.

benign prostatic hyperplasia (BPH): The increase in size of the prostate gland in middle-aged and elderly men that appears to be part of the natural ageing process; it is a non-cancerous condition.

beta-carotene: The molecule that gives carrots and other fruit and vegetables their colour. It is part of a family of chemicals called the carotenoids.

biomass: Plant materials and animal waste used as fuel.

biome: A climatically and geographically defined area of ecologically similar climatic conditions, such as communities of plants, animals and soil organisms, often referred to as ecosystems.

biosphere: All of the ecosystems on the planet, along with their interactions in air (atmosphere), water and land, where living organisms exist.

bitters: Plant products that have a bitter taste, which stimulate the autonomic nervous system, saliva secretions and digestive juices, increasing appetite and assimilation.

botanical (n.): Refers to substances obtained from plants used in food or pharmaceutical products.

British National Formulary (BNF): is a bi-annual publication containing a wide spectrum of information on drugs, drawn from the manufacturers' product literature, medical and pharmaceutical literature, regulatory authorities and professional bodies.

British Pharmacopoeia: The official collection of standards for UK medicinal products and pharmaceutical substances, published each year.

calcareous: Containing or resembling calcium carbonate or calcite or chalk.

calyx: The collective sepals of a flower.

cardiac: From the Greek word kardia (heart), the term means "related to the heart".

cardiotonic: Relating to or having a favourable effect upon the action of the heart.

carminative: A herb or preparation that prevents the formation and induces the expulsion of gas from the stomach or intestines.

caryopsis: A small, dry, one-seeded fruit in which the ovary wall remains joined with the seed in a single grain, as in cereals such as barley and wheat.

cathartic: In medicine, a substance which accelerates defecation.

cephalic: Pertaining to the head.

cholagogue: A drug or other substance that promotes the flow of bile from the gall bladder into the intestine.

choleretic: An agent that stimulates the liver to increase output of bile.

contraindication: A condition or factor that increases the risks involved in using a particular drug or carrying out a medical procedure.

cosmeceutical: A cosmetic product claimed to have medicinal benefits.

cultigen: A plant that has been deliberately altered or selected by humans; the result of artificial selection.

demulcent: An agent, such as an oil, that forms a soothing film when administered onto the surface of a mucous membrane, thus relieving irritation.

depurative: Remedy or agent used to eliminate toxins and purify the blood.

detergent: A cleansing agent, used on wounds, to remove dead and diseased matter.

diaphoretic: A medicine or agent which promotes perspiration.

dihydrotestosterone (DHT): A male hormone that is suggested as the main cause of hair loss; it is formed when the male hormone testosterone interacts with the enzyme 5-alpha reductase.

dissociative (n.): A drug that reduces (or blocks) signals to the conscious mind from other parts of the brain, typically (but not necessarily) limited to the senses. Such sensory deprivation can facilitate self-exploration, hallucinations and dreamlike states.

drupe: A fleshy fruit, such as a peach, plum, or cherry, usually having a single hard stone that encloses a seed.

DVT: Deep Vein Thrombosis.

emetic: An agent that induces vomiting.

emmenagogue: A substance that induces or hastens menstrual bleeding.

emollient: Substances that soften and soothe the skin.

endemism: The ecological state of being unique to a place that is a discrete geographical unit, such as an island, habitat type or other defined area or zone. Endemic species are not naturally found elsewhere.

enteritis: Inflammation of the intestine (especially the small intestine); usually characterized by diarrhoea.

entheogen: A psychoactive substance, primarily derived from plants, used in a religious or shamanic context; it is a term often used to contrast with recreational use of the same substances.

espalier: A tree or shrub that is trained to grow in a flat plane against a wall, often in a symmetrical pattern.

essential fatty acids (EFA): These are polyunsaturated fatty acids, linoleic acid and alpha-linolenic acid, that cannot be made in the body and must be provided by diet.

'Essiac'/Essiac tea: A blend of herbs discovered by a Canadian nurse, Rene Caisse, who named it after her surname spelled backwards; it is used to make a tea that is believed to have cancer-treating properties. The original formula is said to have been given to her by a Canadian Ojibwa. It contains greater burdock root (*Arctium lappa*), slippery-elm inner bark (*Ulmus rubra*), sheep sorrel (*Rumex acetosella*) and Indian or Turkish rhubarb root (*Rheum officinale*).

ethneogen: A psychoactive substance, derived from plant sources, used in a religious, shamanic or spiritual context.

ethnobotany: The study of how people of a particular culture and region make of use of indigenous plants.

eupeptic: Having properties which encourage healthy, functioning digestion.

expectorant: Promoting the expulsion of phlegm, mucus, or other matter from the respiratory tract.

febrifuge: A medication that reduces fever; an antipyretic.

fixative: A natural or synthetic substance used as stabilizing or preservative agent in cosmetics and perfumes.

flavonoids: a group of chemical compounds found in all plants, most notably fruits, vegetables, nuts, seeds and roots. Flavonoids are most commonly known for their antioxidant activity.

formic acid: The simplest carboxylic acid; it is a colourless, volatile acid and skin irritant, contained in fluids emitted by red ants and nettles.

free radical: Any atom or molecule that has a single unpaired electron in an outer shell. Most biologically-relevant free radicals are highly reactive and free radical damage is closely associated with oxidative damage and ageing.

fungicidal: destroys or inhibits growth of fungi.

galactofuge: A medicine to reduce the flow of milk in nursing mothers.

galactogogue: A substance which is used to increase the production of breast milk in humans and other animals.

German Commission E: A committee made up of scientists, toxicologists, doctors, and pharmacists formed by the German government in 1978 to find out if herbs sold in Germany are safe and effective. The Commission has published information on the uses, side effects, and drug interactions of more than 300 herbs.

gingivitis: Inflamed and bleeding gums.

GLA (gamma-linolenic acid): An essential fatty acid (EFA) found primarily in vegetable oils.

glabrous: Having no hairs, projections, or pubescence; smooth.

glossitis: Inflammation of the tongue.

glucoside: Complexes of substances with glucose. The general name for such complexes with other sugars is glycosides.

green manure: A type of cover crop grown primarily to add nutrients and organic matter (humus) to the soil.

haemostatic: A medicine or application that stops bleeding, serving to arrest haemorrhage.

hallucinogen: A pharmacological agent in one of three broad categories: psychedelics, dissociatives and deliriants. They amplify familiar states of mind and induce experiences such as trance, meditation, conversion experiences and dreams.

HDL cholesterol: High-density lipoprotein is a protective type of cholesterol.

hemi-parasite: A parasitic plant, such as the mistletoe, which carries on some photosynthesis, but obtains a portion of its food, water or minerals from a host plant.

hepatotonic: A substance that is tonic to the liver – usually employed to normalize liver enzymes and function.

hermaphrodite: A flower that has both staminate (male, pollen-producing) and carpellate (female, ovule-producing) parts. This condition is seen in many common garden plants.

Hippocratic Oath: An oath traditionally taken by physicians pertaining to the ethical practice of medicine. It is believed to have been written by Hippocrates in the 4th century BCE, or by one of his students.

histamine: A naturally occurring substance in the body that causes allergic reactions (redness, itching and swelling) of the nose and eyes.

homeopathy: A system of medicine based on treating the individual with highly diluted substances that are thought to cause effects similar to the symptoms presented and thus trigger the body's natural system of healing.

hyoscine: An alkaloid; see Scopolamine.

hyoscyamine: A poisonous crystalline alkaloid, used medicinally to treat abdominal pain and similar conditions.

hygroscopic: Substances that attract moisture from the surrounding environment.

hypertrophy: Abnormal enlargement of a body part or organ; the overgrowth can occur in a select area of soft tissue or skeleton.

hypnotic: Drugs or substances whose primary function is to induce sleep.

hypoglycaemic: Having abnormally low blood sugar, usually resulting from excessive insulin or a poor diet.

hypolipidemic: Agents used to lower blood cholesterol when this is elevated (hypercholesterolemia), especially in patients at risk for cardiovascular disease.

hypotensive: Having abnormally low blood pressure.

immuno-stimulant: An agent that stimulates the body's immune system.

indole: A white crystalline compound obtained from coal tar or plants and found in the intestines and faeces as a product of the bacterial decomposition of tryptophan.

inflorescence: A branch, or system of branches, bearing two or more individual flowers.

King's American Dispensatory: First published in 1854, this book covers the uses of herbs used in American medical practice, especially by those involved in Eclectic medicine which was the botanical school of medicine in the 1800s-1900s. The 18th edition, published in 1898, was entirely

rewritten by the most famous and accomplished eclectic pharmacist of the time, John Uri Lloyd.

laryngitis: Inflammation of the mucous membrane of the larynx, characterized by hoarseness or loss of voice and coughing.

LDL cholesterol: Low-density lipoprotein is often called the bad type of cholesterol; If it deposits in the walls of blood vessels, it can lead to atherosclerosis and heart disease.

London Pharmacopoeia: Regarded as the first book on pharmacy to be authorized as the legal standard for a city, *Pharmacopoeia Londinensis* was published in May 1618 by the Royal College of Physicians. Herbalist Nicholas Culpeper translated it into English.

LSD (lysergic acid diethylamide): One of the most common hallucinogenic drugs of the ergoline family, usually a semi-synthetic psychedelic street drug in the West.

macerated: Made soft by soaking in a liquid.

MAOI (monoamine oxidase inhibitor): Part of a class of powerful antidepressant drugs prescribed for the treatment of depression.

materia medica: The body of collected knowledge about the therapeutic properties of any substance that is used for healing.

micturition: The process of disposing of urine from the bladder through the urethra to the outside of the body; also known as urination and voiding.

monoterpenoid: Occurs as a result of biochemical modifications, such as oxidation or rearrangement of monoterpenes; see Terpene.

mycelium: The mass of interwoven threads (hyphae) making up the vegetative body of a fungus.

neotropical: Refers to one of the world's eight terrestrial ecozones, which includes South and Central America, the Mexican lowlands, the Caribbean islands and southern Florida.

nervine: A medicine or remedy that has a beneficial effect upon the nervous system.

neurotransmitter: Chemicals released by neurons to stimulate neighbouring neurons, allowing impulses to be passed from one cell to the next throughout the nervous system.

norepinephrine: A neurotransmitter and a hormone that is released by the sympathetic nervous system into the heart, blood vessels and other organs, and by the adrenal gland into the bloodstream as part of the 'fight or flight' response.

oestrogenic: Having an action similar to that of an oestrogen.

opioid: A chemical substance that has a morphine-like action in the body and may induce a dreamy, relaxed state and, in some people, intense feelings of pleasure; its main use is for pain relief.

Oshara (Northern) Tradition: An archaic culture of the American south-west, c.5500 BCE to c.600 CE.

palmate: having veins, leaflets or lobes radiating from a common central point.

panspermia: The hypothesis that life on Earth originated with micro-organisms from outer space.

parasiticidal: An agent or preparation used to destroy parasites.

paresthesia: A sensation of tingling, pricking or numbness of the skin with no apparent long-term physical effect; known as 'pins and needles'.

pectoral: relating to the chest or thorax. A herb or remedy that relieves ailments of these parts.

perianth: The collective term for the outer parts of a flower, consisting of the calyx and corolla and enclosing the stamens and pistils.

pharmacology: The study of drugs and their origin, nature, properties and effects upon living organisms.

pharyngitis: Inflammation of the pharynx, leading to a sore throat.

phytoestrogen: A naturally-occurring plant compound that acts like the hormone oestrogen.

phytomedicine: The use of plants, parts of plants, and isolated phytochemicals for the prevention and treatment of various health concerns.

phytonutrient: A plant-derived substance that is beneficial to health, especially one that is neither a vitamin nor a mineral.

phytotherapy: The use of plants or plant extracts for medicinal purposes; favoured by those who wish to emphasize the modern potential of traditional remedies.

pinnate: A term used to describe feather-like or multi-divided features arising from both sides of a common axis in plant and animal structures.

placebo: An innocuous or inert dummy medicine or treatment, containing no active ingredients, and therefore of no real benefit, although it may nevertheless make people feel better. It may be given as a pacifier or to the control group in experiments on the efficacy of a drug.

polyphenol: A group of chemical substances found in plants, characterized by the presence of more than one phenol unit or building block per molecule, believed to protect against some common health problems.

Popol Vuh: An epic first written down in the 16th century, but probably based on older traditional material, describing the cosmogony, mythology and history of the Quiché Maya of Guatemala.

potentize: To render latent power available.

protease inhibitors (PIs): A class of medication used to treat or prevent infection by viruses, including HIV and hepatitis C.

psilocin (4-HO-DMT): A psychedelic (hallucinogenic) mushroom alkaloid, found in most psychedelic mushrooms together with psilocybin. Psilocin is a Schedule I drug under the Convention on Psychotropic Substances.

psilocybin: A psychedelic chemical (indole) of the tryptamine family, found in psilocybin mushrooms.

Psychedelic substance: A psychoactive drug whose primary action is to alter the thought processes of the brain and the perception of the mind.

psychoactive: capable of affecting mental activity.

psychonaut: Someone who experiences intentionally induced altered states of consciousness in an attempt to investigate his or her mind, and possibly address spiritual questions, through direct experience.

psychosis: Any severe mental disorder in which contact with reality is lost or highly distorted.

psychotherapy: The branch of psychiatry concerned with psychological methods and treatment of mental or emotional problems by psychological means.

psychotropic: A drug or substance affecting mental activity, behavior or perception.

purgative: Tending to cleanse or purge, especially causing evacuation of the bowels.

qi: Also *chi*. Vital energy, or life force, that is thought to flow through the body in Chinese and Japanese medicine and martial arts.

quinsy: Painful pus-filled inflammation of the tonsils and surrounding tissues; a complication of tonsillitis.

raceme: An inflorescence having stalked flowers arranged singly along an elongated unbranched axis, as in the lily of the valley.

resolvent: Helps reduce swelling by dispersal, or helps the absorption of new growth, promoting removal of abnormal growths such as tumours.

rhizome: The horizontal stem of a plant that is usually found underground, often sending out roots and shoots from its nodes.

rubefacient: Herb or substance that brings blood rapidly to a concentrated area of the skin, thus causing redness of skin - used for pain relief.

sanatorium: A medical facility for the improvement of health, especially for convalescents.

schizophrenia: Any of several psychotic disorders characterized by distortions of reality and disturbances of thought and language.

scopolamine: A chemical compound with anticholinergic effects, used as a truth serum, or with morphine as a sedative in surgery and obstetrics; also to treat nausea and dilate the pupils in ophthalmic procedures.

scrofula: Any of a variety of skin diseases; in particular, a form of tuberculosis affecting the lymph nodes of the neck.

self-fruitful: Capable of setting a crop of self-pollinated fruit.

sepal: Part of a flower, usually green, that surrounds and protects the flower in bud.

serotonin (5-hydroxytryptamine, or 5-HT): A hormone and monoamine neurotransmitter that regulates many functions, including mood, appetite and sensory perception.

Shamanism: A range of traditional beliefs and practices concerned with communication with the spirit world.

sialagogue: An agent promoting the flow of saliva.

specific (n.): A remedy used to treat a particular disease.

spasmolytic: A drug used to relieve or prevent spasms (especially of the smooth muscles).

SSRI (selective serotonin reuptake inhibitor): One of a class of antidepressants used in the treatment of depression, anxiety disorders and some personality disorders.

Stolen Generation: Collectively, the Australian Aboriginal and Torres Strait Islander children, removed from their families by government agencies and church missions, between about 1869 and 1969.

stolon: A horizontal stem or branch from the base of a plant, which grows at or below the soil surface and produces new plants from buds at its tip.

stomachic: A remedy beneficial to increasing appetite or stimulating digestion in the stomach.

stomatitis: Inflammation of the mucous membrane of the mouth.

styptic: A substance that stops external bleeding (usually an astringent).

subshrub: A partly shrubby plant that has woody stems growing new shoots annually at the tips.

sudorific: A substance taken internally to promote or increase sweating.

sympathetic magic: A type of magic, also known as 'imitative magic', based on the belief that a person or thing can be supernaturally affected by its relationship to another thing.

synaesthesia: A neurologically based phenomenon in which stimulation of one sensory pathway evokes the sensation of another. Those affected may, for example, 'see' a sound as a colour.

syncretism: The attempt to reconcile disparate or contradictory beliefs, often while melding practices of various schools of thought.

tannin: One of a group of yellow or brown solid compounds found in many plants and used as tanning agents, mordants and medical astringents.

Taoism: A popular Chinese philosophical system based on the teachings of Lao-tzu, but characterized by a pantheism of many gods and the practices of alchemy, divination and magic.

TCA (tricyclic antidepressant): A class of antidepressant drugs first used in the 1950s.

terpene: A large and varied class of hydrocarbons, primarily produced by a wide variety of plants, though also by insects; they are used in some natural agricultural pesticides.

tonic: A medicinal preparation that improves and strengthens body functions and increases the feeling of wellbeing.

tonsillitis: Inflammation of the tonsils.

topical: A drug or ointment for application to the body surface.

Traditional Chinese Medicine (TCM): Chinese alternative therapies, including herbal remedies, acupuncture and massage.

tranquillizer: A drug that calms without affecting clarity of consciousness.

trefoil: Any of several Old World herbs having trifoliate compound leaves, such as clover, a plant of the genus *Trifolium*.

trichome: A fine outgrowth or appendage on plants; examples are hairs, glandular hairs, scales and papillae.

trifoliate: A pinnate leaf with just three leaflets, such as clover.

tryptamine: The backbone for a group of compounds known collectively as tryptamines; it includes many biologically active compounds, including neutotransmitters and hallucinogens.

umbel: An arrangement of flowers on a stalk, in which a number of short flower stalks of the same length grow from the same point in the main stem, forming a cluster.

Unani system: A system of medicine which originated in Greece and is based on the teachings of Hippocrates, Galen and Avicenna and the concepts of the four humours: Phlegm, Blood, Yellow bile and Black bile. India is now one of the leading countries so far as its practice is concerned.

unitarianism: The Christian doctrine that stresses individual freedom of belief and the oneness of God, instead of the traditional Christian belief in the Trinity.

United States Pharmacopoeia: The first pharmacopoeia published in the US, compiled for army use, which appeared in Philadelphia in 1778. It became the legal standard in 1906 by enactment of the Food and Drug Act.

universal veil: A layer of tissue that completely surrounds a baby mushroom in some species. When the mushroom grows, it pushes through the universal veil, leaving parts of it on the stalk or cap.

urtification: The practice of rubbing or beating the fresh leaves of nettles onto the skin in the treatment of rheumatism.

vasoconstrictor: A drug or agent that causes the narrowing of the walls of the blood vessels.

vasodilator: A drug or agent that causes the expansion of the walls of the blood vessels.

vasoprotector: a medication which alleviates certain conditions of the blood vessels, used, for example, in the treatment of varicose veins and hemorrhoids.

Vedas: Any of the most ancient sacred writings of Hinduism, written in early Sanskrit; traditionally believed to comprise the Samhitas, the Brahmanas, the Aranyakas and the Upanishads.

venous insufficiency: Occurs when there is poor or impaired flow of venous blood from the legs and feet to the heart; often characterized by symptoms such as varicose veins, pain, ankle swelling, feelings of heaviness, itching and leg-cramping at night.

vermifuge: A drug or agent that can destroy or expel intestinal worms.

virucide: an agent that inactivates or destroys a virus.

Voodoo: A charm superstitiously believed to embody magical powers, and (Haiti) followers of a religion that involves witchcraft and animistic deities.

vulnerary: a remedy used to heal or treat wounds.

Wicca: The polytheistic nature religion of modern witchcraft whose central deity is a mother goddess.

wort: The word 'wort' (pronounced 'word', not 'wart') means 'plant'; it forms part of the name of many medicinal herbs.

Index

Acknowledgements

The author would like to thank Mr Bernie Hephrun Cert. Ed., Dip. Rural Ed., F.R.A.S., a pioneer of Essential Oils for Aromatherapy, fount of knowledge, and founder of the Natural Oils Research Association (N.O.R.A.), and Environmental Theorist Prof. Dr David Bellamy O.B.E., BSc., PhD., D.Sc., D Univ. Hon FLS, FIBiol., for his continuous encouragement regarding my plant-oriented research work and information. The author's website is www.herbsphere.com.

Executive Editor Sandra Rigby
Senior Editor Lisa John
Executive Art Editor Karen Sawyer
Designer Sally Bond
Production Controller Linda Parry

AGPix/Bill Beatty 58; **akg-images** 79; /North Wind Picture Archives 173; **Alamy**/Amazon-Images 311; /Helmut Baar/imagebroker 240; /Dr.

Wilfried Bahnmüller/imagebroker 154; /blickwinkel/Koenig 247; /E.R. Degginger 314; /Susan E. Degginger 333; /Foodcollection.com 178; /Paroli Galperti/CuboImages srl 255; /Mike Goldwater 357; /Christian Hütter/imagebroker 91; /ImageDJ 208; /JEVGENIJA 120; /joefoxphoto 371; /Geoffrey Kidd 205; /Lou-Foto 146; /Darlyne A. Murawski/National Geographic Image Collection 327; /North Wind

ACKNOWLEDGEMENTS

Picture Archives 252; /Edward Parker 268; /Photoshot Holdings Ltd 92; /Sebastiano Volponi/MARKA 358; /Michael Wald 139; /Rob Walls 361; /Jay Wanta 321; /WILDLIFE GmbH 46, 57; /yogesh more 258; /Anna Yu 105; **Howard Birnstihl** 354; **Bridgeman Art Library**/Bibliotheque Nationale, Paris 82; /Freer Gallery of Art, Smithsonian Institution/Gift of Charles Lang Freer 11; /Samuel Courtauld Trust, The Courtauld Gallery, London 152; /South Tyrol Museum of Archeology, Bolzano/Wolfgang Neeb 8; /The Putnam Foundation, Timken Museum of Art, San Diego 183; **Corbis**16; /Amit Bhargava 211; /Mark Bolton 293, 298; /Envision 106; /Malcolm Hanes/Etsa 151; /Lindsay Hebberd 322; /Image Source 119; /Sean Justice 376; /Helen King 372; /LWA-Stephen Welstead 363; /Clay Perry 301; /Bill Ross 134; /Schultheiss Productions 375; /The Art Archive 191; /Roger Tidman 291; /Bernd Vogel 169; /Larry Williams 369; **FLPA**/Nicholas and Sherry Lu Aldridge 217; /Nigel Cattlin 352; /Tony Hamblin 297; /Jurgen & Christine Sohns 280; **Forestry Images**/Joseph O'Brien, USDA Forest Service, Bugwood.org 63; **Fotolia**/Hennadiy Androsov 308; /Alexander Bedoya 161; /Chushkin 96; /Peter Cox 263; /DiT 202; /Elenathewise 6; /emer 53; /Frogger 348; /hbriphil 257; /Andreas Karelias 2-3; /Marcin Karpeta 189; /Anne Kitzman 49; /krysek 142; /Anna Kuznetsova 28; /Karin Lau 317; /Lensman300 26; /Chong Lee Lian 33; /LianeM 350; /Yong Hian Lim 39; /Doug Olson 31; /Saied Shahinkiya 87; /snez_4eva 340; /Doug Stacey 344; /sylwia2007 177; /Charles Taylor 235; /Mikhail Tolstoy 199; /Wong Siew Tung 324; /Gautier Willaume 195; /Tomasz Wojnarowicz 265; /Caroline Yoachim 141; /Fabrizio Zanier 164; **Gap Photos**/Pernilla Bergdahl 288; /Mark Bolton 244; /Jonathan Buckley 294; /Elke Borkowski 128; /Sarah Cuttle 218; /Paul Debois 84; /Heather Edwards 81; /Suzie Gibbons 64; /John Glover 212; /Muriel Hazan/biosphoto 229; /Daniel Heuclin/biosphoto 347; /Lynn Keddie 226; /Howard Rice 166; /Friedrich Strauss 42; /Jo Whitworth 283; **Garden Collection**/Derek

St. Romaine 171; **Garden World Images**/Deni Bown 68, 232; /Gilles Delacroix 73; /Arnaud Descat/MAP 334; /Jacqui Dracup 50; /Flowerphotos/Carol Sharp 76; /Paul Nief/MAP 36; /John Swithinbank 179; /Lee Thomas 328; **Getty Images**/Paul Avis 111; /Angelo Cavalli 253; /Ken Chernus 19; /Kaz Chiba 54; /DEA/C.SAPPA 302; /Grant Faint 272; /National Geographic 312; /Alexandra Grablewski 174; /Louis-Laurent Grandadam 15; /Siegfried Layda 9; /Matilda Lindeblad 40; /Manzo Niikura/Neovision 108; /Martin Page 60; /Richard Ross 158; /Ariel Skelley 367; /Still Images 364; /Kazunori Yoshikawa/A.collection 239; **Zoë Hawes** 225; **Dave Lee**, Greenwood Creek Photo 98; **Natural Visions**/Colin Paterson-Jones 338; **Octopus Publishing Group**/Frank Adam 172, 236; /Colin Bowling 23; /Michael Boyes 95; /Stephen Conroy 124, 133; /Laura Forrester 127; /Mike Good 21; /Jerry Harpur 267; /Marcus Harpur 330; /Will Heap 145; /Janine Hosegood 112, 168; /Ruth Jenkinson 306; /Sandra Lane 136; /William Lingwood 200; /Peter Myers 25; /Lis Parsons 153, 163, 182, 222, 243; /Mike Prior 13, 22, 307, 355; /William Reavell 4, 131, 192, 221; /Howard Rice 186; /Craig Robertson 196; /Russell Sadur 14, 251; /Eleanor Skan 207; /Simon Smith 115; /Freia Turland 148; /George Wright 230; **Photolibrary**/Pernilla Bergdahl 279; /Botanica 74; /Linda Burgess 67; /Angelo Cavalli 304; /Carl R. Englander 287; /Berndt Fischer 261; /Goodshoot 248; /Chris L. Jones 123; /JTB Photo 156; /Jerry Pavia 70; /Fritz Pölking 88; /Howard Rice 276, 284; /J S Sira 275; /White Star/Spierenburg 45; /Busse Yankushev 100; /Francesca Yorke 103

Photoshot 37; /BSIP 271; /Eye Ubiquitous 318; **Alan Rockefeller** 343; **Scala, Florence** 162; /Courtesy of the ministero Beni e Att. Culturali 215; **Science Photo Library**/Anthony Cooper 34; /Michael P. Gadomski 180; /Claude Nuridsany & Marie Perennou 337; /Bjorn Svensson 185; **SuperStock**/Silvio Fiore 117; **TopFoto**/Alinari 220; /World History Archive 12